SuperCash

Founded in 1807, John Wiley & Sons is the oldest independent publishing company in the United States. With offices in North America, Europe, Australia, and Asia, Wiley is globally committed to developing and marketing print and electronic products and services for our customers' professional and personal knowledge and understanding.

The Wiley Trading series features books by traders who have survived the market's ever changing temperament and have prospered—some by reinventing systems, others by getting back to basics. Whether a novice trader, professional, or somewhere in-between, these books will provide the advice and strategies needed to prosper today and well into the future.

For a list of available titles, please visit our web site at www.WileyFinance.com.

SuperCash

The New Hedge Fund Capitalism

JAMES ALTUCHER

John Wiley & Sons, Inc.

Published by John Wiley & Sons, Inc., Hoboken, New Jersey.
Published simultaneously in Canada.

For general information on our other products and services or for technical support, please contact our Customer Care Department within the United States at (800) 762-2974, outside the United States at (317) 572-3993 or fax (317) 572-4002.

Wiley also publishes its books in a variety of electronic formats. Some content that appears in print may not be available in electronic books. For more information about Wiley products, visit our web site at www.wiley.com.

Library of Congress Cataloging-in-Publication Data:

Altucher, James.
SuperCash : the new hedge fund capitalism / by James Altucher.
p. cm. — (Wiley trading series)
Includes index.
ISBN-13 978-0-471-74599-0 (cloth)
ISBN-10 0-471-74599-5 (cloth)
1. Hedge funds. I. Title: SuperCash. II. Title. III. Series.
HG4530.A526 2006
332.64'524—dc22

2005034032

Printed in the United States of America.

10 9 8 7 6 5 4 3 2 1

Dedicated to my mom,

Rita Altucher,

for being my hero

Contents

Introduction: What Is SuperCash? 1

CHAPTER 1 Hedge Funds Are the New Banks 9

Subprime Auto Finance 10
Trade Factoring 11
Hard-Money Real Estate Lending 11
Life Insurance Premium Financing 14
Tax Liens 16
Taxi Medallions 18

CHAPTER 2 Activism 21

CHAPTER 3 Buying Delinquent Credit Card Debt 47

CHAPTER 4 Everything You Wanted to Know about PIPEs But Were Afraid to Ask 55

Regulation S 57
Death Spirals 58
Deal Types 59
Common Stock 60
Convertible Debentures 61
PIPE Performance 65

CHAPTER 5 The New New IPO 71

Specialty Acquisition Corporations 72
The Dutch Experiment Is Over 75
The Rise of the Reverse Merger 76

CHAPTER 6 Trade like a Billionaire 79

Mark Cuban 80
Bill Gates 81
Michael Dell 81
Bruce Kovner 82
Peter Lynch 84
George Soros 87
Peter Kellog 87
Carl Icahn 87

CHAPTER 7 Closed-End Fund Arbitrage 91

Discounting Mechanisms 92
Do-It-Yourself Closed-End Fund Arbitrage 93

CHAPTER 8 Short-Selling 99

Pitfalls of Short-Selling 101
When Short-Selling Works 105

CHAPTER 9 The Finer Things in Life 111

Don't Spend All Your Rare Coins in One Place 112
But Can I Afford a $100 Million Painting? 114
Whatever Happened to the Bowie Bonds? 117
Appendix: The 12-Piece United States Gold Coin Type Set 119

CHAPTER 10 Trend versus Countertrend 131

QQQQ Crash Revisited 135
The Christmas System 138
Fading Unemployment 141

CHAPTER 11 The Myth of the Index, or ETFs: Active or Passive? 143

Whatever Happened to the Original Dow Jones? 149

CHAPTER 12 Watch Out! 157

Do-It-Yourself Due Diligence 164
Appendix: Sample Background Check Report 166

CHAPTER 13 So You Want to Start a Hedge Fund? 185

Mistakes Start-Up Hedge Fund Managers Make 185
Getting By on $600,000 a Year 188

CHAPTER 14 Classic Investment Reading and New Media Resources 193

Books about Investment 193
Blogs for Hedge Funds 196

CHAPTER 15 Where to Find the Data 201

Index 205

SuperCash

INTRODUCTION

What Is SuperCash?

During the day, Superman is mild-mannered Clark Kent. He doesn't want to make waves or draw attention to himself. He is safe, calm, and offers no excitement to the adventure-prone Lois Lane. However, when he's out saving the universe, using every power at his disposal, he becomes Superman. Even with his red-sun-enhanced superpowers he often risks his life as he saves the lives of those around him.

The same thing is true of cash. Most cash sits in bank accounts, money market funds, index funds, and shoe boxes, doing whatever it can to just stay alive, not seeking to do more.

But cash can wake up and fill the cracks in liquidity that stretch throughout capitalism. Capitalism is constantly reaching out to fill a much larger universe of possibility and, in doing so, creates opportunity wherever risk aversion has kept out larger institutional players such as commercial banks and mutual funds. It is this risk aversion, and only this risk aversion, that creates the anomalies in liquidity that allow an investor to make money.

As hedge funds and other investors have awakened to the possibilities, they have begun doing more than simply trading stocks in the expectation that they will go up. For every dollar they manage, they attempt to find a customer for that dollar and then charge that customer. Moving beyond stocks, many hedge funds are actively lending money to companies and individuals that banks won't or can't touch, finding arbitrage situations that the larger mutual funds are unable to dip into because of size or regulatory constraints, and putting their dollars in companies where activism could perhaps extract more value from the investments.

These savvy investors are turning cash into supercash where instead of paltry returns of X percent they are seeing returns on their investment of Y percent. Gone are the days of buying a stock and watching it triple in a day. Now every dollar needs to be pushed out the door into a good home, and then the hedge fund manager needs to actively monitor that dollar, making sure maximum value is being sought by the new holders of that dollar.

The question a fund manager has to ask himself is: Why should capitalism reward me with a paycheck? For instance, if a mutual fund manager says to himself, "I'm going to buy Intel today, I think it's going to go up," it is hard for that manager to prove that he has an edge over the other 8,000 mutual funds, or tens of thousands of day traders and analysts out there who are also debating whether to buy Intel. Everyone has the same information and with the Internet, all new information is assimilated instantly. This is efficient market theory in action, and although markets are not perfect and anomalies exist, the market is largely efficient, particularly in the large cap stocks that are so widely followed.

The way to get beyond the inefficiencies that taint most transactions in the markets is to actively control the transaction. In other words:

- With stock picking, either (1) directly negotiate with the company to structure the transaction (see Chapter 4 on PIPEs), or (2) vigorously persuade a management team with poor return on equity to take actions that increase the use of cash (see Chapter 2 on activism).
- With fixed-income transactions, do not simply buy the debt structured by others and let loose on the open market, but actively enter into the arenas the banks are avoiding and structure and lend as if you, the investor, were the bank.
- With arbitrage opportunities, engage in the situations where the investment banks and large hedge funds are simply too big to flexibly and nimbly find and take advantage of the remaining anomalies.
- In cases where any of the above are difficult, find the players who are finding *alpha* and simply piggyback behind them by following their publicly disclosed transactions.

This book can be thought of as the third book in a series on attempting to map out where the gaps and holes are in capitalism. Since the landscape is constantly changing, any road map is just a guide; and since the universe of opportunity is so vast in a global economy, I'm afraid I've only mapped out the space of a few square miles on a world that is millions of miles wide and long. My first book, *Trade Like a Hedge Fund*, attempts to find the basic anomalies and inefficiencies that I feel will recur again and again in the markets. An example is how, when formerly large cap stocks declare bankruptcy (think Worldcom and Enron), their stocks tend to double or even triple within 48 hours of declaring bankruptcy. Another anomaly I explore is the tendency for stocks to reverse direction when they have significant gaps down due to an earnings miss or some other equally bad news. The 19 or so anomalies I look at are perfect for short-term trading accounts and work well with funds with less than $100 million in assets. With too many assets it is hard to be nimble enough to take advantage of the various trading anomalies.

Trade Like Warren Buffett was my second book. Buffett is definitely the world's greatest investor and has demonstrated this again and again over a career that has spanned more than 50 years. But I was dissatisfied with most of the books out there and decided to do my own study of his multifaceted career. For Buffett, the most important aspect of an investment is not necessarily a stock's return on equity, or the P/E ratio, or any of the other familiar valuation metrics. However, with each one of his investments, he always had one, two, sometimes even three "back doors" that assured him he had a margin of safety and would not lose his money. Gillette is a great example. Although that is usually considered one of his greatest stock picks, it never was actually a stock pick. The CEO of Gillette, worried that his declining business (Bic was eating Gillette's lunch in terms of market share) but solid cash flows would attract a predator, approached Buffett about being a white knight. Buffett bought, direct from the company and not on the open market, an interest-bearing note yielding almost 9 percent a year that was convertible into common stock. Buffett knew several things when he made this investment:

- In the worst-case scenario, he would get his money back since he had senior debt, and even in a bankruptcy (which was pretty much unthinkable for Gillette) there would be assets to liquidate.
- Even if the stock went down, he knew he would be making 9 percent a year on it since cash flows at Gillette were very steady. And if the stock was down when the term of the debt was up, he would simply get his money back.
- He knew that if the stock went up, past his conversion price, then he would just convert and have a nice profit on the investment, which is what happened.

In other words, Buffett was able to put a significant amount of money to work, never really worry about getting his money back or even losing a dime of his money, and enjoy the benefits of any stock appreciation—all the time getting paid 9 percent a year while he waited. While this seems like a great deal if you can get it, this is business as usual for Buffett, and I made a conscientious attempt to catalog all such similar margin-of-safety characteristics that Buffett has used over the past 50 years.

SuperCash takes it one step further by examining all of the new types of investments that have been developed over the past few years by the top hedge funds and investors in the world, including asset-backed lending, PIPEs, closed-end fund arbitrage, new types of IPOs, and even securitizing the cash flows from elevator music.

In the following chapters, I will show you how savvy traders and hedge fund managers are turning cash into supercash in today's tough markets. We'll look at the following topics and strategies for supersizing returns:

- Hedge funds as the new banks. Hedge funds are feasting on the scraps from banks. Banks will not do short-term debt, they will not do hard-to-collect loans, they will not take risks on microcap companies, and so on. So hedge funds have become the new banks on everything from subprime auto financing to trade factoring, hard-money real estate lending, tax lien investing, life insurance premium financing, and more.
- Activism. Much has been written about so-called "value traps," stocks that have all the characteristics of value stocks (i.e., low P/E ratios, steady earnings, great balance sheets) but never seem to move higher. Sometimes the reasons for the trap are clear—management has become entrenched and lost whatever competency it ever had in terms of bringing value to shareholders. Or sometimes the reason is more insidious—management is raping the company blind and not leaving much excess cash flow for investors. Activists invest in deep value situations where they think management is, for whatever reasons, refusing to unlock that value. The activists then begin communicating with management, expressing their opinion on how to extract value, and then, in the worst case, attempting to change things forcefully, either by taking over the board of directors of the company or by taking over the entire company. Although it is difficult for the typical retail investor to be an activist investor, it is possible to piggyback on the coattails of larger activists and to learn about their investment philosophies and activities through their very public SEC filings which document their approach.
- Delinquent credit card debt. Hedge funds have become the credit card issuers of last resort. While you can't get a VISA card from a hedge fund, they may be the holder of the outstanding balance on your card. Some banks have been unable to collect on bad debt and are now wrapping up the delinquent debt in securitized paper and selling it off to hedge funds, who then outsource the collection.

- PIPEs. Private investments in public equities (PIPEs) have been quietly replacing the traditional secondary offering as the financing of choice for many small cap and mid cap public companies. Rather than paying an investment bank 7 percent or more in fees, dealing with expensive SEC filings, and going on six-month road shows while everyone shorts your stock, public companies are opting to raise money by going directly to hedge funds, negotiating terms, and closing financings in a matter of days or weeks rather than months. Chapter 4 examines the various deal structures that have become popular and the post-deal performance of these PIPEs.
- A new approach with IPOs. The large banks and brokerages used to have the monopoly on IPOs and the profits that could be gained by investing in those IPOs and then flipping them on IPO day. But a new crop of IPOs has sprung up, simultaneously taking some power away from the blue chip investment banks and giving some power back to the retail investor. Chapter 5 looks at Dutch auctions, pioneered by investment firm WR Hambrecht, and the 90 percent or higher returns garnered by this strategy. I also examine how reverse mergers don't deserve the reputation they've garnered over the years, and look at an unusual innovation combining private equity with the IPO—the specialty acquisitions corporation (SPAC).
- Trade like a billionaire. Where are the world's richest putting their personal money? A look at the portfolios of Bill Gates, Michael Dell, Carl Icahn, Peter Lynch, Mark Cuban, and others.
- Closed-end fund arbitrage. This is one of my favorite "arb" strategies. The idea is to find closed-end funds that may be undervalued when you look at the combined values of the components of their portfolios. Closed-end funds are often fairly illiquid, meaning not enough volume, and hence difficult for the larger institutions (even those with more than $20 million in assets) to be nimble enough to get in and out of without leaving wreckage behind. In Chapter 7 I provide some real-world examples, interview a fund manager who specializes in this approach, and describe how the retail investor can play in this as well.
- Short-selling. I'm not a big believer in short-selling. I think the market does have a tendency to go up over time and, even if it doesn't, the odds are stacked against the short-seller simply by the fact that even fraudulent companies can have stocks that can go up multiples of a hundred percent before they head down. Nevertheless, Chapter 8 looks at the arena and offers a few methods for short-selling that have withstood the test of time.
- Art, music, and rare coins. The finer things in life can also generate cash flows. A great example is the so-called Bowie Bonds developed by David Pullman. This was a bond that allowed David Bowie

to borrow $50 million using anticipated cash flows from his music catalog as the asset backing the loan. The loan remained investment grade throughout its life, and Pullman was able to continue using this innovative structure to provide financing for other musicians. Bowie benefited, the investors got paid, and Pullman created an industry for himself. Chapter 9 also takes a look at Fernwood, a fund set up just to invest in art, and I talk with Sylvano DiGenova about investing in rare coins.

- Trend versus countertrend. John Henry versus Toby Crabel, Richard Dennis versus Monroe Trout, volatility versus consistency. How should one trend-follow? What works in countertrend trading? Over the past 30 years, hedge funds practicing the art of trend following have become increasingly popular, particularly after they avoided the slaughter of the bear market years of 2000–2002 and racked up 20 percent-plus years during that time when other hedge funds failed or closed. We'll look at some of the techniques and results I presented in my book *Trade Like a Hedge Fund* and update some strategies.
- The myth of the index. Most efficient market theorists are big believers in index investing, the idea of investing in exchange-traded funds (ETFs) that broadly represent the market by investing in a basket of stocks such as the S&P 500, the Dow 30, or the NASDAQ 100. In this chapter, I look at how deletions from the NASDAQ 100 and S&P 600 have fared as well as take a look at the grandfathers of all deletions, the fine companies that were deleted from the original Dow Jones Industrial Average.
- Watching out for fraud. Investing in hedge funds is like going out and digging for gold in the Wild West—you might strike it rich, but unless you're extremely thorough and careful in your research, you might get robbed. Chapter 12 looks at some actual cases, including a discussion with a hedge fund manager who uncovered a fraud at her own fund, and describes some ways to avoid fraud when possible.
- Starting a hedge fund? It's not easy to start up a hedge fund in today's environment. I examine the common pitfalls hedge fund managers make, including thinking they can get by on the salary and risk provided by running a moderately successful fund.
- Classic investment reading and new media sources. Turning cash into supercash is not just a style of investing but a way of life. Striving to maximize the value of every dollar, and to find actual customers for the services your dollars can provide, requires nonstop research, patience, courage, and fortitude. Going down the supercash path can be very frustrating as well as rewarding. For me, it is helpful to constantly review the classics as well as read the latest blogs, books, and finance materials out there. In Chapter 14 I provide a reading list that

reviews a few of the information sources, be they books or blogs, that I couldn't live without.

- The data dump. Every investment strategy requires testing and study. Random guesswork and theorizing are fine, but ultimately one needs to find the data and test the theory. Chapter 15 identifies where the best data sources are and how to test using that data.

CHAPTER 1

Hedge Funds Are the New Banks

In testimony before the Senate Banking Committee in February 2004, Federal Reserve Chairman Alan Greenspan expounded on why he thought hedge funds should stay, for now, beyond regulation: "The value of these institutions is to create a very significant amount of liquidity in our system." When he says "liquidity," I don't think he means it in the traditional sense that hedge funds are simply providing more buyers and sellers for stocks in order to make a more efficient stock market. Rather, I think he's referring to all the illiquid areas within traditional banking where, because of risk aversion or just plain fear, the banks are losing valuable opportunities to generate returns and the hedge funds are stepping in to take their place.

Trading strategies obey the same laws that particles do in quantum physics: When you observe them (i.e., index a hedge fund strategy) they change. By definition, funds are alternatives. To institutionalize them is to damage them. The reality is, for fund of funds managers (I'm one of them) looking to diversify into a group of uncorrelated hedge fund strategies, the traditional strategies of merger arbitrage, fixed income arbitrage, and convertible arbitrage are no longer good enough. With market-neutral strategies I'm getting half the return at twice the risk. The market-neutral, trading-oriented hedge funds that have typically been uncorrelated with all other assets are now correlated with a flat line or worse due to the enormous amount of inflows combined with the lack of volatility in the market. However, with the overall decline in interest rates since the late 1990s, the risk aversion of trading-oriented hedge funds and banks alike, and the dot-com bust, which also flushed out many of the third-tier investment banks, many hedge funds have gone from traders to what could be called “alternative banking.”

Can you get a car loan from a hedge fund? a loan to buy a TV? a loan to pay for a life insurance policy? a school loan or financing to fund a movie? The answer is yes. Hedge funds specializing in alternative financing rather than alternative trading have sprung up in every category of asset-backed lending and have taken up the banner in areas where banks have either been too bureaucratic or too risk-averse to make the leap. The end result has been funds that are completely uncorrelated to the traditional financial markets and have so far been delivering above average returns at lower volatility.

SUBPRIME AUTO FINANCE

For example, Centrix Financial, a Denver, Colorado–based hedge fund that provides subprime auto financing, is interesting. Often commanding yields of 15 to 20 percent, each loan is insured via an A-rated insurer to help in dealing with default risk. The typical borrower has limited credit history or impaired credit and is unable to qualify for a loan from the typical bank or auto lender.

The due diligence issues when examining a hedge fund in the auto finance space include examining the loan origination and servicing operation (since a fund could have thousands of loans outstanding and need to service each one) and the relationship between the lender and the insurer. Is the legal agreement regarding defaults lock-tight?

An investment in a pool of subprime auto finance loans has several interesting features:

- Largely a lack of correlation to the traditional asset classes such as stocks and bonds.
- High diversification. The average loan size is $16,000 and loans are diversified both geographically and by risk quality.
- Low volatility. The loans are not really interest rate sensitive since they are starting off at a much higher rate than where interest rates are. Also, since the loans are relatively short-term (two to five years), it is unlikely that any move in interest rates will occur so quickly as to affect the loans. Additionally, the loans have fixed rates and do not change regardless of interest rate levels.

Centrix Capital Management has had no down months since 1999 in its managed accounts. It launched its hedge fund in December 2003, and the returns show the fund's success. Centrix ended 2004 up 9.987 and expects to achieve similar results in 2005.

Why don't banks offer subprime auto financing? "They are simply not set up to collect and service a subprime loan portfolio, as opposed to a prime portfolio," said Clark Gates, president of Centrix Capital Management. "We view these loans as investments and our entire business is set up to service these investments, [whereas] the banks would view them as receivables on their balance sheets in a diverse portfolio of receivables."

TRADE FACTORING

Another example is IIG Trade Opportunities Fund, a trade finance–focused hedge fund with $330 million in assets. An example of a trade finance transaction could occur when a large discount retailer buys a large shipment of electronics from a manufacturer. The retailer doesn't want to pay until the shipment arrives, but the manufacturer doesn't want to ship until the goods are paid for. Enter the trade finance fund, which loans the money for a two- to six-month period while the goods are assembled, shipped, and confirmed delivered. The loan terms are typically 15 percent annual interest. The main due diligence issue is not necessarily that there is default risk (is a Wal-Mart or Costco really not going to pay?) but that the fund manager is clearly aware of all the details of each transaction ("Where are the remote controls we ordered for these TVs?"). Since IIG's inception in August 1998, the month Long-Term Capital Management (LTCM) suffered its collapse, they have not had a down month. In 1999, IIG's first full year doing business, the company ended up 10.982, with results improving even further in 2000 when they ended the calendar year up 13.240. While IIG's results have not since reached the levels they did in 2000, they continue to end each month on the plus side. Palm Beach Finance Partners, another fund in the trade finance arena, also has yet to see red in any month since establishment in 2002. Again, this company shows extraordinary results, finishing 2003 up 12.526 and 2004 up 11.583.

HARD-MONEY REAL ESTATE LENDING

Another area where hedge funds are popping up is in hard-money lending on real estate. Michael Druckman, who also invests in delinquent credit card debt, runs the fund Equity Income Partners, which lends money to credit-impaired individuals using real estate as collateral. An example of this might be a person who has bad credit (perhaps a bankruptcy in the past, perhaps no income) who owns a $2 million home and needs to borrow $1 million. Druckman will lend the $1 million, at a fairly high double-digit interest rate, and the $2 million home will be collateral. If the borrower defaults, Druckman has no compunction about foreclosing on the asset. "I tell my friends not to borrow money from me," Druckman told me, "because I will foreclose and then we won't be friends. Some of my best months are when I foreclose."

Equity Income Partners will never lend more than 67 percent loan to value. In other words, on a $1 million home the maximum they would lend would be $670,000. Why wouldn't banks do this lending? A couple of reasons:

- Banks tend to focus on the individual. They want long-term, creditworthy customers. They don't care as much about the assets because they do not view themselves as being in the business of foreclosing and having to liquidate those assets.
- These hard-money loans tend to be short-term, one- or two-year loans. If banks can't wrap it up into a 30-year piece of paper and securitize it, they aren't interested.

Druckman's results since the inception of his fund in 1989 aren't so bad. The fund has never had a down month, and has ended calendar years up as much as 13.348 in 1990. Similar success was repeated in 2004 when the fund ended up 13.072.

An interview with Michael Druckman of Equity Income Partners on hard-money real estate lending follows.

> ***How do you identify loans?***
> Perspective loans are brought to us by independent mortgage brokers for consideration. Galileo [Druckman's fund] does first position mortgage loans at no more than 67.5 percent loan to value. Careful analysis is done on the liquidation value of the property that is the security for the loan.
>
> ***How do you value property?***
> Liquidation value of properties is provided by an independent third party appraisal and, more importantly, due diligence on my part as to the actual liquidation value.
>
> ***Why aren't banks doing this?***
> The sole reason that we make loans of this nature and banks don't is that the banks' criteria are based upon the borrower's ability to demonstrate that they can service the debt. Although banks require an appraisal and a deed of trust, the actual property is in-

consequential to the loan approval process. They look at the borrower's ability to pay. We, on the other hand, really do not care about the borrower's ability to service the debt. We look solely to the value of the collateral (property). Based on our criteria, one could assume that we are making high-risk loans. Quite the contrary. In the 18-plus years that we have been making these loans, we have had 13 foreclosures. It just so happens that we have made a profit on each of the 13 foreclosures.

What are typical interest rates?
The interest rates that we are able to charge on these loans are not affected by what the Fed fund rate does or what Alan Greenspan does. These are strictly driven by current market forces. In 18 years, the lowest rate we have charged is 11 percent, and the highest is 14 percent. We are currently [mid-2005] loaning at 12.5 percent to 13 percent.

What happens in a Japan-style crash of real estate?
We have been making loans since 1987. From 1987 to about 1994, the Arizona real estate economy was severely depressed. The savings and loan debacle put severe pressure on real estate values and yet we were able to make profitable loans. Current times are much better and we are able to make profitable loans. Because we loan no more than 67.5 percent loan to value, property values would need to drop by 32.5 percent before we would be affected.

Is real estate in a bubble?
Real estate bubbles are generally created by speculators, and the real estate bubble that existed in the late 1980s was in fact due to speculation. I can only speak to the Arizona economy. I cannot speak to other parts of the country, but we don't make loans there. The Arizona real estate economy is driven by demand and it is my feeling that as long as the sun continues to shine, and the aging baby boomers in upstate New York, Chicago, and Wisconsin continue to relocate to the sunbelt, our real estate economy will remain healthy. This is not to say that it is not cyclical, because it is. We have loaned through good times and bad, and I remain optimistic for the future.

What happens when interest rates rise? Do your rates rise along with them?
Our loans are for very short duration—two to three years. They are interest-only loans with a balloon. Increasing or decreasing prevailing interest rates have no effect on us, nor do we have interest rate risk.

Have you ever lost money on a loan?
No.

How did you get into the business?
The hard-money mortgage business represented a viable alternative to the equity and bond markets for my investment clients. One day I was approached by a mortgage broker who was looking for investor capital and we struck up a relationship. I saw the advantages of low correlation, low standard deviation, and high Sharpe ratio, and knew that this would be a positive alternative investment for my clients.

LIFE INSURANCE PREMIUM FINANCING

Much has already been written about the growing secondary market for life insurance policies, but the latest twist in this burgeoning market is an innovative asset-backed lending strategy called life insurance premium finance. Essentially, there is a class of seniors who would like to have life insurance policies for various reasons but acquiring a policy at that age can result in expensive premiums. However, because the secondary market in life insurance policies establishes a market and means for valuing policies, it is possible for the seniors to borrow the money to pay for the premiums and use the policy itself as the asset backing the loan.

Why would seniors want to do this?

- Most of their assets could be illiquid or tied up in other investments.
- They could have large estates for which the death benefit would help pay the estate tax.
- They could be approved for a larger policy than they can afford the premiums for.
- A traditional bank might not allow them to use their policy to back the loan and may force the senior to liquidate assets in the case of a default.

Why would investors want to lend?

- The lender will typically receive 10 to 15 percent interest on the loan.
- The lender is provided with an alternative investment opportunity to traditional asset classes.

However, as with any investment, there are certain risks, which include liquidity in the secondary marketplace, changes in the regulatory environment, and increased life expectancies.

Several hedge funds have started up in this area, on the basic idea that the fund will lend to senior citizens 65 or older the premiums to pay for their life insurance policies. These seniors are often wealthy, looking to protect their estate, and often qualify for large insurance policies. The loans are five-year loans paying 10 to 15 percent interest and are nonrecourse. In other words, if there is a default then the fund can foreclose on the policy and continue paying premiums or sell the policy in the secondary market. If the insured party decides to keep their life insurance policy they would have to pay back the loan plus interest. Should the insured elect not to keep the life insurance policy they can relinquish the policy to the fund instead of paying the interest payments. If the insured dies during the loan period, then the loan is likely to be paid back from the death benefit and the insured's estate will owe a prepayment penalty that is paid out of the death benefit.

In addition, this strategy has numerous barriers to entry for successful implementation and execution. The following skills and capabilities are essential:

- The ability to value and source life insurance policies with set criteria.
- The ability to sell the policies in the secondary market to life settlement firms or institutions at competitive prices.
- The ability to coordinate with medical underwriters, actuaries, and other service providers to assess the mortality rating on individual policies as well as to create a diverse portfolio of policies.
- Expertise in the insurance regulatory environment that differs from state to state.

The secondary market for life insurance has evolved remarkably over the past six or seven years as institutional buyers have entered the market, purchasing pools of life settlements—life insurance policies for seniors age 65 and older. They are investing based on the law of averages and life expectancies. The investors who buy a pool of these policies with the expectation of paying premiums until they receive the death benefit, which averages around $2 million, are aiming to receive a 10 to 15 percent internal rate of return (IRR) over an average holding period of seven to eight years. Investors range from hedge funds to banks to endowments, and all use life settlements not only as a source of (sometimes significant) returns but also as a way to diversify away from the traditional asset classes of equities, bonds, and commodities.

Currently a $15 billion market, it is estimated by Bernstein Research that the life settlement industry will grow to $160 billion within the next several years. Factors driving the growth include:

- Individuals outliving the usefulness of their policies.
- Potential elimination of estate tax may result in the sale of many survivorship policies.
- Low interest rates that result in lower cash values within existing policies.
- Increasing use as a financial planning tool whereby an insured party sells his policy and then buys a new, cheaper policy with the assistance of the cash received from the old policy.

What are the risks in buying life settlements?

- Insured parties may live past their life expectancy, resulting in a lower return as more premiums are paid out. However, this risk is minimized when the investor buys a pool of policies where the law of averages is expected to play out.
- The investor in a pool of life settlements is initially cash flow negative. While all the insureds are still alive the investor is paying out the premiums. Eventually the death benefits become greater than the premium payments.
- Policies on the secondary market are inversely correlated with interest rates. Increasing interest rates will impact the prices that investors are willing to pay for policies.

The value of a policy is determined as a function of several criteria:

- The life expectancy of the insured.
- The type of policy.
- The amount of the premium payments.
- The amount of the death benefit.
- The rating of the insurance company.

As it has matured, this secondary market, which was almost nonexistent 10 years ago, has grown to $15 billion and will continue to grow exponentially. It has ultimately led to new profit opportunities for investors while indirectly allowing more people to afford life insurance.

TAX LIENS

While hedge funds can often be considered the "new banks" due to their ability to take financing risks where banks are either unwilling or unable to, hedge funds can also take on the role of the "new tax collector." The government is often in a position where it effectively lends its citizens money in the form of uncollected taxes that accrue interest. These are not loans in the traditional sense in that no money was ever extended to the citizen. Nevertheless, the amount due on property taxes has all the components of a distressed senior secured loan:

- It usually pays a high interest rate, ranging from 8 to 50 percent depending on the laws of the state or the city where the tax is supposed to be paid. Part of the reason for this is that although the tax is usually a small percentage of the overall value of the property, there is no way to value the creditworthiness of the people who owe the debt to the government. Everybody who owns a property must pay a tax, regardless of creditworthiness.
- It is usually the senior debt on the house, in front of even bank loans. However, IRS obligations may come first and again, depending on the state, a bankruptcy might interfere with the debt being repaid. Most likely, though, if a tax lien is not paid, then the owner of that lien can begin foreclosure proceedings on the property. Since the lien is usually worth between 3 and 7 percent of the value of the house, it is somewhat rare that a house owner will allow a foreclosure just to avoid paying the lien. Hence liens have a high probability of being paid and defaults are rare.

Typically, if a property owner is more than one year late on paying his property taxes, the state may sell the tax lien in an auction. Just as banks are loath to collect on every single piece of credit card debt or subprime auto loan, the government is not really set up to aggressively collect delinquent property taxes and would rather have a portion of the money to immediately use for whatever the taxes were budgeted for in the first place—schools, road development, fire department services, and so forth.

As with any investment, due diligence is required before buying a lien. Here are some of the areas that need to be covered:

- Make sure the auction is not so competitive that your yield goes down to a level where some other investment-grade vehicle might be a better use of your money.
- Although the ratio of the lien to the value of the property is typically so low that the property owner will not want to default, this is not always true. Make sure the property is not sitting on the site of a pollution dump, for example, where the property owner would be ecstatic if it went into foreclosure.

- Although the lien is senior to just about any other debt, make sure the IRS doesn't have a much bigger lien sitting over you, or that the bankruptcy laws of the state don't allow the property owner to drastically delay paying before a foreclosure can happen.
- Determine if there are any lawsuits against the property owner that would need to be settled before the lien is paid.

Tax liens are uncorrelated to any other asset class. Even if interest rates step up, it is unlikely the value of liens will go down because the yields on a tax lien could be upwards of 2,000 basis points, or 20 percent, higher than Treasury bill yields. Real estate values have little bearing on the value of tax liens. Even if the lien is as high as 10 percent of the property value, that's still a steep drop (over 90 percent) that the value of the house would have to fall before affecting the value of the lien. Consequently, hedge funds are quickly entering the arena and making the purchase of tax liens competitive. MD Sass, a New York–based family of hedge funds that has a primary focus in asset-backed securities, has a hedge fund that focuses on tax liens and has racked up returns ranging from 8 to 14 percent annually. Orion Capital, run by former Citigroup vice president Richard Chen, is another hedge fund focused on the tax lien space. Optimum Realty Corporation of Elmhurst, Illinois, offers a fixed 8 percent return and uses the money invested to purchase tax liens.

TAXI MEDALLIONS

Although this chapter is titled "Hedge Funds Are the New Banks," it is not unusual now to see public companies participating in the alternative lending game, particularly in areas that banks would not touch with a 10-foot pole. I've lived in and around New York City nearly all my life, but I don't like to drive. I'll be honest, I drive only a few times a year. I almost always use some form of public transportation. The subway is the fastest way to get from one end of New York City to the other. But in a taxicab you can work, talk on the phone, relax, and so forth, even though it takes longer and is more expensive. In New York City there are 12,187 licensed cabdrivers. Everybody who works in Manhattan, at 5 P.M. on a rainy day, wishes there were 100,000 cabdrivers. But there are not, nor will there ever be. The supply of cabdrivers is limited by law. In order to drive a cab in New York City you need a city-issued medallion.

In 2004 the city decided to add 900 more cabdrivers, 300 per year. The process by which it made that decision took years. The New York City government even commissioned environmental studies showing that an extra 300 cars each year wouldn't result in a massive increase in car pollution. Mind you, there are some 2 million cars driving around Manhattan every day, but this is the kind of bureaucracy it takes to add even 300 cars. So the number of cabdrivers is going to stay largely capped.

Because the supply of medallions is severely limited and the demand is so high (why not take a job with no boss, set your own hours, meet new people all day long, etc.), the price of medallions has soared ever since the first day they were issued. However, many of the people who would like these jobs and medallions cannot afford them. Often they are immigrants looking for work, or people who have become unemployed when other industries have experienced a downturn. These are not the type of people who can typically get loans from the mainstream banks.

This brings us to NASDAQ-traded TAXI Medallion Financial Corporation, which finances taxicab medallions. Medallion prices have gone from $200,000 in 1997 to almost $400,000 now. Since medallions first originated in 1937 they have gone up in value an average of 13 percent per year, beating the Dow's 10 percent per year. A company like TAXI operates by borrowing money and then using that money to lend to the people buying the medallions, typically at 60 percent loan to value (in other words, if a medallion costs $300,000, the most TAXI would lend would be $180,000). Its profits are the spreads between the interest it is being paid and the interest it is paying.

Additionally, TAXI started Medallion Bank so it can take in deposits. Other than creating an insurance company (and one where you can keep cost of float at zero), starting a bank is the best way to get cheap money (think about how much interest you get in your checking account—almost nothing). In fact, during 2004 the margin spread between TAXI's borrowing costs and the interest payments it receives has risen from 372 to 437 basis points. This occurred despite the Fed raising interest rates.

TAXI is run by father and son team Alvin and Andrew Murstein. To say they know the taxicab business in New York City is an understatement. In 1937, their grandfather bought one of the first medallions for $10. They have been in the business in one shape or another ever since. In addition to their business of lending against medallions they also own 150 medallions and will probably increase that inventory with the current release of new medallions. The last time the city sold medallions, in 1996 and 1997, it sold 400, and the price of medallions went up more than 10 percent over the next year, demonstrating that the slight increase in supply did not dampen the demand.

The fact that the city has, in the early 2000s, passed several price increases will also increase demand for the new medallions being offered. An interesting feature of this business is that economic weakness is not immediately bad for TAXI—more people losing their jobs means more people wanting to become cabdrivers who will need medallions.

In later chapters I will cover other forms of financing being taken up more recently by hedge funds.

CHAPTER 2

Activism

The average investor is usually not big enough to take large stakes in a company, approach management teams, and demand changes that will create value for shareholders. However, it is possible to understand the techniques of the successful activist investors, and to piggyback into and out of positions with those investors. Because of the size of the positions these activist hedge funds have to take, the smaller investor can often benefit by being more nimble than the fund that often has to buy up 10 percent of a company in order to have any influence.

The investment world is largely made up of passive investors, and I think the time when passive investors could produce returns greater than 5 percent annually is largely over. When I say "passive" I'm including not only the lawn-chair investors who sit around and speculate how growth in China is going to affect chip demand in the United States (in which case Intel may or may not be a buy, depending on the premise being discussed) but any of the 100,000-plus mutual fund analysts, day traders, and others making theories on the markets, who then try to benefit from investing based on those theories. None of these people have any edge. They are all handing money back and forth to each other. Some days some of the analysts are smart, and they make money on those days, but the very next day other analysts and investors win the game and take their money back. In order to gain an edge, one needs to find a situation that is undervalued and then actively try to create an edge by taking the steps necessary to unlock that value.

It is not enough to know that a company owns valuable real estate that has never been reflected on their balance sheet and hence is undervalued by the stock market. The company has to actually sell that real estate and then take steps to distribute the resulting cash to shareholders, or to somehow use that cash to create a higher return on equity than by simply distributing it. But the company may not want to do it for various reasons. Management is entrenched and they might not want to take chances. They simply like sitting on the valuable assets, taking their salaries, and to hell with shareholders. These are the so-called *value traps*, where there is significant value but shares keep going lower because entrenched management simply wants to spend 100 days of the year on the golf course.

Activist hedge funds try to find undervalued companies, build positions in those companies, and then declare war. Whatever it takes, the activist will attempt to unlock value. As one activist hedge fund manager, Bob Chapman, told me, "It takes a certain type of personality to be an activist. You can't hold back from the battle at all."

The typical modus operandi of an activist is as follows. First, find a situation that is undervalued. *Undervalued* does not necessarily mean the stock is trading for less than book value. This is much different than the Graham-Dodd style of value investing. An activist fund's definition of undervalued might include companies that have steady cash flows but low return on equity, implying that management is not deploying the cash flows into profitable businesses. Hence, those cash flows either could be deployed better by management or might be better off being distributed to shareholders or used for a stock buyback. In other words, by all appearances, the stock might even seem to be overvalued, but the activist investor is digging deeper than the balance sheet.

Second, begin building a position. The activist wants to build a big enough position where he can be heard, but not so big initially that he is forced into filing with the Securities and Exchange Commission (SEC) before he is ready. The SEC requires a form 13D filing whenever an investor or group of investors takes a position in a company that is greater than 5 percent. Many investors will build up 4.9 percent positions in a company and then, in one push, buy as many shares as possible as quickly as possible so that by the time the 13D is filed, the position is now closer to 10 percent than 5 percent. Part of the challenge for a hedge fund that does activism is to pick companies of the appropriate size. If an activist fund is managing $100 million then it makes no sense to be an activist in companies that are over $1 billion in market capitalization since it is unlikely the fund will ever take a big enough position to be able to throw weight around in such a company to the point that management is forced to listen.

Once the 13D filing is made, the activist can state in the filing itself the reasons for taking the position and the steps that need to be taken by management to unlock value. If more shares are bought, the activist can file amendments to his initial 13D filing, further stating or restating the reasons. This is often very effective PR as all major shareholders of the company will read these filings, as will proxy services, such as Institutional Shareholder Services (ISS), which help institutions determine which side of proxy contests to vote on. We will take a look at some successful 13D battles later in this chapter.

The third step is to state what changes need to be made in the company. Typical demands of activists include:

- Hire a new management team. For whatever reason, the CEO has refused to unlock value and now is the time to go.
- Place nominees of the activist on the board of directors. The current board of directors might be filled with cronies of the management team. This is critical since the board has a fiduciary responsibility to the shareholders, and if the management team is not being responsive to shareholder interests then it is important to know if the board is truly independent. Some activists have to resort to detailed background checks and investigations in order to determine if board members are independent. Members of a board can appear to be independent until it is discovered that the board member and the CEO of the company were college roommates 30 years earlier, or they jointly own a chalet in Aspen, or they play golf together three times a week. Basic resume checks in many cases will not determine whether a board member is truly independent.
- Sell the company. Maybe the company is in a declining industry and there is simply no way to unlock further value. The best thing to do might be to sell the company.
- Liquidate the company, or part of it. For instance, let's say a software company happens to own a lot of real estate. Sell the real estate and distribute the proceeds to shareholders.

One of the more successful recent and very public examples of activism was in the case of Disney. For many years Roy Disney, the nephew of Walt, and his partner Stanley Gold had been unhappy with the reign of Michael Eisner as CEO of Disney. Between the $100 million-plus payout of Michael Ovitz after only a year as president of the company, and the enormous $200 million payout of Jeffrey Katzenberg (both situations could have been settled for much smaller amounts had they been done earlier), plus missed opportunities in China, the failure of Euro Disney, and other similar mishaps, Roy Disney and Stanley Gold decided to press for change. They engaged in a proxy fight to remove Eisner from the board and started an enormous PR campaign to rally shareholder support behind them. Eventually Eisner was removed from the board and resigned as CEO.

Although Roy Disney and Stanley Gold had a special interest in Disney, they have also engaged in recent activism over other companies. In the first half of 2005 they took two new positions that required them to file 13D filings. The two companies were iPass and Intrado. These companies had similar features, which allow us to see what type of value Disney and Gold (through their hedge fund, Shamrock Holdings) look for before taking positions. It is not enough to simply piggyback on investors' positions. Rather, it helps to see what philosophy underlies their holdings so that before taking positions ourselves we can see what guideposts to look at and determine whether to build more of a position or to exit. It is also helpful simply to learn the approaches of successful investors.

The two positions Disney and Gold built had several things in common:

- Both companies had consistent cash flows. Revenue and profits had gone up each year in the past three years for both companies.
- Both had great balance sheets. iPass was sitting on $158 million in cash and had no debt, and Intrado was sitting on $40 million in cash and had only $4 million in debt.
- Both had low and inconsistent returns on equity, suggesting that cash used on outside ventures was not being used productively.
- Both companies had single-digit ratios when looking at enterprise value divided by cash flow from operations. iPass had an enterprise value (market cap minus net cash) of $219 million, and cash flow from operations over the previous 12 months was $35 million. Intrado had an enterprise value of $213 million with cash flow generated from operations of $27 million.

Both companies are also peripherally in the wireless space, suggesting that Shamrock has a macro-based opinion on the wireless sector that is driving their bottom-up investing.

iPass provides the software that lets enterprises enable their mobile workers to connect up wirelessly to corporate databases. Intrado provides outsourced emergency calling services. For instance, if you have a phone from Cingular Wireless and dial 911, then your call is being handled by Intrado, which routes you to the appropriate public safety agency, providing all your ID and number information.

Both iPass and Intrado also operate in growing sectors of the economy. Each year, more workers are going wireless, because of outsourcing, increasingly mobile sales forces, or simply work conditions that allow people to work outside the office, benefiting iPass. Intrado, because of Federal Communications Commission (FCC) rules requiring phone companies to meet certain 911 standards, has become increasingly in demand to help voice-over-Internet protocol (VoIP), wireless, competitive local exchange carriers (CLECs), and other carriers meet the FCC standards.

In May 2005, Shamrock filed that it owned 4.5 million shares of iPass at an average price of $5.30, costing it about $27 million. Shamrock did not make a statement as to why it had made this investment, although it did make the investment from its activist fund.

With Intrado, Shamrock first filed a 13D on May 26, 2005, saying it owned a little more than 1 million shares, or about 6.2 percent of the company, at an average price of around $12.50. On June 26, Shamrock filed another 13D, detailing its concerns and recommendations for the company and also suggesting that the company has not been responsive. Specifically, it said:

> *In May, I contacted George Heinrichs to request that he arrange an introductory meeting for me with the Lead Director of Intrado. Subsequent to that request, Shamrock filed a Schedule 13D disclosing our 6.2 percent interest in the Company. Eventually, the requested meeting was arranged for June 23rd in Longmont. Unfortunately, at the last minute, you cancelled, and now have agreed to meet with us on July 27th.*

And then later:

> *I am taking the liberty of sending a copy of this letter directly to your fellow Directors because it appears that my prior correspondence with George was not forwarded to them as requested.*

As is common with activist letters, they provide great insight into how to extract more value from a company. Shamrock's main concern with Intrado was that although customers and revenue were steady, return on equity had not been doing well; this indicated that there could be a better use of money. Among the suggestions, Shamrock advocated including a diagnostic review to assess the success of all of its initiatives:

> *The primary areas of focus for this review would be a detailed and thorough assessment of historical financial performance, including profitability of major project initiatives and capital allocation decisions. It has been our experience that, with the assistance of management, such a review could be completed within 60 to 90 days and at a modest cost.*

These statements also suggest that the company might not need all of the cash on the balance sheet, since the customers are all long-term and cash is being steadily generated. Specifically:

> *Because the Company has a solid customer base, steady and recurring subscription revenues, and very little debt, it appears to us that the Board ought to consider returning to shareholders a significant amount of the Company's excess cash balances. We believe an overly capitalized balance sheet often results in sub-optimal capital allocation decisions. Write-offs and losses associated with the commercial database initiative (CDB), Palladium, and the bmd wireless acquisition, that collectively total approximately $30 million, represent specific examples justifying our concerns.*

And finally, these statements suggest that company compensation, particularly option grants, be tied to performance.

Piggybacking on top of Shamrock's SEC filings would have resulted in great initial success. When they first filed a 13D the stock price was at $12.50. Three months later the stock price was at $16.50, over 30 percent higher. The stock went up as a combination of market excitement that activists were getting involved and building positions as well as anticipation that management was possibly going to respond to the activist demands.

Although, as can be seen in Figure 2.1, there was a short jump up

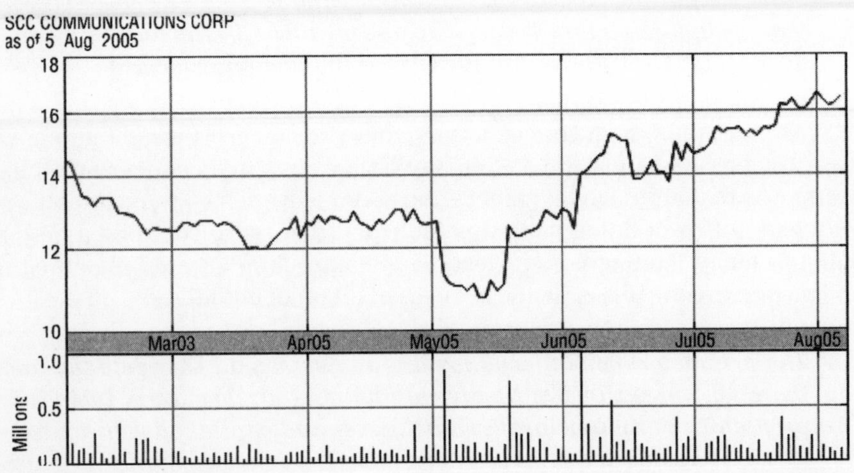

FIGURE 2.1 Intrado
Source: http://finance.yahoo.com/. Reproduced with permission of Yahoo! Inc. © 2005 by Yahoo! Inc. YAHOO! and the YAHOO! logo are trademarks of Yahoo! Inc.

when Shamrock initially filed a 13D, there was still plenty of time to enter into the position (at better prices than Shamrock's) and then continue the ride up. This example underlines the main reasons for following the latest 13D filings, reading them, and potentially acting on them. Some of the best 13D writers include activist funds Chap-Cap Partners, run by Robert Chapman, and Third Point, run by Dan Loeb, and it is worthwhile reading through some of their filings, sometimes called "extreme 13D filings." Here are some of the reasons I like these filings:

- I can get the insights of a great investor. Shamrock, Chap-Cap, and Third Point all have enviable track records, returning 20 percent or more per year to their investors. Their 13D filings usually contain brutally honest assessments of the results of their due diligence, both the positives and negatives—what they like about the companies (after all, they have bought up more than 5 percent of the company) and what they don't like (hence the reason for their activism). Learning the extent of their due diligence is always a fruitful lesson.
- When a CEO is accused of all the things these activists accuse their respective CEOs of, it would normally seem to be a red flag: Oh, a CEO is paying off all his friends through advisory fees—*don't invest*! And yet these guys not only invest, they back up the truck. These guys go where the fires are burning hot and attempt to put them out.
- These letters are a step-by-step guide on how to turn around a company. It is refreshing to get these thoughts and not the bland cheerleading that usually accompanies SEC filings. Whenever a retail investor can get hold of a snippet of honesty in a public document, it is well worth the read.

In some of the following examples I include the entire filing, somewhat against the request of my editor at Wiley. In the case of Shamrock and Intrado, it was possible to summarize the salient points and move on. In the cases of "extreme 13Ds" it is a bit more interesting to see the approach these investors take throughout the entire filing. Every paragraph in their filings hammers home their arguments about why they are investing, what is going wrong with the company, and what the activists plan on doing about it. Additionally, the filings are entertaining in their entirety.

In December 2002, Robert Chapman accumulated a 7 percent position in Misonix, a maker of ultrasonic medical devices. The stock had fallen from a high near 10 to below 4 when Chapman decided to take issue and get involved. He started off with a letter to CEO Terrence Cassidy, which I excerpt here. It is a rather large excerpt, but I wanted to include the full filing, not only for the entertainment value but to understand the level of detail that went into investigating the company and CEO, the attempts at communication with the company prior to filing the 13D, and the recommendations and analysis that go along with making an investment in a company that may not have many redeeming qualities on the surface but ultimately has value that can be unlocked.

> For months on end, Chapman Capital attempted to garner your attention to the stagnating market value and persistent undervaluation of NWH's [National Wireless Holdings] shares. Finally, after being redirected by your administrative assistant Carl Nicola on October 10, 2002, I was blessed with the sound of your soothing voice when I caught you at home around 10:30 A.M. EST during an apparent "sick day" away from your duties at NWH. Your reputation for shareholder disgust preceded you, leaving me somewhat prepared for something other than a "red carpet reception." However, nothing outside of reading your second ex-wife's publicly available divorce filings could have prepared me for the execration that you delivered that morning. Within seconds, you managed to attack one of NWH's largest shareholders using some of the most profane language I have ever heard during such a brief period of time. I was treated to a variety of boasts and blasphemy, including your claims that you were "the best God damn telco investor alive," "I don't give a shit about the fuckin' shareholders," and my personal favorite, "I'm going to come over there and kick your fuckin' ass." I have trouble comprehending how you could have determined this to be proper executive comportment, especially with such a large institutional shareholder as your audience. So X-rated was your onslaught that I doubt that even rap stars Eminem or Ice Cube would allow such verbiage to reach their children's ears unshielded. However, should you decide to change careers from what we view as a failed corporate executive to a Wall Street rapper, we recommend that you name your band "E.W.A.," standing of course for "Executivz Wit' Attitude." Furthermore, given that a rapper's zip code is considered to be crucial to his standing in "the hood," I can think of no better name for your debut CD than "E.W.A.—Straight Outta Hampton."
>
> So mesmerized was our firm by your most beguiling behavior that we immediately began an investigation into your background in a quest to better understand the root of your apparent dereliction at the helm of NWH. We figured that your brutish behavior, though never excusable for a public company CEO, might find some rational explanation in a resume replete with accomplishment and wealth creation. However, our inquiry revealed a career with a rather mixed pedigree.
>
> Though much of the criticism contained herein is the opinion of Chapman Capital L.L.C. and other past/current shareholders, I am

confident you will recognize that we have provided substantial evidence to support our views.

It seems that you endured a 15-year tenure at Allen & Co. before decamping after reaching the less-than-impressive "vice president and principal—corporate finance" title. This departure seems to have preceded an extremely brief stint as "chief financial consultant and investment banking adviser" of Touchstone Video Network (TVN) in the fall of 1988. Inexplicably, the TVN experience is not mentioned in your biographical background section of NWH's recent proxy statements. Your apparently forgettable TVN employment came and went around the time that you served on the board of directors of Eagle Telephonics Inc. (last traded at 5c/share on the Pink Sheets). After stumbling upon news of your second divorce on the Internet, we considered giving you the benefit of the doubt by ascribing your volatile behavior to marital remorse. However, after reading your then-wife's court pleading that she "vacated the marital residence because the husband emotionally and verbally abused" her, we concluded that your contumely was likely the cause rather than effect of apparent marital and professional setbacks.

The September 21, 1998, *Palm Beach Post* article on national wireless holdings seems to have sealed your reputation for repugnance, arrogance, and delusion. The article contains many mind-boggling lines, the lowlights of which follow:

- "Now, that BellSouth deal [that "turned nearly a ninefold profit on its investment"] is what Terrence Cassidy, the CEO and president of National Wireless, cites to attract investors. He tells them he is capable of other such coups"—fallaciously implying that the BellSouth "coup" was of Terry Cassidy's doing and not the brainchild and result of Mr. Michael Specchio, and lacking any real predictive power in hindsight given NWH's performance since the article's publication.
- " 'He's an investor's investor,' said Richard Koe, general partner at Astoria Capital Partners, in Portland, Oregon, owner of 7.1 percent of National Wireless stock as of May. 'The product is Terry Cassidy and his ability to find opportunity.' " Koe would later come to his senses and lead the successful opposition to your proposal for a lavish amendment to the 1997 Equity Incentive Plan. In an apparent allergic reaction to your managerial cooking, Astoria vomited its investment in NWH in the fall of 2001, creating a six-year low tick for the stock.
- "Cassidy said in April that he scheduled the shareholders meeting in Miami so that New York analysts and investors wouldn't come.

> He could not be reached for comment for this article. His New York office said for a month that he was traveling." The idea of a public company's CEO locating his shareholder meeting so that shareholders wouldn't attend is unimaginable, and the arrogance that accompanies that CEO insouciantly disclosing this to a reporter, the year after being paid $420,000 but before taking off for a month of travels, inconceivable.

Chapman Capital's discovery of your involvement in the Pine Top Insurance scandal of 1985 deepened our suspicions of ineptitude. On March 22, 1985, Greyhound Corporation sold the domestic units of Pine Top Insurance (Pine Top) to Whitney Financial Group Inc. (Whitney) for about $28 million, the book value of the units as agreed to by Whitney. Whitney, a Delaware corporation based in Phoenix, Arizona, was controlled by one Terrence S. Cassidy, who owned 100 percent of its voting stock. Accompanying Mr. Cassidy in this management buyout of Pine Top were partners Glenn Herbst (President of Pine Top), Robert M. Brown, George M. Powers (Chairman) and H. Loren Hawley (Vice Chairman). The apparently ill-conceived Pine Top deal masterminded by you began to unravel almost from day 1. According to the July 4, 1988, issue of *Business Insurance*, Greyhound resumed control of Pine Top only a few months after Whitney took control "because of internal problems at Whitney resulting in litigation among its owners, directors, and officers." We reviewed with horror the litigation between you and your partners at Whitney, especially the allegations of fraud, deception, and boardroom manipulation as competing parties fought for control. Shockingly, Pine Top, the target of what one would hope was extensive due diligence, was apparently already insolvent by over $100 million (over three times the book valued apparently estimated by your investment group) at the time your acquisition was announced. By June 1986, Pine Top had been placed in voluntary rehabilitation. Had Bryan Burrough not been occupied writing *Barbarians at the Gate*, the classic story of the RJR Nabisco LBO [leverage buyout] battle, I feel he could have written a comic version about the story of Whitney Financial, starring you as the bumbling corporate tycoon, entitled *Buffoons at the Gate*. Perhaps you and your partners should have invested more time understanding the business you were attempting to acquire rather than suing each other over who would control the company and the cash allegedly diverted from it.

While dismayed by your litigation against your business partners in the Pine Top deal, we were even more stunned to learn that you served as defendant as well as plaintiff in this financial meltdown. According to the July 4, 1988, issue of *Business Insurance*, Illinois insurance director John E. Washburn sued you and other parties, charging responsibility for the insurer's collapse. Indeed, the suit, which sought an unspecified amount of damages, alleged Pine Top's insolvency "was directly and proximately caused by the negligence and mismanagement of its directors and officers." Specifically relating to your own actions, the suit accuses Pine Top's former parent, Whitney Financial Group of Phoenix, Arizona, "of misappropriating funds during its brief ownership of the insurer in 1985." The suit accused three officers of Whitney—Robert A. Brown, Terrence S. Cassidy, and H. Loren Hawley—of negligence for "improperly withdrawing" $253,000 of the insurer's assets and asked the court to order the three to return this sum plus any additional damages the court deemed fair. Apparently so disgusted by the behavior exhibited in this matter was Judge William T. Marony of the Superior Court of Arizona that in a filing dated December 18, 1985, he gave you and your partners the unflattering label of "promoter."

We believe the credit for NWH's rich net asset value legitimately belongs to Michael J. Specchio and Joseph D. Truscelli, the respective founder/developers of the company's since-liquidated South Florida Wireless cable and existing electronic claims/transaction processing (ENS [Electronic Network Systems]) businesses. Contrary to your numerous reported professions of greatness for the not-so-incredible accomplishment of "not going broke while everyone else went to zero," we view you as nothing more than a Wall Street pretender who specializes in boisterously bullying the very shareholders to whom you owe a fiduciary duty. Though you have changed your tune in the wake of a public rebuke by NWH's largest public shareholder, when there was more praise to spread around you gave due credit for the highly-successful South Florida Television (MMDS) division to Mr. Specchio some two and a half years ago, saying at the time of his unfortunate resignation, "We wish Mike well in his other pursuits. He made a valuable contribution in developing and disposing of our wireless cable interests."

Indeed, we found reprinted on NWH's message board a 1986 article from the *Business Journal of Milwaukee* chronicling Mr. Specchio's now-legendary building from the ground up of a wireless cable empire that preceded his repeat performance at NWH. Mr. Truscelli, who you reportedly drove away as ENS CEO and president through a Machiavellian combination of dilution and derision, started this NWH division on a shoestring budget in his garage before Mr. Specchio brought it to NWH's attention some seven years ago. Just so that you do not feel left out, I suppose you should be given "boasting rights" to

NWH's 1995 abortive purchase of TLC Productions, Inc. ("The strategic decision to purchase the teleport and uplink company was motivated by the synergies of the two companies' technologies and the fact that TLC Productions is financially sound and produces positive cash flow."—Terrence Cassidy, May 3, 1995; in April 2001, NWH closed TLC Productions, Inc., leaving its net assets at a mere $91,000).

It seems to Chapman Capital that serving as one of Terrence S. Cassidy's business partners is a one-ingredient recipe for financial and emotional pain. Included in such a group of apparently abused parties are (a) your partners in the Pine Top Insurance fiasco (with whom you became embroiled in litigation), (b) your second ex-wife Caroline (with whom you battled over the custody rights to LuLu, a Yorkshire Terrier reportedly given to her as a Christmas present), (c) Joseph Truscelli (who left ENS, the company he founded, after his ownership stake was massively diluted), and (d) numerous other NWH shareholders, potentially including Richard Koe (head of former shareholder Astoria Capital Partners), Lawrence Zimmerman (a "brash New Yorker" who, according to the August 2, 1998 issue of the *Sunday Times*, "took the advice of a friend, Terry Cassidy, to concentrate on telecoms and has since made 'successful' investments in National Wireless and Winstar Communications"), and, of course, the current shareholders of NWH (who hold shares valued near the 1994 IPO price despite a 145 percent increase in the S&P 500 since that time). The only parties we can find who have profited in association with you are former NWH shareholders such as wireless pioneer Michael Specchio, who reportedly sold NWH shares into the delusional and brief mania driving the Internet/telco bubble of 2000.

I find it difficult to believe that your insulting behavior toward NWH's owners is condoned by the company's board of directors, which until now has been perceived to be comprised of prestigious members of the New York business community. When NWH was so unfortunate as to lose Michael Specchio as Chairman of the Board (shoes filled vacuously by you soon thereafter), former New York State Director of Economic Development Vincent Tese filled the vacated Board seat. Tese, "an experienced lawyer, investment adviser, and cable television executive," may be unaware of your deportment as NWH CEO given his being spread quite thin between reported directorships of no less than eight companies and virtually nonexistent (5,000 shares) ownership stake in NWH. Michael A. McManus Jr., former assistant to both Presidents Ford and Reagan and one-time lieutenant to New York financier Ronald Perelman, obviously has placed his own reputation in jeopardy if he has consented to your perturbing management style at NWH. I find it unlikely that Mr. McManus desires a repeat of the disaster that followed his time served as director of RGB Computer & Video (a.k.a. Saf T Lok Incorporated, the highly controversial company whose shares last traded for $0.0001 each). Additionally, Mr. Thomas R. DiBenedetto, president of Junction Investors, part-owner of the Boston Red Sox, and trustee of Massachusetts General Hospital and Trinity College, potentially could be embarrassed by your potentially erratic actions. Mr. Louis B. Lloyd, president of Belfinance Securities, Inc., former CEO of Republic New York Securities Corporation, and former senior executive of Shearson Lehman Brothers and Morgan Stanley & Co., may find that the potential upside of his mere 10,000-share position in NWH is capitated by his association with a man of your apparent character.

With HIPAA [Health Insurance Portability and Accountability Act] gaining momentum and set to crash on the shores of U.S. health care customers in the next few months, the full value of NWH's ENS division should be apparent to any potential buyer. ENS's customers, both current and prospective, must become compliant through software and IT solutions like those offered by ENS or face major repercussions. These HIPAA-compliant solutions must limit access to protected data and provide audit trails about those who access files for privacy and security rules. More relevant to NWH's Electronic Network Systems (ENS) division, any health care company must ensure HIPAA compliance with any provider or intermediary payer directly (EDI) connected to their systems for eligibility inquiry, claim status inquiry, remittance, and advice distribution. ENS's PASS (Pre-Adjudication Software System), which assists payers to improve the ratio of electronic claims that can be auto-adjudicated, is simply in the right place at the right time. It has been incumbent upon you, ever since you began the rumored auction process for ENS many months ago, to find the buyer willing to offer NWH the highest price and thus capitalize on the demand spike created by HIPAA's looming deadline. To date, you appear to have failed to accomplish this task, despite rumored interest (Yahoo! Finance: http://messages.yahoo.com and enter symbol "NWIR") from the likes of Proxymed, Inc. (NASDAQ: PILL) and others.

Since Michael Specchio's propitiously timed development and sale of South Florida Television to BellSouth for some $50 million in stock six years ago, NWH has to its credit very little that has elevated the Company's shares. I am not sure how much longer you expect NWH's shareholders to tolerate your disrespectful nonperformance in maximizing shareholder value. However, I can tell you that Chapman Capital L.L.C., overseeing an initial investment position in NWH that the IRS deems "long term," has reached its threshold of pain. As a result, we demand that you either (a) sell NWH, as a whole or through a two-step transaction led by the auction of ENS, to the highest bidder, or (b) submit your resignation immediately. Should you gracefully fall on your sword by choosing the latter option, NWH shareholders should rest comfortably knowing that Chapman Capital has lined up several CEO candidates with far more experience in the affairs of ENS than the man they would supersede. Regarding the all-too-familiar subject of litigation, it would not surprise our firm in the least if your knee-jerk reaction to this dispatch were to phone one of your many legal counselors to initiate spurious litigation against NWH's own shareholder. Please be on notice that our firm salivates at the idea of commencing the discovery process on NWH's records as we seek to confirm other suspicions we have regarding your tenure at the Company.

Very truly yours,
Robert L. Chapman, Jr.

This letter was followed up by another 13D filing on May 6, 2003, excerpted below.

On April 28, 2003, Mr. Chapman telephoned Mr. McManus to invite him to visit the Los Angeles headquarters of Chapman Capital, the general partner of one of the Issuer's then largest shareholders. Mr. McManus countered by stating that he already had invited Mr. Chapman to visit the Issuer's headquarters for a "plant tour." Mr. Chapman responded that it was public knowledge that Mr. McManus had traveled to visit other sizable shareholders of the Issuer, and that he would expect the same of Mr. McManus in the case of Chapman Capital. A brief digression followed regarding Mr. Chapman's making Mr. McManus aware that sources close to WebMD Corporation had communicated their views that such company was not interested in acquiring NWH, Inc. (on the board of directors of which Mr. McManus sits and in which Chap-Cap had a 13D position). Then, after Mr. Chapman asked Mr. McManus if Chapman Capital would be well advised to place a full page "Help Wanted" advertisement in the Wall Street Journal *for a replacement CEO of the Issuer, the latter became silent for several seconds before eerily inquiring of Mr. Chapman, "I would like to know if you are Satan." Disquieted by Mr. McManus' unholy interrogation, Mr. Chapman asked why Mr. McManus would ask such a question. Mr. McManus responded that he had read on the Yahoo! Finance message board that a poster had identified Mr. Chapman as "the Overlord of Hell" and that such poster had instructed Mr. McManus to "bow down before Satan." Mr. McManus questioned as to whether Mr. Chapman expected Mr. McManus to genuflect before him. Mr. Chapman, seeking to terminate such blasphemous blabber, replied, "Well, Mr. McManus, I am not an expert in the occult but if you would like to come out here, hold me down, and shave my head to check for three sixes burned into my skull, please let me know so that we can put this matter to rest." Mr. McManus declined Mr. Chapman's offer, and the conversation concluded.*

On May 9, 2003, Mr. Chapman received a telephone call at the offices of Chapman Capital from Mr. McManus. After several inane comments from Mr. McManus relating to his apparent fascination with the Yahoo! Finance message board, Mr. Chapman asked Mr. McManus if he was at that time within the Issuer's plant (as Mr. Chapman could hear background noises sounding like an assembly line). Mr. McManus responded, "Misonix doesn't have a plant." Mr. Chapman responded by asking Mr. McManus, if that were true, then why Mr. McManus had invited Mr. Chapman "to visit the plant." Suddenly, Mr. McManus seemed to remember that the Issuer did in fact have a plant "connected to Misonix's main building." Mr. Chapman asked Mr. McManus if he had ever actually "stepped foot" in this plant, rather than remain in his executive suite insulated from the Issuer's proletariat-class workers. Moreover, Mr. Chapman asked if Mr. McManus could please attempt to spend more time in this quasi-mythical plant to reduce the odds of the Issuer experiencing additional problems with the Food and Drug Adminstration. Mr. McManus replied that Misonix "never had any problems with the FDA." Mr. Chapman, startled by this second discrepancy from the truth in as many minutes, reminded Mr. McManus of a December 20, 2001, FDA "Warning Letter" sent to the Issuer by FDA District Director Thomas A. Allison and carbon copied to Issuer subsidiary President and CEO G. Wayne Moore. Seemingly flustered, Mr. McManus then became incoherent in the view of Mr. Chapman, leading to the conclusion of the conversation.

The CEO remained but the company did cut costs, reported better revenues and earnings, and the stock recovered accordingly to a high of 12.34 in April 2004 before settling down to its current level in the 6s. (See Figure 2.2.)

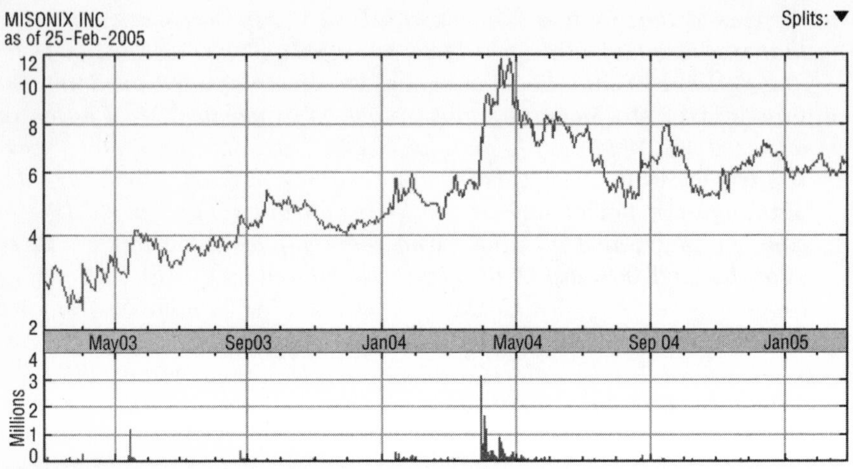

FIGURE 2.2 Misonix Inc
Source: http://finance.yahoo.com/. Reproduced with permission of Yahoo! Inc.

In March 2004 Chapman closed his fund after recovering from a surfing accident. He then proceeded to travel the world, settling down in mid-2005 to prepare to relaunch his fund.

Dan Loeb, from Third Point, doesn't shy away from a battle. In early 2005, Loeb became an activist in Star Gas (SGU), an oil and gas utility. On February 14, 2005, Loeb wrote to the CEO, as reported through SEC filings, documenting his concerns with the company and how he felt shareholder value could be unlocked. My favorite part of the letter is this:

> *Sadly, your ineptitude is not limited to your failure to communicate with bond and unit holders. A review of your record reveals years of value destruction and strategic blunders which have led us to dub you one of the most dangerous and incompetent executives in America. (I was amused to learn, in the course of our investigation, that at Cornell University there is an "Irik Sevin Scholarship." One can only pity the poor student who suffers the indignity of attaching your name to his academic record.)*

The entire letter is as follows and is worth reading not only for the humor but to see the level of due diligence that Loeb applies. Most investors, I think, would shy away from a company with these red flags. But Loeb clearly feels that the sins of the father should not be borne by the child, or, in this case, the company, which has legitimate oil and gas assets. Three weeks after SGU received this letter, CEO Irik Sevin resigned his post. Two months after that, the CFO resigned. In the subsequent quarterly reporting in May 2005, the company beat all expectations on revenues and earnings and the stock soared upwards. Here is the letter:

Mr. Irik P. Sevin
Chairman, President, and CEO Star Gas Partners L.P.
2187 Atlantic Street
Stamford, CT 06902

Dear Irik:

Third Point LLC ("Third Point") advises certain entities that hold 1,945,500 common units in Star Gas Partners L.P. ("Star Gas" or "the Company") (NYSE: SGU). Our 6 percent interest in the common units of the Company makes us your largest unit holder. Unlike the poor, hapless retail investors "stuffed" with purchases at the $24 level (many of whom are party to class action lawsuits against you personally and against the Company), we purchased our stake around these levels and took profits on about 500,000 shares near the $7 per unit level. Since your various acquisition and operating blunders have cost unit holders approximately $570 million in value destruction, I cannot understand your craven stance with respect to shareholder communications. We urged you to hold a conference call to discuss the Company's plight and to set forth a plan of action.

We have also tried to reach you on innumerable occasions only to be told that your legal counsel advised you against speaking to bondholders and shareholders due to the torrent of shareholder litigation currently being brought against senior management and the Company. We did receive a call from Company CFO Ami Trauber (who I was interested to learn previously worked at Syratech (NASD: SYRA) which currently trades at 6 pennies a share and is undergoing a restructuring of its debt). How peculiar that Ami, who is named in virtually all the same shareholder class action complaints that have been filed, is not subject to the same gag order mandated by Company counsel. Since you refused for months to take our numerous calls, I must regrettably communicate with you in the public forum afforded us by Section 13(d) of the Securities Exchange Act of 1934.

Sadly, your ineptitude is not limited to your failure to communicate with bond and unit holders. A review of your record reveals years of value destruction and strategic blunders which have led us to dub you one of the most dangerous and incompetent executives in America. (I was amused to learn, in the course of our investigation, that at

Cornell University there is an "Irik Sevin Scholarship." One can only pity the poor student who suffers the indignity of attaching your name to his academic record.) On October 18, 2004, Star Gas announced the suspension of its common unit dividend, causing an 80 percent crash in unit price from $21.60 on October 17 to $4.32 on October 18 and destroying over $550 million of value.

On November 18, 2004, after a modest recovery in the stock price, Star Gas announced the sale of its propane business, causing the common units to decline in price from $6.68 on November 17 to $5.55 on November 22. Management evidently felt this would create shareholder value when in fact it did the exact opposite. The Company apparently did not feel a fiduciary obligation to maximize value for unit holders, and elected not to return calls from major unit holders prior to the sale of the propane segment. Had you been more responsive, we could have warned you that this action would not create value. Shockingly, the Company also indicated that unit holders would be "passed through" a taxable gain on sale of up to $10.53 per share even though unit holders may have suffered a loss of over $15.00 a unit.

To add insult to unit holder injury, and to ensure you a dazzling place in the firmament of bad management, we learned that two members of the Company's special committee assigned to evaluate the sale of the propane business, Stephen Russell and William P. Nicolletti, received a one-time fee of $100,000 each! Was that really necessary given that you paid advisory fees to Lehman Brothers (your former employer), paid additional advisory fees to KeyBanc Capital for advising the special committee, and paid significant legal fees associated with the transaction? The dereliction of fiduciary duty is truly astounding and we demand that all fees paid to the special committee be repaid immediately by Mr. Russell and Mr. Nicolletti.

On December 17, 2004, Star Gas closed on a $260 million JP Morgan working capital facility. As of December 31, 2004, the Company was already in violation of its fixed charge coverage ratio of 1.1× to 1.0×. As a result, the Company has been forced to use $40 million of the $143.5 million in excess proceeds from the propane business sale for working capital purposes in order to maintain minimum availability on the working capital facility of $25 million to prevent a violation from occurring under the credit agreement. Clearly, JP Morgan did not expect EBITDA of $0 million (before nonrecurring items) for the quarter ending December 31, 2004, given that the deal closed December 17, 2004. I also presume that Peter J. Solomon (the Company's restructuring adviser) was not marketing a refinancing based on such projections.

In its Form 10K filed December 14, 2004 (with 17 days left in the quarter), the Company stated that heating oil volumes were down 7.2 percent year-over-year for the two months ended November 30, 2004. However, in its Form 10Q for the quarter ended December 31, 2004, the Company indicated that heating oil volumes were down 15 percent for the entire quarter. This would mean one of three things: (1) volumes were down over 50 percent in the last part of the year (hard to believe), (2) management does not have an accurate picture of where the business is heading, or (3) management felt it was unnecessary to update its unit holders on material information regarding its customers heading into the all-important winter season.

As mentioned above, for the quarter ended December 31, 2004, EBITDA declined to $0 million from $26 million the prior year. Heating oil volume was down 15 percent, gross margin per gallon was down over $0.05 or approximately 10 percent, but fixed costs (delivery, branch, G&A) were up 8 percent. This is unacceptable and will cause a death spiral. How are you rationalizing the cost structure of the business? Ami Trauber indicated to us that the Company believes it can improve EBITDA margin per gallon to historical levels of $0.12 (some of your competitors are at an approximate 50 percent premium to that). As your largest common unit holder, we insist that you provide a plan of action on how you will achieve that goal.

Furthermore, we would also like to understand why, even at its peak performance, the Company's margins are significantly lower than those of your competitors. We do not see any reason why a properly managed heating oil distribution business should not operate at least at your historical margin levels, if not at levels similar to the 17 percent margins enjoyed by your competitors. We would like to form a special committee of unit holders and would like to retain an independent consulting firm to evaluate the Company's operations and management performance; we are prepared to sign a confidentiality agreement in order to have access to the necessary Company data.

The Company received $153.5 million of net proceeds from the sale of the propane business. Star Gas has indicated it has until the end of the year to make use of this cash. However, the Company must pay interest on the MLP Notes of 10.25 percent per year, amounting to $15.7 million in annual costs (or almost $0.50 a unit) if the Notes are not repurchased immediately. We urge you not to destroy more value for unit holders than you already have; we believe that, unless there is a better use for the cash, the Note holders should be repaid as soon as practicable before that cash is burned away. However, if you think there is a better alternative than repaying the Note holders, such as tuck-in acquisitions, we would like to understand that strategy before cash is deployed.

The Company's expenditure on legal and banking fees is completely inexplicable and out of proportion to the Company's size, resources, and scant earnings. We estimate the Company has spent approximately $75 million in fees over the last four months (approximately 50 percent of SGU's market capitalization) related to make-whole payments, bridge financing, debt refinancing, advisory professional fees, and legal costs.

Furthermore, a careful reading of the small print in the Company's most recent Form 10K reveals a further record of abysmal corporate governance. In particular, your $650,000 salary for a company your size is indefensible given the spectacular proportions of your failure as an executive. Furthermore, given the magnitude of your salary, perhaps you can explain why the Company paid $41,153 for your professional fees in 2004 and why the Company is paying $9,328 for the personal use of company-owned vehicles. We questioned Mr. Trauber about the nature of this expense, and I was frankly curious about what kind of luxury vehicle you were tooling around in (or is it chauffeured?). He told us that you drive a 12-year-old vehicle. If that is so, then how is it possible that the Company is spending so much money on the personal use of a vehicle that is 12 years old?

Additionally, your personal use of a Company car appears to violate the Company's Code of Conduct and Ethics, which states that "All Company assets (e.g., phones, computers, etc.) should be used for legitimate business purposes." We demand that you cease accepting a car allowance for personal use of a Company vehicle, in apparent violation of the Company's Code of Conduct and Ethics. We also demand that you voluntarily eliminate your salary until dividend payments to common unit holders are resumed.

The Company's Code of Conduct and Ethics also clearly states under the section on Conflics of Interest, that "A conflict occurs when an individual's private interest interferes or even appears to interfere in any way with the person's professional relationships and/or the interests of SGP. You are conflicted if you take actions or have interests that may make it difficult for you to perform your work for SGP objectively and effectively. Likewise, you are conflicted if you or a member of your family receives personal benefits as a result of your position in SGP. . . . You should avoid even the appearance of such a conflict. For example, there is a likely conflict of interest if you:

"1. Cause SGP to engage in business transaction with relatives or friends; . . ."

By this clearly stated policy, how is it possible that you selected your elderly, 78-year-old mom to serve on the Company's board of directors and as a full-time employee, providing employee and unit holder services? We further wonder under what theory of corporate governance does one's mom sit on a Company board. Should you be found derelict in the performance of your executive duties, as we believe is the case, we do not believe your mom is the right person to fire you from your job. We are concerned that you have placed your greed and desire to supplement your family income—through the director's fees of $27,000 and your mom's $199,000 base salary—ahead of the interests of unit holders. We insist that your mom resign immediately from the Company's board of directors.

Irik, at this point, the junior subordinated units that you hold are completely out of the money and hold little potential for receiving any future value. It seems that Star Gas can only serve as your personal "honey pot" from which to extract salary for yourself and family members, fees for your cronies, and to insulate you from the numerous lawsuits that you personally face due to your prior alleged fabrications, misstatements, and broken promises.

I have known you personally for many years and thus what I am about to say may seem harsh, but is said with some authority. It is time for you to step down from your role as CEO and director so that you can do what you do best: retreat to your waterfront mansion in the Hamptons where you can play tennis and hobnob with your fellow socialites. The matter of repairing the mess you have created should be left to professional management and those who have an economic stake in the outcome.

Sincerely,
Daniel Loeb

One of the more successful recent activist funds has been the aptly named Pirate Capital. Started in 2002 by former Goldman Sachs executive Tom Hudson, the firm's assets have risen from $2 million to $800 million in less than three years and have notched in incredible returns during that time. In 2004 assets rose 30.02 percent, and through July 2005 Pirate Capital's assets were up 10.65 percent.

Piggybacking on top of their 13D filings would have resulted in several successes. For instance, they first filed a 13D on golf sportswear maker Cutter & Buck in July 2004, to report that they had amassed a greater than 5 percent position. (See Figure 2.3.)

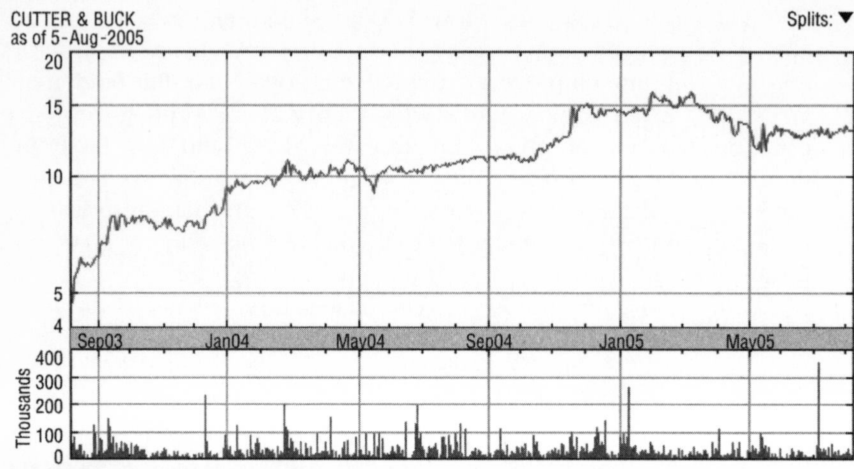

FIGURE 2.3 Cutter & Buck
Source: http://finance.yahoo.com/. Reproduced with permission of Yahoo! Inc. © 2005 by Yahoo! Inc. YAHOO! and the YAHOO! logo are trademarks of Yahoo! Inc.

They bought their shares between 9.40 and 10.60, and at the time of the filing, shares were around 10.50. One year later the shares were 25 percent higher at 13.09 despite the fact that sales were sluggish, and although they were cash flow positive throughout the year, guidance was continually lower. However, Pirate's repeated calls for management to sell the company were probably inspiring other piggyback activists to jump on board and wait for things to happen.

Another Pirate position was Gencorp. In this case, Pirate itself piggybacked on top of the research and filings done by another activist firm, Steel Partners, a New York City–based firm run by Warren Lichtenstein. Lichtenstein had several prior successes, including one of the first examples of activism in Japan. In December 2003, he launched a takeover battle against Yushiro Chemical, a company trading on the Nikkei index that had about $100 million cash, $193 million market capitalization, and other assets, bringing the liquidation value of the company substantially above the market capitalization. Although Lichtenstein didn't succeed in taking over the company, the company did dividend out a large chunk of their cash and the stock ended up going up another 50 percent during Lichtenstein's holding of the investment.

Another Steel example is that of United Industrial Corp. In September 2002 the management team sent a letter to shareholders, pleading with them to reject an attempt by Lichtenstein to nominate another board member of his choosing. They wrote:

> We think the choice is clear:
>
> 1. Your Board's nominees, Dick Erkeneff and Page Hoeper, two experienced defense industry executives—one of whom, Dick, has led the Company in creating substantial shareholder value, and both of whom are actively engaged in current efforts to sell the Company; or
> 2. Steel Partners' nominee, an employee of Steel Partners with no apparent defense industry experience."

They lost the battle. Lichtenstein is now chairman of the board and, fortunately for stockholders, the stock is about 50 percent higher.

In November 2002, Steel started accumulating shares of Gencorp at an average price of $7.50 a share. They continued to accumulate throughout 2003 and 2004 until on November 11, 2004, they made an offer of $17 a share to acquire the company. Pirate Capital, which had also begun accumulating shares in Gencorp, also sent a letter to the company, echoing the points stated in various filings by Steel:

- The company owns 12,700 acres which management has stated is worth $50,000 per acre unfinished and anywhere from $600,000 to $1 million per acre finished. Pirate's conclusion is that the real estate alone could be valued anywhere from $82 per share to $154 per share.
- The company is selling its fine chemicals business by the end of the year for about $120 million, or about seven times the earnings before interest, taxes, depreciation, and amortization (EBITDA) of that business.
- The aerojet division, with EBITDA of between $75 million and $85 million, can reasonably be valued at $520 million, or about $11.45 per share.
- The company has announced that it expects to be cash flow breakeven by the fourth quarter and cash flow positive in 2005.

Although the company rejected the offer, the repeated filings by both Steel and Pirate alerted the investment community to the hidden value within Gencorp and the result was a huge success for both funds as well as any investors that were piggybacking on their filings. (See Figure 2.4.)

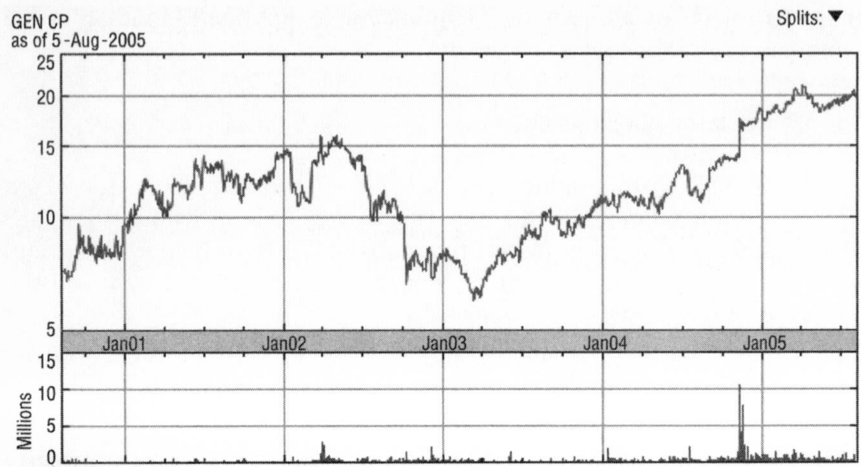

FIGURE 2.4 Gencorp
Source: http://finance.yahoo.com/. Reproduced with permission of Yahoo! Inc. © 2005 by Yahoo! Inc. YAHOO! and the YAHOO! logo are trademarks of Yahoo! Inc.

"The day before I file an SEC filing, I call the CEO and tell him, 'Your life is about to change forever,' " Bob Chapman told me while he was on his initial trip to line up support for his relaunched activist hedge fund, Chapman Capital. Known as "the terminator," and as can be seen from the filings just outlined, Chapman has built up a reputation as perhaps the most aggressive of the activist funds. As part of his fundraising drive for his newly-launched fund, he put together a document outlining the risks and pitfalls of activist hedge fund management, reproduced below.

TIME AND MONEY SINK

Successful activism stipulates an exhaustive commitment of time/resources.

- Iraq War in Pinstripes: Activist must wage both political (media "spin"; shareholders/judges = voters) and strategic (e.g., proxy fights/acquisition proposals) offensives while researching and trading balance of diversified portfolios; assistance in regulatory matters of Target both positive and negative.
- Target Management Fighting with Activist's Own Money: Executives and Board of Directors defend their jobs/honor (vs. the Target itself), squandering "shareholders' own cash" in their defense campaigns.

THE "REMORA EFFECT"

Passive hedge/mutual funds and private investors crowd the entrances/exits.

- Position Accumulation More Onerous: Number of "wise guy," public market buyers for security proliferates, essentially expunging "averaging down" opportunities.
- Position Distribution Strained: Similarly thinking/behaving remora engage in profit taking alongside Activist, with the eventual "cut-stake 13D/A" often provoking fierce selling.
- El Niño Effect: "Temperature" of money in the security escalates, exacerbating hedge fund's mark-to-market pricing volatility for NAV reporting purposes.

ILLIQUIDITY

Fund is married to the investment—due diligence must embody sedulous investigation.

- Marriage versus Dating: Divorce (13D/14A/TO public announcement required) is fraught with malignant financial and reputation risk versus breaking up's (sub-13D quiet selling) benignity.
- LTC Million Scenario: Avoid becoming "bigger than the market" in each activist investment.
- Eschew "Fast Money": Performance-unrelated redemptions can disrupt Activist's campaign.

THROWING STONES IN GLASS HOUSES

Target will paint truculent Activist in Satanic light.

- Terminators Only: "Doesn't feel pity or remorse or fear . . . and absolutely will not stop. Ever."
- Limited Partner Name Disclosure: U.S. District Court ruled against in January 2004 (Ronson).

PRIVATE EQUITY/LONG-SHORT HEDGE FUND

"Highly confident" of 1980s-style convergence.

- Hands-On Involvement Similarity: "Help" shape management decisions and indecision.

- Kick Starting Auctions with Unsolicited Bids: Force Targets into "Revlon/ Unocal modes."
- Drexel Style Financing: Funding sources for "raiders" is expanding in number and dollar commitment.
- LBO versus MBO Disparity: Activists typically do not extend equity participation to incumbent CEO.

Source: Chapman Capital LLC.

To become an activist hedge fund one has to deal with all of these risks and pitfalls. However, as much as I hate being a part of the "remora effect" described by Chapman, it does seem worthwhile to piggyback and learn from the activist positions being undertaken every week. To mimic the activists, one can:

- Review recent 13D filings at www.10kwizard.com or www.sec.gov.
- Look for other articles on activism, including "The Activist Track" articles I write every Monday at Realmoney.com, or the "13D Filings" section that comes out in *Barron's* every Saturday.
- Study the reasons for the activism. Fortunately those reasons are probably spelled out in detail in the filings, perhaps the only times the thoughts of hedge fund managers are so clearly elucidated for investors.
- Build positions but keep track of form 4 filings (which detail increases or decreases in the hedge fund managers' positions) or DFAN14 filings or 8K filings, which may contain letters from the management to the managers.

CHAPTER 3

Buying Delinquent Credit Card Debt

I love the credit card business. Every year paper money is being replaced by ones and zeros, transmitted with the permission of plastic cards containing more ones and zeros on them. When I was a freshman in college (1986) the first business I ever started was in the debit card business. With Wende Biggs (daughter of Barton) and Rick Arons (now at Pokèmon and, additionally, the one who came up with the idea), we started a business called CollegeCard in Ithaca, New York. At that time very few college kids had credit cards, so we decided to set up charge card accounts for the students and compete with the "CornellCard" that the university offered. Parents of students would send us money and we then issued the student their CollegeCard.

We arranged for about 90 different stores and restaurants in the Ithaca area to accept our card. Each place offered a 10 to 20 percent discount for all transactions using our card. In exchange for this they would get free advertising since they were in our network, and students with the card would be more likely to eat, for instance, at the Greek restaurant that accepted our card than at the Greek restaurant that didn't. We charged each student a flat $21 a year for our card. As far as I know we were the first charge card company to sell advertising on our cards. Both Q104 Radio and Citizens Savings Bank purchased advertising on the card. About 1,000 students signed up for our card.

I signed up a good chunk of the businesses to accept our card during each day, and at night I would be busy trying to figure out how to program a Verifone machine to accept our cards, dial into the PDP-11 sitting in my bedroom (it was loud and about one-fourth as powerful as a Blackberry), and then go through all the secure protocols to confirm that the student did have money in the account. Additionally at night, Wende, Rick, and I would take turns delivering food from the places that accepted our card that we also offered delivery service for, a forerunner to failed businesses Kozmo and Urban Fetch. For some reason, I would never get any tips from the customers although Wende, who I had a crush on, cleaned up. Our margins on the delivery side of our business were negative, and on the charge card our gross margin was probably 90 percent but we never covered our fixed costs of about $50,000.

As an aside, I have a vivid memory of Wende's dad, Barton, visiting us one weekend. While Wende and her mom would spend time together, Barton basically spent the entire weekend sitting on the staircase leading up to our apartment (we all lived together and worked together) with a stack of magazines, economist reports, analyst reports, and SEC filings. The stack was about five feet high (I was tempted to exaggerate here and say it was taller than me but it was actually slightly shorter), and with a yellow highlighter Barton would go through each report, highlighting the things he felt were important. Then he left the highlighted stack for Wende to read.

In any case, after a semester Wende went off to business school at Duke, Rick went to work at MasterCard, and I decided to go through with my sophomore year after debating whether to quit school in order to continue the business.

We noticed a couple of things in our one semester in business. Not all debt is created equal. For instance, parents love it when their kids use credit cards (debit or credit) so they can see on a monthly statement exactly where their kids are spending the money. In the late 1980s and early 1990s credit card companies realized this and started issuing credit cards to college kids without any regard to credit history since there was none. The proliferation of credit cards led to an entirely new asset class: charged-off credit card debt.

Banks are a godsend to the hedge fund. Forget the normal hedge fund strategies like merger arbitrage or convertible arbitrage. Always there are opportunities when picking up scraps thrown away by the megabanks. When a credit card issuer like Citigroup decides that credit card debt overdue by 90 days is too difficult for them to collect they wrap it all up in one big security and auction it off. Credit card debt that is only overdue by 90 days typically can be collected at a rate of 20 to 25 cents on the dollar. The banks usually sell it off to the highest bidder around 8 to 10 cents a dollar. Why do this? Why flush good money down the toilet?

The answer is: Why not? They are simply not set up to collect credit card debt. Nor do they want to. We've seen throughout this book several things that banks do not want to do:

- They do not want to loan money to people who don't have checking accounts.
- They do not want to give short-term, one- to two-year loans, no matter if the loan is asset-backed and paying 15 percent interest.
- They do not want to lend money to penny stock companies.
- They won't lend money based on assets that are difficult to quantify, such as, for instance, a taxi medallion, or future receivables from a movie.

Whenever a bank doesn't want to do something, this is an opportunity for a hedge fund manager to dress up and play banker, take advantage of the opportunity, and grab the extra points of interest that the banks don't feel like taking. Now, that said, the banks are more than happy to provide leverage (i.e., lend money) to the hedge funds that are taking these risks. But playing collection agency they won't do.

Hence the opportunity. Hedge funds are, in effect, becoming the credit card issuers of last resort. Not directly—they won't actually issue you a VISA card. But they allow the banks to take more risks than they otherwise would since the banks know if a student is a bit lackluster on paying the bills then, no problem, let's securitize the debt and sell it off to one of the many hedge funds that are cropping up to take advantage of the opportunity.

First, let's look at Figure 3.1. It really doesn't get much better than

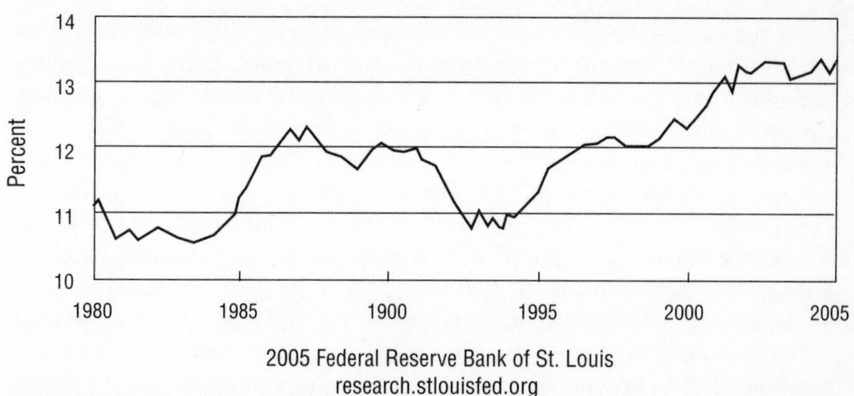

FIGURE 3.1 Household Debt Service Payments as a Percent of Disposable Personal Income
Source: www.research.stlouisfed.org; Board of Governors of the Federal Reserve System

this: the ideal crooked smile that venture capitalists (VC) would kill for when looking at a business opportunity. Every business plan put in front of a VC has the same characteristics: $0 sales in year 1, $1 billion sales in year 5 (give or take). It's a rare business that actually does what it says it will do. Nevertheless, if credit card debt were a business, then . . . oh wait, it *is* a business.

This is an industry that isn't going away. Student loan issuer Nellie Mae has stated that the percentage of students with credit cards rose from 67 percent in 1998 to 78 percent in 2000. Average student credit card debt rose from $1,879 to $2,748 over the same period of time. Similarly, bank credit card loans in the United States went from $568 billion in 2000 to $607 billion in 2001. These numbers are going to keep increasing for a long time. At the end of 2001 there were 158 million VISA and MasterCard credit cards in circulation, according to Talisman Partners and Creditweb.

Here are some more statistics from Talisman Partners, a hedge fund that buys charged-off debt and then outsources the debt to collection agencies:

- More than 6,500 collection agencies and 1,600 credit reporting agencies service an estimated $135 billion in delinquent consumer debt placed for collection in 2000. This is nearly double the $73 billion placed for collection in 1990 (source: *The Kaulkin Report*, August 2001).
- The debt collection market generates approximately $13 billion in revenues for United States companies (source: *The Kaulkin Report*, August 2001).
- Contingency collection activity makes up 58 percent of the total market revenue. These annual contingency revenues amount to $7.5 billion divided among six segments: health care, financial services, government and student loans, telecommunications, utilities, commercial, and other (source: *The Kaulkin Report*, August 2001).
- The Kaulkin Ginsburg Company expects the overall collection industry to grow approximately 14 percent by 2004.
- According to ACA International's *2000 Top Collection Markets Survey*, the auto industry (sales and service) has the highest recovery rate with 65 percent, while child support collections has the lowest recovery rate with only 2 percent.
- The average recovery rate for accounts placed between 30 and 60 days is 27.55 percent, compared to 13.41 percent for accounts placed beyond 181 days (source: ACA International's *2000 Top Collection Markets Survey*).
- It is estimated that there were five sellers of delinquent debt in 1992. By 1998, that number had grown to 225, and it is projected that there

will be 300 major sellers of delinquent debt by 2005. The face value of all such debt sold in 1993 was $1.3 billion. By 1997, that number had grown to $15 billion and sales reached $25 billion in 2000.

According to Talisman, issuers of VISA and MasterCard credit cards are willing to sell delinquent debt for about a quarter of the collectable value of the debt. In Figure 3.2, the horizontal axis represents the number of months the debt is delinquent before being sold.

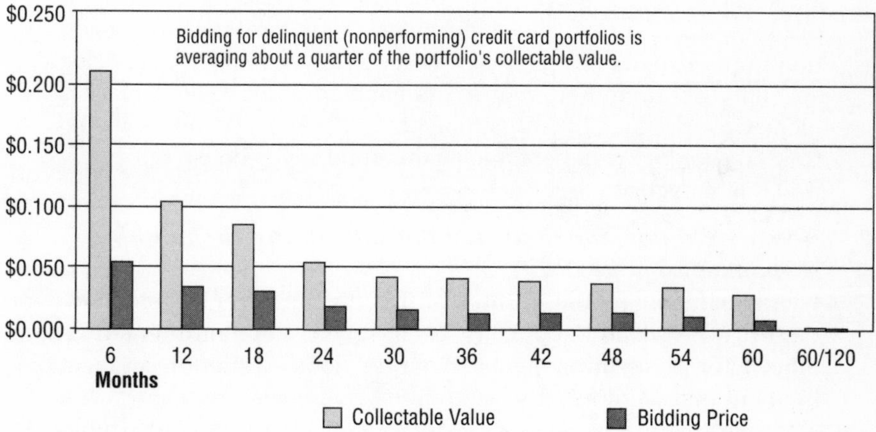

FIGURE 3.2 What Purchasers Are Paying for Portfolios
Source: Envision Capital Management, Ltd.

Talisman, run by Michael Druckman, expects to recover 2.5 to 3 times its invested capital within 24 to 36 months from placement with a collection agency. Because Talisman is among the top 30 or so purchasers of debt, it is able to get attractive pricing from the issuers, bypassing the collection agencies that often resell debt they can't collect. The primary purchasers of debt are the collection agencies themselves, but if they can't collect quickly they usually immediately resell. By bypassing this channel, Talisman is able to produce better returns than otherwise.

Talisman, like any portfolio manager of a complicated asset class, attempts to diversify its portfolio. The fund will buy debt portfolios ranging across geographic regions, average balances, and the type of consumer debt (credit card, student loan, retail, utility, telecom, etc.). The results are very consistent. Since its inception in April 2002 through May 2005, the monthly percent change has ranged from 0.560 percent to only 1.340 percent, showing very stable conditions.

Druckman, the portfolio manager, recently did an interview with HedgeFund.net (HFN). It is reprinted here with permission from Druckman and HFN.

Hedgefund.net: Your fund does not quite fit neatly into a tightly defined pigeonhole hedge fund strategy. Could you begin by describing what the fund invests in and how you manage your portfolio?

Michael M. Druckman: Very simply, we purchase written-off consumer debt and outsource it to collection agencies for a return on our investment. Primarily we purchase credit card debt; however, other opportunities have presented themselves to us. Bad checks, specialty retail, and student loans enabled us to exploit market niches overlooked by other players. Although we use the distressed category as a benchmark this fund really doesn't fit easily into that category.

How would you characterize the initial and the ongoing responses to your fund?

We had a huge amount of interest initially; however, potential investors viewed us skeptically because we were different than other alternative investments. What we do is different than most funds in that we don't deal in equities. I've been very happy with what we've gotten using this strategy. Our investors come to understand what it is that we do and the benefits that can be derived. We have created a great diversifier and a worthy addition to a portfolio.

What does your fund do that distinguishes it from others?

I would guess that the vast majority of funds on your site deal with equities, which we don't do, which is why we have predictable returns. With our strategy, we've seen a high Sharpe ratio and low correlations to equity indices so we don't have the same variability and the same volatility of people who deal in equities. The very nature of what we buy and what we do results in very low volatility.

What is your absolute return target?

I believe that this fund could ultimately generate returns in excess of 15 percent annually. We were at a little over 11 percent last year. This year I expect the return to be roughly the same, maybe just a tick more. The reason for this is that we've got a $17 million fund, but we've got about $5 million in cash. Cash has hurt our returns—not because we've made bad purchases or bad investments, but because of the amount of cash we've been carrying. So, as we continue to purchase larger portfolios, I expect our cash balances will go down and our returns will start picking up. If we can earn 12 percent this year, I'm a happy guy. Next year I'd like to see it at 13, 14, 15 percent, and I think we have the capability to do that. Talisman Partners now generates about $1 million a month in free cash flow. That's in a $17 million fund, not bad but it compounds our too much cash problem.

What kinds of risks do you encounter with your strategy, and how do you manage them?

Because we don't deal with equities, our risks are different. We have certain business risks. We could, for example, buy a bad portfolio. We currently have about 1.6 million accounts. That means we have 1.6 million people who owe us money. We deal in the law of large numbers. Right now, about $1 billion is owed to Talisman by these individuals. We believe that enough of these individuals will pay us to make the whole business worthwhile. We have, I think, currently 56 separate debt portfolios, about half of which we've gotten all our money back from and are now just generating sheer profit.

Another approach to the credit card collection/hedge fund business is taken by Ted Dumbauld from Asset Investors. Similar to Talisman, they attempt to buy what they consider undervalued delinquent debt. However, instead of attempting to collect the debt, they divide the portfolios into slices based on state. Within each state there will be lawyers or niche collection agencies that specialize in collecting debt just from that state. Lawyers are familiar with the specific laws on seizing assets or collection in their respective states and are able to achieve a higher rate of return than a collection agency that focuses on debt portfolios consisting of debt spread nationwide. Buying debt for 3 to 6 cents on the dollar, slicing it up, and then immediately reselling it to local experts, often for double what they paid for it, is Dumbauld's strategy. In the following interview I asked Dumbauld about this strategy.

How do you find the portfolios that you buy?

Our portfolio manager has nearly 10 years of experience in the business and has built an extensive network of contacts that provide proprietary deal flow. We are also periodically active in some of the public auctions, for example National Loan Exchange (www.nlex.com), where we can find value where other players don't see it.

What happens in a rising interest rate environment to the pricing of these portfolios?
Our business is to own the portfolios for relatively short periods of time (buy wholesale, sell retail within three months) and so we haven't observed sensitivity to interest rates during our holding periods. In general, however, while interest rates may be a factor, the dominating factor in the value of the portfolios is the supply/demand equation.

What is the effect of the new bankruptcy laws?
While the real effects remain to be seen (the law was signed April 20, 2005), the general consensus is that it should increase the value of the charged-off debt as debtors will have a more difficult time in filing bankruptcy. The prices for bad debt portfolios have been rising over the past year, and while it is hard to know the causes for sure, it seems likely the new law has had an influence.

How come the Astas or PRAAs of the world (public companies in the same space) don't compete with you?
They clearly are competitors in that we all want to buy attractively priced charged-off consumer debt. However, our business model is much different than theirs—they buy and hold and collect while we buy to resell. Their infrastructure consists of a large number of collectors, ours is a large number of collection firms, and so we may find value where they don't, and vice versa.

What do you think is the capacity?
We recognize the strategy is a niche strategy. We are targeting initially $100 million in capacity, but hopefully as the charged-off consumer debt market continues to grow, we'll grow along with it.

When you slice the portfolio into states and resell them, what's the cheapest state and why?
Those states that are the most debtor friendly—short statute of limitations, restrictions on creditors to aggressively contact debtors, and so on—will have debt trading at the cheapest level, at times one-third to one-fifth the value of the good states. Southern states like Texas, Florida, Georgia are typically "bad" states; northern states like Ohio, Michigan, Illinois are traditionally among the "good" states.

CHAPTER 4

Everything You Wanted to Know about PIPEs But Were Afraid to Ask

Most of the topics I cover in this book revolve around the theme of how the retail investor, the hedge fund, and the smaller banks and brokerage houses are taking away the monopolies once held by the larger, well-entrenched investment banks. Similarly, private investments in public equities (PIPEs) have been quietly replacing the secondary offering as the financing mechanism of choice for up-and-coming companies. The PIPE mechanism has also been a very successful hedge fund strategy, providing consistent returns in both bear and bull markets.

For better or for worse, several thousand companies went public in the late 1990s and early 2000s that probably should have stayed private. Companies like Pets.com should probably have never opened up their doors, let alone gone public (although online sales of pet products worldwide across all companies are expected now to top $3 billion this year—that seems like a viable market to me). Consequently, when the market crashed from 2000 to 2002, the investment banks that bravely brought these companies public and dumped shares on willing buyers either dropped research and coverage of the companies or actually went out of business. Robbie Stephens, one of the biggest dot-com banks of the 1990s, shut its doors, Hambrecht & Quist (H&Q) got absorbed upwards into the mother ship of JP Morgan, Donaldson, Lufkin & Jenrette Inc. (DLJ) got sucked into Credit Suisse First Boston (CSFB), and so on. Over 6,000 public companies were left orphaned with no banking coverage or support.

And, like many companies, both good and bad (even General Electric and Berkshire Hathaway occasionally raise money by issuing debt), many if not all of these 6,000 orphans, need money at some point. A biotech firm, for instance, that might be operating without incoming revenues as it works its way through the FDA trials for its drug will probably need money to sustain it as it makes its way from Phase I to Phase II to Phase III of its trials. It will then need to build a manufacturing facility to produce its drug. Or an oil and gas company will need money to drill wells. Or a chain of restaurants will need money to make acquisitions in a rollup.

In the late 1990s, life was easy. If you needed money, no problem. Just start a dot-com initiative for your company, hire Goldman Sachs or Morgan Stanley, and do a $200 million secondary offering. I'm being a bit facetious at the expense of these two white-shoe investment banks, but even they would admit that at the peak of the market, they brought many companies in front of the public that only a short while later proved deeply disappointing. A half decade later they would never even touch companies remotely similar to the ones they touted during the dot-com heyday.

Five years after the NASDAQ crash, if a company without banking support needs money, and they do not have the stable cash flows required for a bank to do a debt deal with them, then the private investment in public equity mechanism is the only way to go. An example PIPE is Genitope, a biotech company, which did a PIPE in December 2004. Genitope is a company that avoided the mainstream bankers every step of the way. They did their initial public offering (IPO) in November 2003 with Dutch auction advocate WR Hambrecht at $9. Then, to complete their FDA trials and raise money to build a manufacturing facility, they decided to go out into the market and raise money again. They hired WR Hambrecht to help them raise the money through a PIPE.

On December 13, 2004, their PIPE transaction closed. The stock was at $15 on that day. The company sold $60 million worth of stock in a private transaction at $14.25 per share, a 5 percent discount to where the stock was trading that day. WR Hambrecht charged a 5 percent fee, bringing the total cost of the transaction to 10 percent. This is commensurate with, or perhaps even better than, the costs of a secondary transaction, which often costs about 7 percent in fees to the bank, another 5 to 10 percent discount in the secondary price, and a 10 to 20 percent slide in the stock during the three- to six-month period that the company's management team is on the road. So we see two reasons why a company might choose the PIPE option over the secondary route:

1. Speed to market. There is no road show necessary and usually the filings are less cumbersome. All in all, it is a faster route to bring in needed financing.

2. Less cost. This isn't always true. Sometimes a PIPE can be quite expensive, particularly if a company has no choice but to offer a very significant discount. That said, the companies that do those PIPEs usually do not have secondaries as an option.

The PIPE funds that participate in these deals benefit in a variety of ways. The most important, of course, is that they are getting terms that are not available to the retail investor. In the case of Genitope, they were able to purchase stock at a nice discount to the market. We will go over other deal types later in this chapter, but suffice it to say that the deal terms usually help to significantly reduce risk in the transaction. Another benefit to PIPE investors is that they can get significantly more shares in the transaction than if they bought stock on the open market. Genitope, on the day the deal closed, had an average volume of 200,000, or about $3 million worth of shares traded every day. To buy $60 million worth of stock on the open market would have pushed the stock up much higher than $15. Genitope traded as high as $17 over the next few months, allowing investors in the PIPE to exit the transaction successfully if they were so inclined.

This is a simple example of a PIPE. The company sold stock at a discount to where it was trading. There are many other types of PIPEs, mostly involving some sort of convertible debt feature. Before exploring the different types of PIPEs, it is worth mentioning that PIPEs often have a negative connotation. Many investors, often quite correctly, assume that if a company needs to do a PIPE rather than a secondary, then there is something wrong with it, or that the funds involved in the PIPE will start selling the stock nonstop, causing the stock to go down in what is commonly referred to as a "death spiral."

A lot of the negative views about PIPEs came about out of 1990s practices. In the 1990s, any company using a pet stock to sell cat food online was given the privilege of associating with Goldman Sachs, doing an IPO, advertising on the Super Bowl, doing a secondary, getting bought, and so forth, so who would need to do PIPEs? Further, as with anything, there have been some abuses.

REGULATION S

The abuses in PIPEs started with something called Regulation S, an obscure loophole the SEC had which allowed companies to issue freely trading stock (stock issued in a private transaction is normally not freely trading but restricted) to foreign entities. This was supposed to encourage foreign investment in U.S. companies. What happened was that micro cap public companies would issue stock at an extreme discount to their buddies, who often used bogus offshore entities in order to qualify for their purchases under the Reg S rule. Then boiler-room style operations would pump and dump the stock while the management teams and their investors would split the proceeds of dumping this newly issued stock on the unsuspecting public. Many of these original Reg S promoters are now in jail and the loophole has since been plugged.

DEATH SPIRALS

If a company needed to do a PIPE in the late 1990s or early 2000s instead of making use of the hundreds of banking operations that would have loved to wine and dine them for the honor of doing their secondary, then there must have been a problem. Many of the deals that were done during this period were not straight equity deals, like the Genitope deal previously described, but were deals more commonly referred to as death spirals.

I can best describe the beauty of a death spiral by relating a personal story. In the mid-1990s, my brother-in-law and I started a company, Reset, Inc., that specialized in making web sites for Fortune 500 companies. In particular, we specialized in the entertainment industry and built web sites for Miramax, Sony, BMG, HBO, New Line Cinema, Universal, and Warner Brothers, among others. When we started the business, in 1995, there were maybe only a dozen people in New York City who knew how to build a web site, so our hourly charge reflected this. By August 1998, we realized that high school freshmen were learning this skill set and we decided to sell the business, hoping that a larger company could take our client list and strengthen the relationship by piggybacking other IT services to our clients. We sold our company to a public company, which then proceeded to buy about 12 other similar companies around the country—a classic rollup. In early 2000, companies were still charging $1 million or more to build web sites that my 6-year-old daughter can now do for $2. This was a business destined to fail, and the rollups like USWeb, Razorfish, Agency.com, and the company that bought my company were about to meet their destinies.

My acquirer (which I will call Company X) decided to weather the storm by doing a PIPE. Bear Stearns had been courting them for a while to do a secondary but then, for reasons still unknown to me, backed off. So on January 14, 2000, Company X, when its shares were at $43.75, sold $30 million worth of convertible debt in a structure now commonly called a "death spiral."

The $30 million was issued as five-year debt, paying a 4 percent interest rate. But the three funds that participated in the PIPE did not buy this debt because they were excited about a 4 percent interest rate. Rather, they liked the terms of the convertible—any time they converted, they got the lesser of $36 or the 10-day average of the lowest daily price each day. In other words, if the stock went from $40 to $10 and the average daily low in the prior 10 days was $8, they would convert at $8, sell at $10, and pocket their 25 percent profit. For funds participating in a death spiral, it's more important that the company have volatility (if it goes straight down then they won't get a favorable conversion price) and volume (else they won't be able to sell their shares). A fund participating in a death spiral can keep shorting or selling shares, however, knowing that if the selling pressure keeps up, then the stock price will go lower and they will convert lower, and then use the shares they got on conversion to cover their other shares.

Company X stock fell from $43 to $7 over the next four months, and shortly thereafter, not able to raise any more money, the company went bankrupt. Many other stories like this occurred among the death spirals, and the stigma attached to those structures continues to this day, perhaps unjustly, as we will see.

DEAL TYPES

Before getting into the discussion of different types of PIPEs, it is important to note that the average retail investor often cannot participate in these transactions. These transactions are directly negotiated between companies, their agents (WR Hambrecht in the aforementioned Genitope example), and institutional investors. That said, having an awareness of PIPEs, their common structures, and an understanding of the regulatory landscape involving PIPEs is helpful when making an investment decision on a company that has done a PIPE.

Who else can benefit from a thorough reading of this chapter?

- Hedge funds. In a world where the markets are choppy and trendless, and even good-quality, growing companies often go through periods where they trade at single-digit price/earning ratios (P/Es), a knowledge of PIPEs as a possible hedge fund strategy is critical in today's environment for long/short funds. Why not have a strategy that allows you to buy stock at a discount to where a stock is trading, with other possible features attached to the deal?
- Companies. Why choose a top-tier investment bank to do a secondary for you when it will cost more, take more time, and no longer garner

the benefits that banks once offered but no longer do—namely, a research report with a top analyst loudly proclaiming the company a "strong buy." Those research reports, we now realize, were hardly worth the paper they were printed on, and the costs to companies, shareholders, and ultimately the banks (through massive fines and lawsuits) were too much for the dot-economy to handle at the time. The PIPE mechanism provides fast access to capital that can be used for acquisitions, technology development, and so on.

- Banks. Despite my criticism of banks, I do think that there is a role for a bank to play in the PIPE space: introducing companies to quality institutions that can participate in PIPEs. Having a bank, or placement agent, facilitate the process (at a nonegregious cost) can make the experience smooth for a company.

COMMON STOCK

Most PIPEs are done in the form of common stock, such as in the case of the Genitope deal. A company trading at a price of, say, $10 will sell stock to private investors at a discount, say at $9. The investors will typically get stock that they are restricted from selling for a certain period of time, usually three to six months. Often, investors will get an additional "equity kicker" in the form of warrants.

Here are four other examples of PIPEs that were common stock deals:

Deal Type: Common Stock

Company Name: Napster Inc. (NAPS)

Date Closed: 1/20/05

Size: $52 million

Summary: A $270 million market cap company with stock trading near $8 and volume of over 1 million shares per day. The company sold 7.1 million shares of common stock at a price of $7.35 for a net proceed of $52,185,000. The transaction price at the time of deal closing represented an 8.35 percent discount to where shares were trading in the open market. Investors agreed not to engage in any short transactions or hedging with the company's common stock.

Deal Type: Common Stock

Company Name: Cadence Resources Corporation (CDNR)

Date Closed: 1/31/05

Size: $9.7 million

Summary: A $79 million market cap company with stock trading at $1.55 the day the deal closed and volume of over 20,000 shares per day. The deal called for 7.81 million shares to be sold at a price of $1.25, which at the time of deal closing represented a 19.35 percent discount to where the shares were trading.

Warrants: A total of 14.05 million shares worth of warrants were issued at a strike price of $1.75 and a term of 48 months. The company can call the warrants if the market price of the common stock exceeds $5 per share for 20 consecutive trading days and there is an effective Registration Statement.

Deal Type: Common Stock

Company Name: TRW Automotive

Date Closed: 3/8/05

Size: $142 million

Summary: A $2 billion market cap company with stock trading at $20.71 the day the deal closed and volume of 154,000 shares a day. The deal called for 7.256 million shares to be sold at a price of $18.65, representing a 5 percent discount to where shares were trading at the time the deal closed. No warrants were issued with the transaction.

Deal Type: Common Stock

Company Name: Protein Polymer Technologies (PPTI)

Summary: A $41 million market cap company whose stock trades around $0.68/share with volume over 200,000 shares per day. Deal called for 19,950,164 common stock shares to be sold at a price of $0.33/share, which at time of closing represented a 67 percent discount to where existing shares were trading.

Warrants: There were 9,975,082 shares worth of warrants issued at a strike of $0.50 and a term of 48 months.

Antidilution Clause: None.

CONVERTIBLE DEBENTURES

There are several flavors of convertible debt that are issued in PIPE transactions. The most common is debt that is convertible at some fixed price, usually at a discount to wherever the stock is trading. Additionally, the debt will pay a coupon (like any bond) and the PIPE will usually have some warrants to provide a little more of an equity kicker. Here are two examples of convertibles where the conversion price is fixed:

Deal Type: Convertible, Fixed

Company Name: NASDAQ Stock Market

Date Closed: 4/22/05

Size: $205 million

Summary: The NASDAQ is public under the symbol NDAQ. They needed to raise money to buy Instinet. Knowing a thing or two about financing, they elected to do a PIPE transaction with a fixed convertible structure. The stock was at $10.65 the day the deal was done. The debt paid an interest rate of 3.75 percent, had a duration of 84 months, and was convertible at $14.50 (representing a 40 percent premium). One month later the stock was at $17. The deal also had 2.2 million warrants with a strike price of $14.50.

The following example includes a reset provision, meaning that under certain circumstances there would be a one-time reset of the conversion price:

Deal Type: Resettable Convertible

Company Name: Consolidated Energy, Inc. (CEIW)

Summary: A $36.35 million market cap company with stock trading near $4.50 and volume of over 60,000 shares per day. The deal, which closed on February 22, 2005, called for $7 million in convertible notes paying an interest rate of 6 percent for 36 months. Initially the notes started with a fixed conversion price of $1.70, which at time of closing represented a discount of 55 percent to where the shares were trading. If the 30-day average closing price of the common stock ending on the earlier of (1) the effectiveness of the Registration Statement or nine months after the closing date, whichever comes later, and (2) one year after the closing date is less than the conversion price, then the conversion price will be adjusted to equal this 30-day average closing price, but only until a hard floor of $1.00 for conversion.

Warrants: A total of 2,058,824 shares worth of warrants with a strike price of $1.70 and a term of 60 months.

Antidilution Clause: In the event the company issues or sells any equity securities or securities convertible into equity for less than the market price, then the exercise price will be adjusted downward to fully account for the dilutive effect of the issuance.

Although the conversion price could be reset lower, there is the $1 floor which avoids the so-called "death spiral" nomenclature, which is a floorless convertible.

Another type of PIPE is a floating convertible that also has a floor. A floating convertible has similar characteristics to a resettable convertible, except for the fact that the reset can occur any day, not just once.

Deal Type: Floating Convertible

Company Name: Rentek, Inc. (RTK)

Summary: A $142 million market cap company with stock trading near $1.54 and volume of over 450,000 shares per day. The deal, which closed on April 14, 2005, called for $9 million in convertible preferred stock paying an interest rate of prime plus 2 percent for a term of 120 months. The preferred stock is convertible at the lesser of a fixed price of $1.39 per share or the variable price of 80 percent of the volume-weighted average price of the company's common stock during the five trading days immediately prior to the conversion date. The variable conversion price is subject to a hard floor of $0.80.

Warrants: A total of 5,921,910 shares worth of warrants were issued at a strike price of $1.61 for an undisclosed term.

The floating convertible allows a company that may not be creditworthy for financing by any other means to provide significant downside protection to the investor. If the company executes on all of its goals then everything will go fine and the investor will end up converting at the maximum conversion price. But if the company fails to execute, then the floating aspect kicks in to provide downside protection to the fund doing the financing. In the case of RTK there is a floor of 80 cents, which at the time the deal closed was a discount of about 40 percent to where the stock was trading.

We'll now look at a PIPE that is convertible at a fixed price. However, the principal needs to be paid back each month, and it can be paid back in stock (this is known as PIK or "paid in kind"). Since many of the companies that do PIPEs are cash-starved (hence the need for the PIPE) it is likely that when they pay back the principal they will be doing so in stock. In these cases, as in the next example, the stock is priced depending on where it is trading the day that payment is made. Hence, although this deal is considered a fixed convertible, there are aspects of it that make it a floating convertible.

Deal Type: Self-Termination Convertible Notes with Fixed Convertible Price

Company Name: Veridicom International (VRDI)

Summary: A $26.6 million market cap company whose stock trades at $2.80 and trades around 4,000 shares per day. The deal, which closed on February 25, 2005, was for $3.4 million in convertible notes which convert at a fixed price of $0.89. The investors may convert only if the average of the closing bid prices of the common stock for the preceding five trading days is greater than $1.27. The company must redeem 1/33 of the notes every month beginning on May 25, 2005, at a redemption price equal to the face value plus accrued and unpaid interest. If the company chooses to repay the amount in the company's common stock, the number of shares will be equal to the portion of the monthly amount to be paid in shares of common stock divided by the conversion price

Warrants: Investors received 3.4 million shares worth of warrants with a strike price of $3.00 and a term of 60 months, and another 3.4 million shares with a strike of $5.00 and a term of 60 months. The company can call the first set of warrants if the market price of the common stock exceeds $4.50 per share for 10 consecutive trading days, at a redemption price equal to the closing price on the redemption date minus $3.00. The company can call the second set of warrants if the market price of the common stock exceeds $7.50 per share for 10 consecutive trading days at a redemption price equal to the closing price on the redemption date minus $5.00.

Antidilution Clause: The investors retain a pro-rata Right of First Refusal over any equity securities or securities convertible into equity offered by the company during the period beginning on the closing and ending 18 months following the effectiveness of the Registration Statement.

Structured Equity Line

A third type of PIPE is the structured equity line. The basic idea is that a hedge fund will say to Company XYZ, "We will provide you with up to $10 million in financing but only in ten $1 million tranches, and you can only draw down a maximum of $1 million a month." Company XYZ will give five days notice when they plan to draw down, and the price of the stock purchased by the amount being drawn down will be determined based on some formula of how the stock trades over the ensuing five days. During those five days the fund will hedge its exposure so that by the time the drawdown occurs, the risk to the fund is minimal.

Deal Type: Structured Equity Line

Company Name: HouseRaising Inc (HRAI)

Summary: A $50 million market cap company with stock trading at $1.45 with average volume of 50,000 shares per day. The deal is a $12 million equity line, which means that the company can draw down up to $1 million with notice in exchange for shares at an effective discount of 15 percent. More specifically, the deal has the following terms: The purchase price is 95 percent of the lowest closing bid price during the last five days after the drawdown notice. The company can elect to terminate the drawdown in the event that any closing bid price during the five trading days following a drawdown notice is less than 75 percent of the average of the closing bid prices for the 10 trading days prior to the drawdown. The company may elect the drawdown amount to be either (1) 200 percent of the average daily volume of the common stock for the 10 trading days prior to the drawdown, multiplied by the average of the three closing bid prices immediately preceding the drawdown; or (2) $100,000. The deal is effective for 36 months.

Note that the drawdown amount is in part limited by the volume of the stock. This further insures that the fund will be able to hedge its exposure during the five days leading up to the drawdown. By the time the drawdown occurs, the fund has to make sure it has basically sold stock at a price higher than 95 percent of the lowest closing bid price during the previous five days. It has to sell enough stock to equal the amount being drawn down.

PIPE PERFORMANCE

There is a blanket assumption that when a company does a PIPE the stock will go down afterwards as the hedge funds who participated in the PIPE sell their shares to hedge their positions. Here are a couple of points to be aware of:

1. Many transactions taking place in the current market do not allow any hedging or shorting. For regulatory reasons it is not possible to hedge before a deal is announced. Nor can you sell short with the idea that you will then use your restricted stock to eventually cover the short. But even beyond the regulatory landscape, most deals now include restrictions saying the investors cannot hedge or short.

2. PIPEs are no different from secondaries in that ideally the company finds investors who believe in the fundamentals and participate in the PIPE because they want a way to build a larger position than the volume in the stock would otherwise allow.

Every year the deal landscape changes, so it is difficult to provide a meaningful five-year analysis of PIPEs. However, from May 30, 2004, to May 30, 2005, I took a look at all the deals that occurred (as tracked by placementtracker.com) and their performance is as follows:

Common Stock Deals

Number: 1,179 deals

Average performance 1 month later: +8.56 percent

Average performance 3 months later: +11 percent

Average performance 6 months later: +26 percent

Structured Equity Lines

Number: 118 deals

Average performance 1 month later: +24 percent

Average performance 3 months later: +20 percent

Average performance 6 months later: +8.94 percent

When the structured equity line deal is first struck it doesn't necessarily mean any money has been drawn down yet. Investors feel comfortable that the company has its financing in place, so they bid the stock up, and then it could fall when the drawdowns occur. The after-deal performance of an equity line has no bearing on the performance of the hedge funds providing the financing since they hedge their positions during the drawdown notice period.

Convertible Fixed Price

Number: 410 deals

Average performance 1 month later: +10.5 percent

Average performance 3 months later: +18 percent

Average performance 6 months later: +20 percent

Because the convertible deals have more downside protection (in addition to the usual discount there is also an interest payment associated with the debt as well as antidilution privileges) the funds have less risk if the underlying stock goes down. These provisions likely explain the slight six-month underperformance when compared with common stock deals.

Convertible Floating

Number: 77 deals

Average performance 1 month later: +2.29 percent

Average performance 3 months later: –12 percent

Average performance 6 months later: –29 percent

The floating convertible (the "death spiral") is not the optimal way for a company to go, for obvious reasons: The price of the stock has no bearing on the returns of the investors. In fact, in some cases, the returns of the investors can be greater if the stock goes down. That said, some companies cannot obtain financing except through this form of financing. While the performance as a group has not been great, some companies have secured financing through a floating convertible and gone on to achieve great success.

Let's look at an example.

Company Name: Isonics Corporation

Date Closed: 10/4/04

Size: $3.3 million

The day the deal closed, the stock was at $1.31 and traded 250,000 shares a day. The deal was convertible debt paying an 8 percent interest rate. The conversion price was the lesser of $1.24 or 85 percent of the three lowest intraday bids of the company's common stock during the five trading days immediately prior to the conversion date. The conversion price was subject to a floor of $1.00. Additionally, the investors received 307,000 warrants with a strike price of $1.24 and 307,000 warrants with a strike price of $1.35.

The addition of the hard floor at $1.00 probably gave investors comfort that the hedge fund that did this deal wouldn't crush the stock. Figure 4.1 shows the company's stock price during that time. Shortly after the deal was completed the stock began a straight-up move as investors were confident that the company had the financing in place to achieve its deals. In February 2005, the company did another round of financing, this time for $22 million. Some pressure on the stock resulted from that financing.

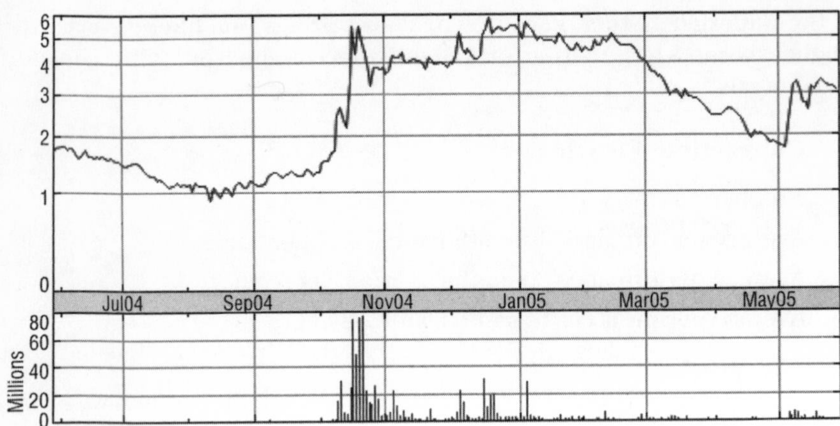

FIGURE 4.1 Isonics CP as of May 27, 2005
Source: http://finance.yahoo.com/. Reproduced with permission of Yahoo! Inc.

PIPEs are usually associated with micro caps, and many investors are nervous about investing in stocks other than blue chips or Dow components. However, this book shows that some of the world's most sophisticated investors (Warren Buffett, Peter Lynch, etc.) like to play in the micro cap sandbox, and that nontraditional investment strategies that take the shape of more direct investments can be highly profitable.

The after-deal performance of micro caps engaging in PIPEs is significantly higher than the larger-cap PIPE transactions.

Common Stock PIPEs on Companies with Market Caps Less than $10 Million (May 2004 to May 2005)

Number: 217 deals

Average performance 1 month later: +33 percent

Average performance 3 months later: +40 percent

Average performance 6 months later: +72 percent

Common Stock PIPEs on Companies with Market Caps between $10 Million and $100 Million

Number: 717 deals

Average performance 1 month later: +3.3 percent

Average performance 3 months later: +5.49 percent

Average performance 6 months later: +18.45 percent

Common Stock PIPEs on Companies with Market Caps between $100 Million and $10 Billion

Number: 245 deals

Average performance 1 month later: +2.74 percent

Average performance 3 months later: +5 percent

Average performance 5 months later: +8 percent

While the PIPEs performance of larger-cap companies is not so bad (positive 8 percent is certainly better than negative, and is a better return than most of the indices in the first half of the 2000 decade) the fact that this category significantly underperforms its smaller brethren could be related to the fact that investors are naturally suspicious of PIPE transactions, particularly when the company is big enough to participate in more traditional secondary financing transactions.

Interestingly, secondary transactions fare the worst, except when compared with floating convertibles. From May 2004 to May 2005 there were 81 secondaries:

Average performance 1 month later: –9.41 percent

Average performance 3 months later: –14 percent

Average performance 6 months later: –5.4 percent

Secondaries are usually shopped around by the larger banks, with prime allocations given to the funds that generate a lot of business for the banks. These funds then move the stock once they get their freely trading shares, pressuring the stock and often causing a selling panic. In May 2005, three multibillion dollar funds were fined by the SEC for shorting ahead of a secondary transaction and using the shares garnered in the deal to cover their shorts. In my opinion, the secondary game is the same old game we've been seeing from the larger banks and their cohorts for decades. PIPEs, like Dutch auctions, specialty acquisitions corporations (SPACs), asset-backed lending, and reverse mergers, take a little bit of the monopoly away from the larger middlemen and return some power to the smaller investors and the smaller companies.

CHAPTER 5

The New New IPO

I admit it: I'm jealous. There's a hedge fund strategy developed in the late 1990s called "playing the calendar" which I wish I had been savvy enough to participate in at that time. Unfortunately, this strategy is largely over and we all completely missed it except for the select few who are now sitting in their $20 million mansions or winging across the country in the comfort of their private jets. The strategy was very simple and didn't require a PhD in chaos theory or complicated formulas based on interest rates in India and how they correlate to the price of coffee in Brazil.

Specifically, playing the calendar consisted of looking at each month's calendar of initial public offerings (IPOs). "Oh," you say to yourself, "Goldman Sachs is planning on bringing a small Internet outfit called Akamai, with no profits and minimal sales, public in the middle of the month. Great!" Then you call your broker at Goldman Sachs and start doing mindless trading of millions of shares. It doesn't matter what you are trading, whether you are making or losing money (heck, it's always good to lose a little and let the market makers at Goldman make a little money off of your spreads), or what you are paying for commissions. Because right before the IPO you're going to call your broker at Goldman and get whatever allocation you want, depending on your trading. In the late 1990s when stocks were going from 20 to 200 in the IPOs, hedge fund managers literally made hundreds of millions of dollars overnight. Riches never before seen were created in a day.

Well, Eliot Spitzer and the attorney general are all over it. Banks have been fined, brokers fired, bankers gone to jail. But the strategy still continues, only in a milder form. The reality is, the big banks control the IPO process. Initial public offerings usually go higher (maybe not 200 percent higher anymore, but they are still usually higher 1 day, 5 days, 60 days after the IPO), and the underwriters still control whom they let in the IPO. If you are a customer of the bank, and a good one, you'll get in; otherwise, you won't.

I think the beauty of capitalism is that when there is an inefficiency like this, caused by corruption and monopolies, then the free market takes over and finds alternatives. In the past five years three alternatives have developed. All of these alternatives have been around since the dawn of markets but have only recently found their advocates, who have cleansed these approaches and made them accessible not only to hedge funds but often to retail investors as well.

SPECIALTY ACQUISITION CORPORATIONS

A very profitable strategy for private equity firms over the past 20 years is to do as follows: Find an executive who has successfully built a (insert favorite widget here) public company and is now retired from that company with reputation and relationships completely intact. Bring him on board and tell him he essentially has a blank check to go out and buy 10 of the widget companies, combine them, eliminate back-end costs, and then the private equity firm will take the whole thing public. The private equity firm makes money by owning most of the shares in the new public company and also by having debt with the company that usually gets paid back in the IPO. One private equity shop that has done this successfully in many different sectors is Chicago-based GTCR. One of their recent successes is Coinmach Corp. which was built from a single laundry facility on Long Island Sound to now being the largest laundry service provider in the United States.

With a new creative structure being pioneered by a few innovative smaller banks, the retail investor now has the opportunity to participate in these types of rollup strategies. A SPAC, a specialty acquisitions corporation, is a blind pool of money that is raised from the public in an IPO. A SPAC cannot have any business operations at all. All it has is a management team, usually with a significant degree of success in a particular sector—for instance, health care, IT services, and so forth. A portion of the cash, usually 85 percent of the amount raised in the IPO, is held in escrow. The 15 percent not held in escrow is used to pay IPO fees and the salaries and expenses of the management team while they hunt for a company to buy and merge into the new public entity. Once the management team finds a company to buy, the shareholders decide whether they like the company, and if they vote yes, the money is released from escrow to buy the company, which is then merged into the public company. If the shareholders vote no, the money is returned to the shareholders. If 85 percent of the money was held in escrow, then the maximum downside for a shareholder who invested in the IPO is 15 percent. If a SPAC does not make an acquisition in a specified period of time, usually 18 months, the money is returned to shareholders.

There's more. Each SPAC usually comes to market not only with stock but with one or two additional warrants. I'll describe what happens with these warrants with a specific example. Aldabra (ALBAU on the OTCBB exchange) went public on February 14, 2005, and raised $55 million in the IPO. They were formed just three months prior. In an SEC filing they state:

> *We were formed on November 22, 2004, to serve as a vehicle to effect a merger, capital stock exchange, asset acquisition, or other similar business combination with an operating business. We intend to utilize cash derived from the proceeds of this offering, our capital stock, debt, or a combination of cash, capital stock, and debt, in effecting a business combination.*

The chairman, Nathan Leight, and CEO, Jason Weiss, both come from Terrapin Partners, a private equity firm. Shareholders buying the IPO, or buying the stock now on the open market, have to believe that Leight and Weiss have the experience and skill to identify an acquisition, negotiate a deal favorable to shareholders, and then integrate the bought company into the SPAC. Ninety percent of the proceeds of the IPO were moved into an escrow account, either to be released on the consummation of a merger or, if the shareholders voted no, to be released back to the shareholders, making the risk on the deal 10 percent.

Every investor in the Aldabra IPO got one share of stock and two warrants. Each warrant had a strike price of $5. The unit, the combination of the one share of stock and the two warrants, sold for $6. If 10 percent of the IPO was being used for expenses then theoretically the stock could trade down 10 percent, perhaps a little more. In fact, the stock was trading at $5.20. The warrants, however, were trading around 60 cents each, valuing the entire package at approximately $6.40, significantly higher than the IPO price despite a poor market. Potentially, one could buy a SPAC at the IPO and hedge the position by selling the warrants in the open market. This is made easier by the fact that the management team of a SPAC such as ALBAU is required to buy the warrants out of their own pockets on the open market post-IPO. In other words, there are two safety mechanisms for the investor in the IPO:

1. The stock will only go down to the level of the cash being held in escrow and probably not go lower.
2. The management team is usually required to buy warrants on the open market, allowing some degree of hedging post-IPO.

I looked at the 12 most recent SPACS that have had IPOs, done by banks such as Early Bird Capital, Morgan Joseph, Broadband Capital, Maxim, and Sunrise Securities. They all have names like "Great Wall Acquisitions Corp.," "Rand Acquisition Corp.," and so on. Most of them went public in 2004. The average one-week return post-IPO was 4 percent. One month later it was 4.7 percent, four months later 6.6 percent, and six months later 10 percent. All 12 are higher now than at their IPO price.

One of the companies, Millstream Acquisition Corp., which went public in August 2003, consummated an acquisition in September 2004 and is now trading under the name NationsHealth. The stock has remained near the IPO price. The companies that have gone public more recently have not yet consummated a deal.

Where is the downside? I called Jay Kaplowitz of the law firm Gersten, Savage, Kaplowitz, which was involved in the legal work of several SPACs. He said: "I think the downside risk starts when a deal is announced. If the market views it negatively, even before a shareholder vote is taken, the stock price could drop below the escrow. And of course, once a deal is done, the company is subject to full market risk." Since a deal is not usually announced for the first 8 to 12 months, the market is really betting on the quality of the management team, and the quality of the structure of the deal, which allows the investors to hedge.

I asked an executive at one of the banks that handles these kinds of IPOs what he views as more important—the management team or the structure of the deal. His view is that ultimately the management team is more important, but he also noted that at one of the pre-IPO road shows a hedge fund manager walked up to the CEO of a SPAC, held the CEO's wrist for a few seconds, and then announced, "He has a pulse, we'll buy shares in the IPO." These deal structures may change as demand rises, but for now the SPAC is an intriguing way for the retail investor, and even hedge funds, to get in on the private equity game but have additional liquidity and risk protection.

THE DUTCH EXPERIMENT IS OVER

The experiment is over. Dutch auction IPOs have proven to be win-win for the companies raising money, the funds and individuals investing in them, and the bank, WR Hambrecht & Co., that first introduced the Dutch auction in 1999 and has since successfully concluded 11 of them, with another two, Morningstar and Bank of The Internet, currently in process.

For decades, traditional investment banks have had a lock on IPO allocations, completely controlling the book of who gets into an IPO and who doesn't. During the 1990s, when IPOs of technology companies were often doubling or tripling in the first hour, there was often a desperate frenzy of funds pleading with the banks to get into each IPO. The way funds would curry favor was by generating commissions with that bank. This technique of culling IPO favor ultimately crossed the line into abuse of the system, and banks have paid hundreds of millions in fines as a result. In other words, everyone lost in the traditional IPO. Companies raised less than they could because the banks had to price the IPO in a way that would allow their favorite funds (the ones generating the most commissions) to flip. Individual investors lost because they tended to enter into stocks when they were peaking on IPO day, right when the funds in the IPO were flipping them. And the funds and the banks ultimately lost with the fines and lost business that it eventually cost them.

The Dutch auction largely removes the bank from the process of determining who is in the IPO and who isn't. Investors bid, much like in a traditional auction, for what price they would be happy to pay to own the shares of the company going public. A computer system then determines the "clearing price" that sells the correct number of shares given the size of the offering.

The thought of doing Dutch auction IPOs first occurred to Bill Hambrecht when he was going through the IPO process with Hambrecht & Quist (H&Q) in 1996. "One part of me was getting increasingly uneasy with what was going on in the IPO process," Bill Hambrecht told me. "This peaked when H&Q went public in 1996. Retail and medium-size institutions that were the lifeblood of H&Q were missing out because they were not big enough commission generators for the big banks. IPO allocations were being decided on the basis of commission flow. The economic agenda of the underwriter had taken over the allocation process. Stock was no longer allocated to people who you thought were the best long-term holders of the stock."

He started up WR Hambrecht in 1999, and the first IPO done in the Dutch auction mode was Ravenswood.

"I felt like the designated driver at a New Year's Party. People just couldn't understand why I wanted to change something they were making so much money at. I ran into one old friend of mine, a top guy at a bulge-bracket bank. He looked at me and said, "I just don't understand it. I thought you were one of us.' "

The first IPO, Ravenswood, came out on April 9, 1999, at $10.50 a share and raised $11.5 million. A year and a half later it was acquired by Constellation for $30 a share. If the IPO had tripled out the gate like many of the IPOs in April 1999, then the retail investor would never have made a dime on it.

The Dutch auction process was covered in the media, of course, with the IPO of Google when they decided to use it to go public in 2004, selling shares at $85 and now trading around $190. But Google is Google. The big question for retail investors and smaller institutions (hedge funds, small mutual funds, etc.) is, "How can I make money on the Dutch auction IPO with a less well-known name than Google?"

The results speak for themselves. If you had invested in every Dutch auction IPO since April 1999, you would be up approximately 95 percent per trade, despite the bear market years of 2000–2002 and despite the fact that the S&P 500 and NASDAQ are down 5 percent and 20 percent, respectively, since that first Dutch auction IPO. This return happens despite two complete losers.

First let's look at the losers. Briazz went public on May 2, 2001. It raised $16 million and started trading at $8 per share. By mid-2005, it is trading for less than a penny. Salon.com went public on June 22, 1999, for $10.50 a share when it raised $27 million. Mid-2005 it is around 33 cents a share.

But the winners stand out. In addition to Ravenswood and Google (300 percent and 150 percent returns so far, respectively) perhaps the most famous company brought public through the Dutch auction process has been Overstock.com. It went public at $13 per share on May 29, 2002, when it raised $39 million, and in mid-2005 it is at $40 after reaching a 52-week high in December at $77. Another company, New River Phamaceuticals, went public August 2004 at $8 and in mid-2005 trades at $26.50. In 2005, Morningstar went public at $18.50, and after three months was trading at $32.

THE RISE OF THE REVERSE MERGER

In late 1999 I helped start a company, Vaultus, which provided wireless software to large enterprises. Typical for those times, we raised $30 million in a split second from the likes of CMGI, Investcorp, Henry Kravis, and others. In early 2001 we were exploring our options, and the option that seemed most likely to succeed was to do a reverse merger with a public shell. A reverse merger is sort of considered the bastard younger brother of IPOs. A public company (usually an empty shell with no operating assets) buys a private company and renames itself with the name of the private company. The private company assumes control of the public shell and is now, for all practical purposes, newly public. So around May 2001, we found ourselves a shell that had $10 million in cash in it but no operating assets. Previously the shell had been the home of an Internet portal that had itself been a reverse merger several years earlier. The stock of the portal in 1999 had gone from $1 to $30 before finally facing reality and settling down between 20 and 40 cents and winding down the operations of the portal.

When debating the merits of whether to do a reverse merger, one of our board members posed the question, "But has a reverse merger ever worked before? Because I don't want to base a decision on 'this time things will be different.' " With no solid answer to his question, we eventually passed on the opportunity, only to watch the stock we were going to consummate our merger with do another deal and then proceed straight to over $5 a share on heavy volume, where it trades today.

Why do a reverse merger as opposed to a traditional IPO? Three reasons: (1) Avoid paying the exorbitant fees that the investment banks charge; (2) it is faster (no road show, less SEC review of the filings); (3) it is often easier for a smaller company to go public through a reverse merger than by attracting a larger investment bank—particularly in 2001, when not only was the market cruising toward its eventual 2002 bottom, but also investment banks were starting to come under scrutiny for questionable IPO practices. A reverse merger conveniently skips all of that.

Why go public at all? The downside of a reverse merger is that if your business plan does not succeed and you fail to attract investor attention it will be impossible to ever raise money again through the issuance of shares, and all your faults and failures will be on public display through SEC filings. The upside is that it can provide potential liquidity to your early investors and you now have currency (your stock) with which to do acquisitions and potentially raise money through either secondaries or PIPEs (private investments in public equities).

So the question is, as the board member of Vaultus so aptly asked, does it work? For one thing, we could ask (if he were still alive) Armand Hammer, who brought his little company Occidental Petroleum public in 1950 (after making millions selling pencils to postwar Russia) through a reverse merger. Or Ted Turner, who took his billboard company public in 1970 when he merged into a publicly traded failed TV company, Rice

Broadcasting, changed the name of the new public entity to Turner Broadcasting, and took over the company. Or Muriel Siebert, who took over public furniture company J. Michaels in 1996, renamed it Siebert Financial, and the public company is now a financial services company. Other companies that have used the reverse merger vehicle to go public and then gone on to fame and fortune include Waste Management Inc. and Blockbuster Video, before it was acquired by Viacom. Arguably the most famous reverse merger is Berkshire Hathaway, the old-school Maine textile manufacturer that was taken over by Warren Buffett when he bought controlling interest in the company and then merged his insurance empire into it. The only thing he didn't do was change the name.

To be fair, probably more than 90 percent of reverse merged companies fail. This is not because the process is bad but because, like with IPOs or any area of life that touches the investing (read: gullible) public, there are those who abuse and take advantage of the system. And, like anything else in investing, good, profitable, growing companies will eventually shine. The beauty of the reverse merger process is that diligent work can uncover these gems before the investing public is told about them by the larger banks. Recent examples of successful reverse mergers include RAE Systems, which did a reverse merger in 2002 at approximately 20 cents a share and three years later was cruising near $7. Intermix, which merged into Motorcyle Centers of America, a business with no operations, in 1999, went through several years of pain and below $1 prices before now emerging as a successful e-commerce player; by mid-2005 it was at $5.70. Global Sources LTD reverse merged with assetless shell Fairchild Corp. and now has a market cap of $341 million, $60 million cash, no debt, $17 million in EBITDA, and is a business-to-business (B2B) player with a focus on China.

The way to invest in reverse mergers is to find companies like these that have been through the process but have not yet been touched by the larger banks and hence receive no analyst coverage and very little media coverage—in other words, legitimate, growing, perhaps profitable companies that nobody knows about. Eventually the banks will come sniffing around when they smell the scent of merger and acquisition (M&A) fees and secondary offerings. But for the moment, these untouched beauties will have room to rise.

CHAPTER 6

Trade like a Billionaire

Money doesn't solve all your problems, but it certainly solves your money problems.

—Sam Vitiello, my father-in-law

If you are a billionaire there are a lot of things you could do in your spare time. You could race 747 jets around the world, you could have 37 kids and not worry about affording their college educations, you could quit everything and try to start a career in standup comedy, or you could do what most billionaires do and try to make a little more money. Money isn't always the goal but it's certainly a method of measuring success. Normally when a private investor, billionaire or not, buys stock, it's a private affair, not worthy of notice. But when someone with a billion dollars or more tries to make a decent return on their investment they are like a bull in a china shop. Using a small portion of their net worth to invest in a public company can often cause them to cross the line in the sand that requires them to file an SEC filing, revealing to the public their interest in the stock. That line in the sand is when their buys cause them to own more than 5 percent of a company. At that point, each new purchase or sale needs to be reported *within 10 days*, according to the SEC, which conveniently allows us to follow the investment strategies of our favorite high-net-worth individuals.

The most interesting and telling point of investors such as Warren Buffett, Bill Gates, or Peter Lynch is that they don't seem to buy for their personal accounts large caps such as Cisco or GE, but instead regularly dabble in small cap and micro cap stocks since that is where the most potential for large gains exists. One doesn't even need to look further than the indices for large caps versus the indices for small caps. In mid-2005 the Russell 2000 small cap index was at an all-time high while indices such as the NASDAQ or the S&P 500 were between 20 and 70 percent down from their all-time highs.

I like to follow billionaire investors Mark Cuban, Michael Dell, Bill Gates, Bruce Covner, Carl Icahn, George Soros, Peter Lynch, and Peter Kellog, among others. I look from a macro perspective (what types of investments, what size companies, and what sectors are they interested in) as well as micro (what are the specific investments). Similar to the activists mentioned in Chapter 2, it is often worthwhile to piggyback alongside of these investors, particularly since you have the edge of knowing exactly when they are making their big purchases or sales (since they have to file within days of acquiring or selling), and this allows you to nimbly trade around their positions.

If there's a billionaire you are interested in following, you can use various services to keep track of their filings, such as www.sec.gov and www.edgar-online.com. Specifically, you want to look for these types of filings:

- Form 4. This details if they are making a significant change to their holdings. If they own more than 5 percent of a company and they sell shares, they must file a Form 4 within 10 days.
- SC-13D. A 13D schedule needs to be filed whenever they hold more than 5 percent of a company or if they go from owning more than 5 percent to less than 5 percent. This form has to be filed within 10 days of the "acquisition event" that took the filer above the 5 percent ownership level in a company.
- 13F-HR. This is filed to list all of the holdings of an institution that needs to file within 45 days of the close of a quarter. For instance, Michael Dell is not an institution but he funnels all of his money through a family office called MSD Capital, which does have to file the 13F-HR filing.

Let's take a look at the investors I like to follow.

MARK CUBAN

Even successful dot-com cowboys diversify. Perhaps they know better than anyone the need to explore unpopular investment options. Cuban, perhaps most famous for his impeccable timing in selling his company, Broadcast.com, to Yahoo! and then selling his Yahoo! shares at the very peak when they were worth upwards of $3 billion, recently posted his stock positions, both long and short, on his blog, www.blogmaverick.com.

His long positions include Lion's Gate Entertainment (his comment: "The only indie film library available, willing to leverage new media for revenue"), Rentrak ("Only independent source advertisers can use for tracking Video on Demand and Online Video on Demand"), and domain name registrar Tucows ("Good management, low PE, sells to growing market segment"). His shorts include Imergent, which makes software to help people build e-commerce sites ("I don't like companies that sell products that consumers shouldn't buy. It catches up at some point") and Interoil, an oil and gas company ("Appears to have cash issues").

BILL GATES

Even billionaires occasionally need to diversify their portfolios, and Bill Gates' massive $40 billion investment in Microsoft is a case in point. Through his investment vehicle, Cascade Investments, Bill Gates buys the stocks of traditional brick and mortar companies. For instance, he owns 2.4 million shares of manufacturing, plastics, electric, health-care company Otter Tail. While the stock hasn't gone up much in recent years, it is currently paying a very steady 4.5 percent dividend and is trading at a low double-digit P/E, providing a decent cushion for Gates and his heirs.

Other stocks Gates owns include 5.1 million shares of Pan American Silver, one of the largest public silver mines; 441,000 shares of Four Seasons Hotels; and 18 million shares of trash collector Republic Services. The rest of Gates' holdings can be found in the SEC filings for Cascade Investments.

MICHAEL DELL

When he's not churning out computers, a look at his stock portfolio (as managed by his investment vehicle, MSD Capital) suggests he spends a lot of time eating pancakes and drinking milkshakes. He owns 2.1 million shares of International House of Pancakes and 2.3 million shares of Steak 'n Shake. He also owns over 9 million shares of Darling International. And what does Darling do? From their description found on Yahoo! Finance: "The Company collects and recycles animal processing by-products, and used cooking oil from food service establishments." Mmmm.

From the 13F-HR report for MSD Capital, Dell's holdings as of December 31, 2004 include:

Company	Number of Shares
Darling International	9.2 million
Dollar Thrifty Automotive Group	2.3 million
Greenfield Online	868,000
IHOP	2.1 million
Steak 'n Shake	2.2 million
Tyler Technologies	3.2 million
USI Holdings	4.4 million

BRUCE KOVNER

Bruce Kovner, founder of hedge fund Caxton Associates, was profiled in Jack Schwager's book *Market Wizards*. He has consistently demonstrated 40 percent-plus annual returns and is regularly on the annual list of top hedge fund managers, with his pay often topping $500 million. His stock picks, and often his reasons for those picks, are often worth following.

For instance, in September 2002, he submitted a 13D filing announcing that he was now a 5 percent holder in GP Strategies (GPX), a management consulting and engineering services company. (See Figure 6.1.) In

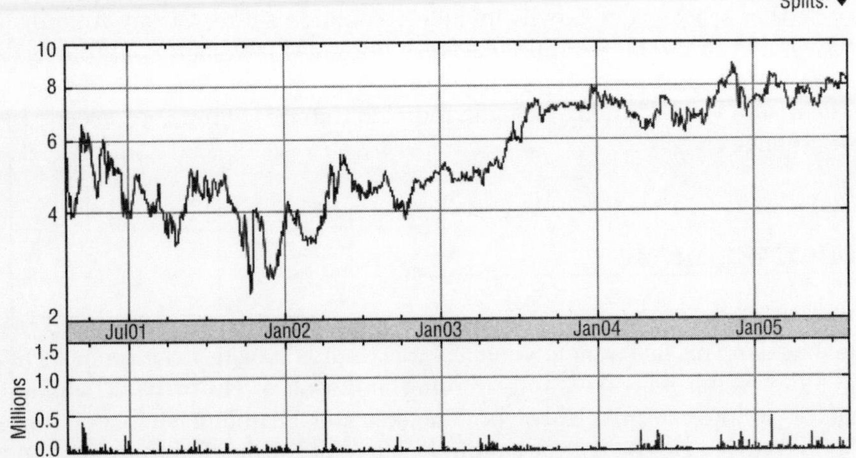

FIGURE 6.1 GP Strategies Corporation as of August 5, 2005
Source: http://finance.yahoo.com/. Reproduced with permission of Yahoo! Inc. © 2005 by Yahoo! Inc. YAHOO! and the YAHOO! logo are trademarks of Yahoo! Inc.

his first 13D filing he stated that he had accumulated his shares at an average price around $4.50 and that he was also concerned about the company's lack of profitability despite significant asset holdings that could be distributed to shareholders. He expressed concern.

> *. . . about actions taken by the Company to restore its profitability and (a) continue to believe that the Common Stock is undervalued, (b) believe it is necessary that management take further steps to improve the quality of the Board of Directors (including changing of the Chairman), and (c) believe changes must be made to the Company's senior management team. We also continue to believe that the Company should consider additional steps to enhance shareholder value including: (1) the sale of the Company in its entirety, (2) the distribution of all shares held in publicly traded companies that have not been sold for the specific purpose of paying down debt, (3) that all outstanding loans to members of management should be paid off in full, or any stock secured by such loans should be forfeited in return for eliminating the debt, and (4) that the Class Billion Supervoting stock should be abolished as a class, as it is only available to select members of management and, we believe, acts as a continued detriment to attracting either new investors or potential buyers for the entire Company.*

The company then proceeded, in November 2004, to spin off National Patent Development Corporation (NPDC). A shareholder of GPX would receive one share of NPDC for each share of GPX as a dividend. (See Figure 6.2.)

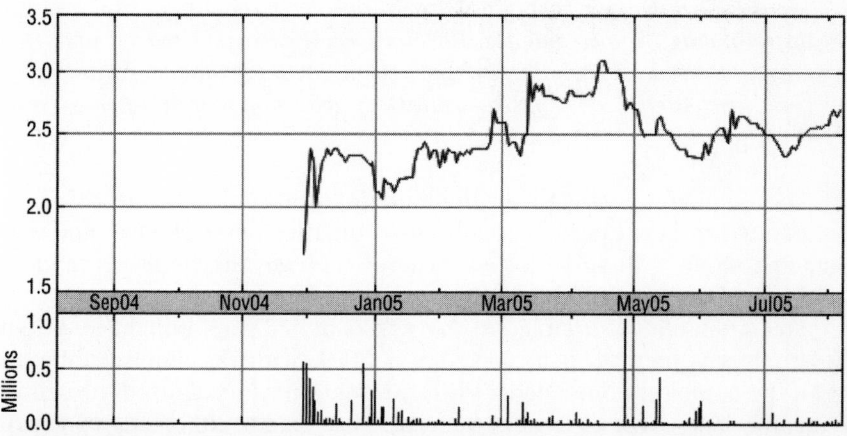

FIGURE 6.2 National Patent Development Corporation as of August 5, 2005
Source: http://finance.yahoo.com/. Reproduced with permission of Yahoo! Inc. © 2005 by Yahoo! Inc. YAHOO! and the YAHOO! logo are trademarks of Yahoo! Inc.

The resulting return (the price of GPX, which was at $8.25 in mid-2005, plus the price of NPDV, $2.70 in mid-2005) was Kovner's return for the $4 per share that he paid in 2002.

Other large holdings of Caxton Associates include:

- Aquantive, the Web services company that was built out of the combination of web site developer Razorfish and online ad network Avenue A.
- Microcap mining companies Oglebay Norton and Regalito Copper.
- Checkers Drive-In Restaurants.

Caxton files a 13-HR filing with the SEC every quarter, detailing its holdings.

PETER LYNCH

Known for the 2,700 percent-plus return Fidelity Magellan mustered during his tenure from 1977 to 1990, Peter "10-bagger" Lynch is now quietly building a portfolio of micro cap stocks. On January 6, 2004, he filed with the SEC that he owned 1.5 million shares, or 8.9 percent, of micro cap company Segmentz.

From its company description on Yahoo! Finance:

> *Segmentz, Inc. is a provider of transportation and logistics services, specializing in time definite delivery in support of specific supply chain requirements. Services include expedited transportation, deferred airfreight transportation, local cartage, aircraft charters, dedicated delivery, consolidation, warehouse management and fulfillment.*

The company is traded on the American Stock Exchange (AMEX), sports a $31 million market cap with growing revenue each year, and was chugging along with small losses. When Lynch got in, the stock made a move in response, as can be seen from Figure 6.3.

The stock almost doubled in the weeks after Lynch bought in. When the stock was near its peak, on May 5, 2004, with the stock trading at $2.51, the company concluded a PIPE transaction which caused the selloff that can be seen over the rest of the year. They sold 6 million shares to private funds and investors at $1.75 a share and also issued warrants at $2.20. Peter Lynch also participated in the PIPE through his Lynch Foundation, putting in $224,000.

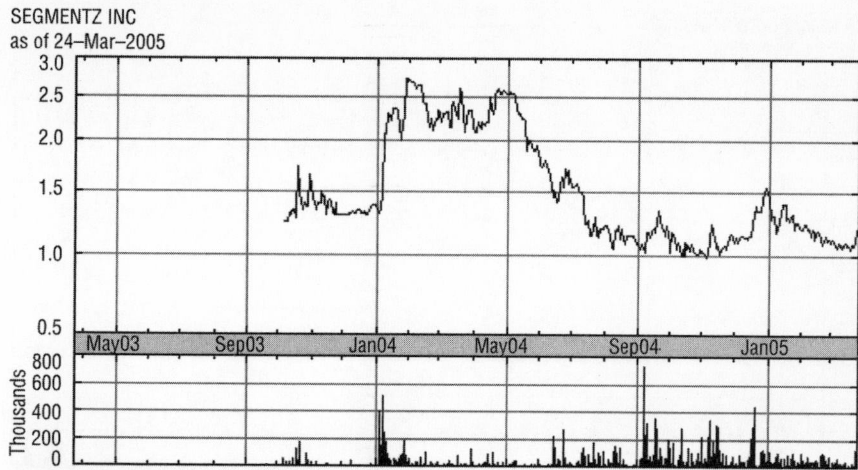

FIGURE 6.3 Segmentz Inc.
Source: http://finance.yahoo.com/. Reproduced with permission of Yahoo! Inc. © 2005 by Yahoo! Inc. YAHOO! and the YAHOO! logo are trademarks of Yahoo! Inc.

At the time of this writing, the stock is trading at $1.13, slightly below Lynch's initial purchase price. But he is probably in no rush.

On March 15, 2005, Lynch filed with the SEC that he owned 3.65 million shares of penny stock Rainmaker Systems. Rainmaker is a $24 million market cap maker of CRM software and services.

This stock has also had a rough ride over the prior year before Lynch bought, as shown in Figure 6.4. It reached a high of $3.50 in April 2004, only to begin a slow and steady ride down to the point where Lynch bought it, at around 50 cents a share. With a $24 million market cap, $10 million in cash, and no debt, and generating $2 million a year cash from operations, Lynch probably figured this was a safe bet. Time will tell.

Lynch is known for buying stocks based on simply observing what people are buying in the malls. According to an SEC filing on July 24, 2003, Lynch bought 238,000 shares of barbeque maker Barbeques Galore, which owns 38 stores selling barbeques and equipment in Australia. Perhaps he smelled a trend.

The stock has had a nice run since he bought his shares, as can be seen in Figure 6.5. With a $17 million market cap, $229 million in revenue, and $3 million in net income, Lynch probably feels he has a pretty safe cushion and any improvement in margins will be reflected in their earnings and market cap. Additionally, they pay a 5.2 percent dividend at the time of this writing so he can get paid to wait.

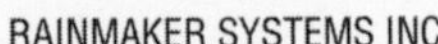

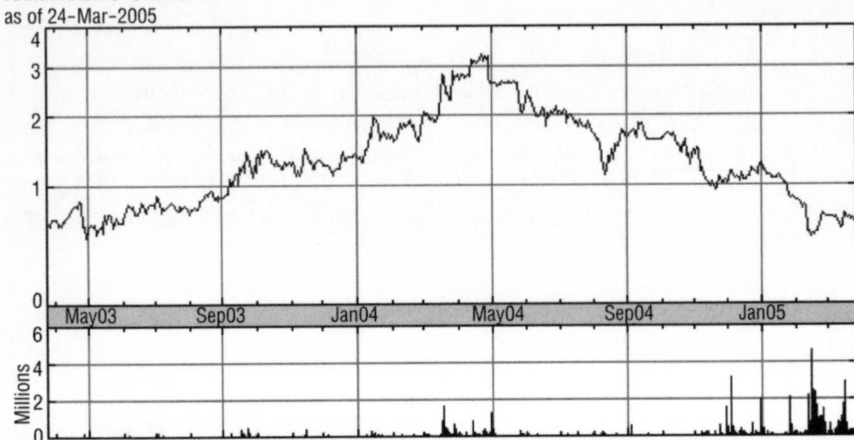

FIGURE 6.4 Rainmaker Systems Inc.
Source: http://finance.yahoo.com/. Reproduced with permission of Yahoo! Inc. © 2005 by Yahoo! Inc. YAHOO! and the YAHOO! logo are trademarks of Yahoo! Inc.

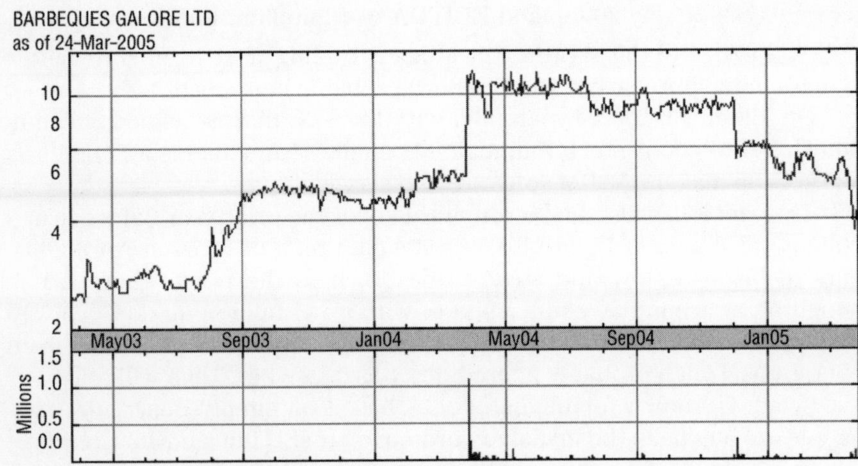

FIGURE 6.5 Barbeques Galore Ltd.
Source: http://finance.yahoo.com/. Reproduced with permission of Yahoo! Inc. © 2005 by Yahoo! Inc. YAHOO! and the YAHOO! logo are trademarks of Yahoo! Inc.

GEORGE SOROS

Soros takes a macro view of the world economy and then makes his stock choices accordingly. The top investors seem to be converging on silver. Bill Gates owns 10 percent of Pan American Silver mines and Soros owns 400,000 shares of Apex Silver mines. Additionally, his brother Paul owns 240,000 shares of Apex.

Soros also owns 5.8 million shares of JetBlue and 652,000 shares of Integra Life Sciences.

PETER KELLOG

Peter Kellog is the founder of the firm Spear, Leeds, Kellog, which he sold to Goldman Sachs. Spear, Leeds, Kellog is a market maker and specialist in thousands of small cap and micro cap stocks, so I like to follow his personal stock picks through his SEC filings.

Elxsi Corp. is a pink-sheet company that owns a chain of restaurants throughout New England. It has a $15 million market cap, $97 million in revenues (as of May 2005), and EBITDA of $3 million. Kellog owns more than 20 percent of the company.

Integramed is a network of 23 fertility centers across the United States. They offer a range of products, services, and financing, in the fertility industry. Kellog, with 500,000 shares, owns about 15 percent of the $33 million market cap company, which has $107 million in revenues, $10 million in cash generated from operations, and $6 million net cash in the bank.

CARL ICAHN

Known as a corporate raider, activist investor, hostile takeover artist, and proxy fight master, Carl Icahn is almost always engaged in one sort of battle or another. Right now, looking through the business news, the past year has seen headlines with Carl Icahn in battles with the boards and managements of Blockbuster (where he just took over the board), Hollywood Entertainment (where he made a nice profit on a merger arbitrage activist play), and Kerr-McGee.

It's interesting to see which companies he buys where he's not an activist. Certainly the management teams of these companies have to wonder what he's up to, even if he hasn't said a word about his investments. Is he planting the seeds for his future takeover attempts? Is he going to wage a proxy fight and try to take over the board? It's worth looking at each company and determining what Icahn might see in them.

Icahn owns 5 million shares of Time Warner (TWX), one of my favorite companies, with a value of approximately $88 million. At $16.96 a share, TWX is priced almost exactly where it was at the market bottom in July 2002, despite a complete management shakeup (including a renaming from AOL to Time Warner) and successful restructuring of their cable and music lines. Because of the guilt-by-association with AOL, the dot-com bubble burst had its effect on the stock, as shown in Figure 6.6 comparing TWX performance over the past five years with the performance of several of its traditional media peers: News Corp (NWS), Viacom (VIA.B), and Disney (DIS). [Since this was written Icahn has begun an activist play on Time Warner, trying to get them to unlock value by selling off the cable company, AOL, and other divisions.]

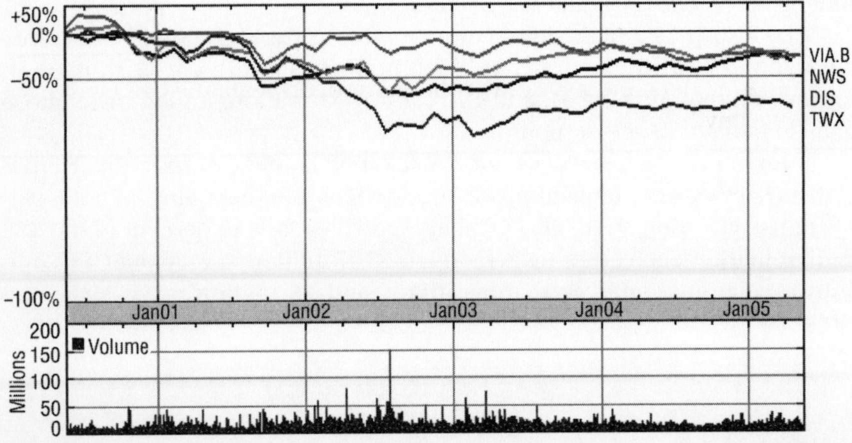

FIGURE 6.6 Time Warner Inc. as of May 13, 2005
Source: http://finance.yahoo.com/. Reproduced with permission of Yahoo! Inc. © 2005 by Yahoo! Inc. YAHOO! and the YAHOO! logo are trademarks of Yahoo! Inc.

The company has also steadily increased cash flow and paid down debt, but investors still don't trust it.

I was surprised to see Icahn owning 4.5 million shares of SEBL, valued at approximately $41 million. I don't really think of him as a tech guy. However, with four CEOs over the past year, SEBL has definitely been a company that has trouble unlocking its potential, despite a war chest of $2.2 billion in cash, $280 million in cash flows, and zero debt, on top of a

$5 billion market cap. With consolidation in the software industry occurring at a rapid pace and even private equity firms getting involved, Icahn is probably making a bet that SEBL is soon to be consolidated. And at the very least there is the safety cushion of the $2 billion in cash to keep things afloat while he waits.

Another technology stock he bet on was HWP, Hewlett-Packard. Icahn has also made a bet on the energy industry, not only with Kerr-McGee but with holdings in Pogo Producing Corp., Noble Energy, and Pioneer Natural Resources.

What is interesting to me is that looking at the broader scope of Icahn's picks is like seeing a who's who of what stocks were in the news over the past year. While some investors like to find stocks that are out of the mainstream and maybe represent pockets of hidden value (Buffett is usually thought of in this category), Icahn seems to dive right into the headlines:

> "Oh, Hewlett-Packard stock is tanking, profits are going down, the CEO is getting fired, it's page one news every day. Let's buy!"
>
> "Time Warner is the biggest media company in the world, plagued by lingering debt and dot-com problems and, oh yeah, the CEO was fired. Let's buy!"
>
> "SEBL has a stubborn, driven chairman, who, by the way, fired several CEOs this year. Let's buy!"

It's almost like a magic trick. While companies get in the news through the firing and hiring of CEOs, Icahn tries to figure out what's going on with the hand hidden behind the back, where the profits are being generated.

For more on his picks, check out this web site: http://www.sec.gov/Archives/edgar/data/1317365/000092847505000136/icahnmanagementlp13f.txt.

Certainly all of these individuals can afford to lose some money on some of their investments. But it is worth noting that these savvy investors and businesspeople have included quite a bit of small cap and micro cap investments.

CHAPTER 7

Closed-End Fund Arbitrage

Closed-end funds (CEFs) are similar to mutual funds in that they are companies formed just to buy and sell securities of other companies. The managers of the fund raise money by going public on an exchange. They then use the proceeds of the offering to make investments. This is different from a mutual fund, where investors purchase shares in the fund directly from the fund itself.

A mutual fund always values itself based on its net asset value (NAV), which is basically the fund's total assets minus its total liabilities. For example, if XYZ Fund has $100 million in stocks and no debt, then its NAV is $100 million. When a mutual fund investor wants to redeem shares, he will be able to sell his shares back to the mutual fund at the NAV price. A closed-end fund investor sells his shares on the open market, so the shares may or may not trade at NAV.

Closed-end funds can invest in anything from bonds to illiquid stocks to private equity investments. At the time of this writing, many private equity firms, such as Kohlberg Kravis Roberts and Apollo, are starting up business development companies, which are a form of closed-end fund.

Closed-end fund arbitrage is one of the few arbitrage strategies that I think will continue to flourish and do well despite the mass-indexing of almost every arbitrage strategy out there. The primary reason for this is the lack of liquidity in most arbitrage strategies. Closed-end funds do not attract a lot of volume, so the larger mutual funds and institutions are usually not players in this arbitrage strategy. Even the multibillion-dollar hedge funds will tend to shy away from this approach. Additionally, this strategy usually requires an activist bent. A closed-end fund might have a huge discount but there also might be no clear catalyst that's going to unlock the value in the situation.

Personally, I think an attractive business is to start a single-strategy fund of hedge funds that only invests in managers that focus on closed-end fund arbitrage.

DISCOUNTING MECHANISMS

Typically, a fund begins trading at a premium to its net asset value. Then, over time, a discount sets in so that the closed-end fund is trading at a lower price than that suggested by the net asset value. There are many reasons to discount results:

- Closed-end funds aren't popular investments. Many people do not even know they exist. After its initial IPO release, a closed-end fund might languish and the shares slowly drift down on nothing but ignorance.
- If a closed-end fund begins to underperform its indices, investors will begin to stop trusting the managers and sell the shares accordingly despite the discount to NAV.
- The NAV might include capital gains that have yet to be taxed. The shares will properly reflect this tax liability by trading at a discount.
- Illiquid or hard-to-value securities may be in the portfolio. For instance, many private equity firms will not be able to properly evaluate their portfolio and this will cause investors to take a more conservative approach when evaluating the NAV.

The benefit of investing in closed-end funds is that they often pay high dividends, even more so because many of the funds trade at a discount to the NAV. Closed-end funds typically dividend out all or most of their profits much like a real estate investment trust (REIT) does.

There are, then, two reasons for investing in a closed-end fund that is trading at a steep discount to its NAV:

1. That discount may narrow. For instance, if an activist buys many shares and then liquidates the fund, the discount will instantly narrow.
2. One gets at a discount a high dividend.

As of mid-2005 many CEFs that specialize in owning municipal bonds ("munis") are trading at a much more severe discount than normal. The reason is twofold:

1. With the dividend tax cut, the fact that munis are not taxed is less relevant when deciding to buy them.
2. With interest rates going up, the funds that use leverage are going to command a less attractive spread between their borrowing costs and the interest being paid by the munis.

When they are trading at a severe discount, however, it could be that the market has more than discounted the problems.

Although closed-end funds usually trade at a discount, the discount normally stays consistent and seldom varies. In the paper "Evidence on the Mean-Reverting Tendencies of Closed-End Fund Discounts," by Dominic Gasbarro and J. Kenton Zumwalt of Murdoch University and Richard Johnson of Colorado State University, the authors discuss that while the discount remains, it does tend to mean revert. In other words, if the discount quickly gets larger, it has a tendency to snap back to historical norms.

However, discounts in closed-end funds do not always eventually narrow (unless they hit an extreme, as described in the previously referenced paper). In the 2004 paper "Arbitrage in Closed-End Funds: New Evidence" Sean Masaki Flynn of Vassar College says that blindly playing a portfolio of going long discounted funds and going short funds trading at a premium is not a successful strategy and often offers negative returns. The trick is to find the funds that are trading at an unusually large discount or an unusually large premium.

Taken one step further, I think it is important to look for the funds that are not only trading at a huge discount (as suggested by the academic research) but where there is a fundamentally driven catalyst that might close the discount.

So the question is, given that many CEFs trade at a discount and that the discount, particularly when it is higher than its historical average or the discount of its peers, tends to mean revert, how does one develop a strategy for trading around these discounts?

DO-IT-YOURSELF CLOSED-END FUND ARBITRAGE

Step 1: Go to www.etfconnect.com. At this site you can find all the data you need about any closed-end fund: NAV, assets under management, date of IPO, management bios, historical NAV performance, historical price performance, top holdings, and so on.

Step 2: At that web site there are links that allow you to list all the closed-end funds ordered by discount, by premium, by year-to-date (YTD) return, and so on. For instance, on April 10, 2005, I came up with the list in Table 7.1 when I ordered by the size of discount. Z-Seven was trading at a 17 percent discount. Clicking on the symbol, I can find out more about the closed-end fund, as shown in Table 7.2. I can also look at a graphic of the stock's premium and/or discount to NAV at which it has traded since inception (see Figure 7.1).

TABLE 7.1 Closed-End ETFs

Fund Name	Ticker	Discount	As of Date
Equus II	EQS	–23.62%	4/7/2005
Canadian World Fund Limited	T.CWF	–23.57%	4/7/2005
Canadian General Investments Limited	T.CGI	–23.21%	4/7/2005
Z-Seven Fund	ZSEV	–16.97%	4/7/2005
Tuxis Corporation	TUX	–16.76%	3/31/2005
NAIC Growth Fund, Inc.	GRF	–15.81%	3/31/2005
Tri-Continental Corporation	TY	–15.65%	4/7/2005
Central Securities Corporation	CET	–15.35%	4/1/2005
Van Kampen Invmt Grade Muni	VIG	–15.16%	4/7/2005
Herzfeld Caribbean Basin Fund	CUBA	–15.02%	4/7/2005
Neuberger Berman Realty Income Fund	NRI	–14.91%	4/7/2005
AIM Select Real Estate Income Fund	RRE	–14.88%	4/7/2005
Investment Grade Municipal Income Fund	PPM	–14.87%	4/1/2005
First Trust Value Line Dividend Fund	FVD	–14.79%	4/7/2005
Neuberger Berman Dividend Advantage	NDD	–14.68%	4/7/2005
RMR Hospitality & Real Estate Fund	RHR	–14.58%	4/7/2005
Castle Convertible Fund	CVF	–14.49%	4/1/2005
Seligman Quality Municipal Fund	SQF	–14.46%	4/7/2005
Bancroft Convertible Fund	BCV	–14.44%	4/7/2005
Swiss Helvetia Fund	SWZ	–14.43%	4/7/2005
Salomon Brothers Fund	SBF	–14.34%	4/7/2005
Gabelli Global Multimedia Trust	GGT	–14.33%	4/7/2005
Insured Municipal Income Fund	PIF	–14.30%	4/1/2005
Van Kampen Trust for Inv FL Muni	VTF	–14.30%	4/7/2005
First Trust Value Line & Ibbotson Equity Income & Growth Fund	FVI	–14.29%	4/7/2005

Source: Etfconnect.com.

TABLE 7.2 ZSEV: Z-Seven Fund

Pricing Info As of:	4/7/2005
Closing NAV:	$5.48
Closing Share Price:	$4.55
Premium/(Discount):	−16.97%
Current Market Yield:	—

Additional Fund Information

- SEC filings
- Intraday pricing and news
- Fund sponsor daily pricing
- Fund sponsor web site

Category:	Global equity
Fund Sponsor:	Top fund management
Portfolio Manager:	Barry Ziskin
NASD/Symbol:	ZSEV
NASDAQ Symbol:	—
Cusip Number:	988789103
Inception Date:	12/30/1983*
Inception NAV:	$4.60
Inception Share Price:	$5.00

Investment Objective

Z-Seven Fund is a closed-end management investment company. The Fund's primary objective is capital appreciation. The Fund invests primarily in common stocks. The Fund intends to use a variety of investment strategies, including investing in foreign issues, lending portfolio securities, writing covered call options, investing in restricted securities, and borrowing to purchase securities. The Fund may invest up to 25 percent of its assets in the securities of a single issuer.

*The actual inception date of this fund is 12/29/1983. Historical data prior to the inception date listed above is being sought for this fund. Please check back soon.

Source: Etfconnect.com.

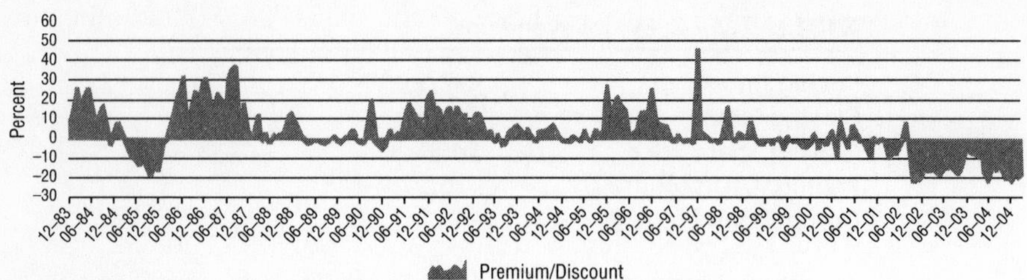

FIGURE 7.1 ZSEV Premium/Discount Chart
Source: Etfconnect.com.

Since it looks like it is trading at an unusually large discount to NAV relative to the discount since its inception (in fact, it was often traded at a premium), it could be an interesting buy. One way to play it is to outright buy the stock. Another way is to buy the stock and then short its top 10 holdings, which are revealed once a quarter. These were Z-Seven's holdings as of December 31, 2004:

Name of Company	Percent of Total Portfolio
Rathbone Brothers PLC	9 percent
Factset Research Inc.	7.8 percent
Barratt Developments PLC	7.5 percent
Techne Corp.	6.8 percent
VT Holding A/S	6.11 percent
Balchem Corporation	5.9 percent
TIS Inc.	5.6 percent
UCB	5.3 percent
Roxboro Group PLC	4.6 percent

If the value of the stocks falls, then you will win on your short and, since the CEF is already trading at a 17 percent discount to NAV, it shouldn't fall as fast as its underlying components. And if the stocks go up, then the bet is that the CEF will go up faster since whatever reasons people had for discounting the stock so much might be moot when its components begin to go up.

Another resource is www.cefa.com, which allows you to search on, for instance, all taxable bond closed-end funds, ranked by their discount to NAV.

A fund that has generated consistent positive returns from closed-end fund arbitrage is Camelot Capital Management, based in Philadelphia and run by Thomas Rosato. Rosato has specialized in the trading of closed-end funds for over 15 years and in 1995 started Camelot. Year-end returns have been positive since its inception in 1995, with Camelot ending 2003 up 22.525, its best year to date.

Another successful fund using the closed-end fund arbitrage approach is Brookdale Global Opportunity Fund, run by Andrew Weiss. Weiss went on leave as a tenured professor at Boston University in order to launch his fund. His results since its inception in mid-2000 have not been as consistent as those of Camelot, though he continues to end each year in the black. And while Brookdale has been in the negative some months, the year-end results have been successful; 2004 ended up 30.883 percent for the fund.

Another approach to take is similar to the approach discussed in Chapter 2 on activism: Piggyback on the shoulders of the activist investors who specialize in closed-end fund arbitrage. Interestingly, Sowood Capital Management, run by Jeffrey Larson, which was seeded with about $700 million from Harvard Management Corporation when Larson left Harvard's employ to start Sowood, specializes in closed-end fund arbitrage.

In March 2005, for example, Harvard/Sowood submitted a 13D filing stating that it felt the Korean Equity Fund (KEF), of which it owned 29 percent, should be turned into an open-end fund, which would immediately close the discount to NAV and result in a liquidation of the fund. It felt that KEF was too small to be cost-effective and too small to amortize the fixed costs of managing the fund. David Nierenberg, manager of the Nierenberg Family of Funds, also filed a 13D supporting Harvard's move.

Harvard has also applied this strategy in the past to other funds. From 2000 to 2002, Harvard had accumulated 23 percent of the Asia Tigers Fund, which was trading at a 25 percent discount to its NAV when Harvard first began buying. Harvard pressured the fund into periodically buying back its shares in order to reduce the discount. By the time Harvard had sold its shares in November 2003, the discount had been reduced to 7 percent and the stock had risen 45 percent since they had first begun buying shares.

As can be seen from Figure 7.2, the discount to NAV of KEF went from approximately 9 percent to 3 percent shortly after Harvard filed its 13D, resulting in the lowest discount to NAV for KEF since 1999.

Closed-end fund arbitrage is one of the most reliable strategies out there for either hedge funds or individual investors and there are various ways to approach it. Sites like www.etfconnect.com or www.cefa.com

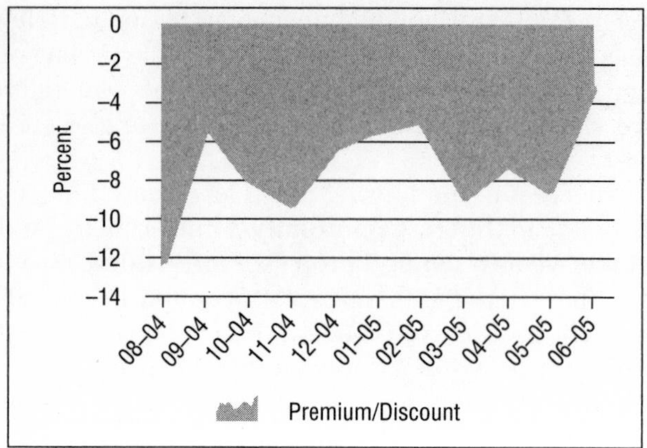

FIGURE 7.2 KEF Premium/Discount
Source: Etfconnect.com.

offer valuable statistics on which closed-end funds are trading at abnormal discounts either relative to their own history or to their peers. Additionally, by perusing the 13D filings of closed-end funds, one can see which funds are potentially being accumulated by activist funds itching to get into a fight over the discount. Meanwhile, there are various ways to hedge closed-end funds—for instance, in the KEF battle just described, one could have hedged by shorting the exchange-traded iShares MSCI South Korea Index Fund (EWY), which mimics the Korean Composite Stock Price Index (KOSPI). And with most closed-end funds there is the added benefit of getting a dividend while you wait for the discounts to close. The consistent results of the hedge funds that apply this strategy attest not only to the skills of those managers but the reliability of closed-end fund arbitrage as a strategy.

CHAPTER 8

Short-Selling

Short-selling is probably the worst method out there for making money, and it's a shame that many funds of hedge funds consider short-selling an asset class or, at least, a hedge against the long bias of other strategies. The basic economics of shorting are just horrible. The best case when you short a stock is that the stock goes down 100 percent. But that's unlikely, even in a bankruptcy, as evidenced in Chapter 3. When you go long a stock, there's opportunity for much greater moves than 100 percent, even in a bear market—in fact, as we will discuss, a bear market is when those multiple 100 percent moves to the upside are most likely to occur.

In this chapter we examine some of the pitfalls and look at several methods that have historically worked and that I use. Even in the vicious bear market that occurred from 2000 to 2002, the worst bear market in 60 years, it was not easy to make money from the short side. The biggest mistake one can make is thinking that just because the trend is down, all one needs to do is short and make money. It's just not true. The CSFB Tremont Dedicated Short Bias Index is a great illustration of this point (see Figure 8.1).

Since its inception the Dedicated Short Bias Index has offered an average annual return of –2.36 percent. Hardly the place where you want to put some money. But okay, given that, one can argue that hedge funds with a dedicated short bias are a decent hedge against disaster or against widescale corporate corruption that might occur in the stock market. For instance, in 2001 the U.S. stock market, as represented by the S&P 500,

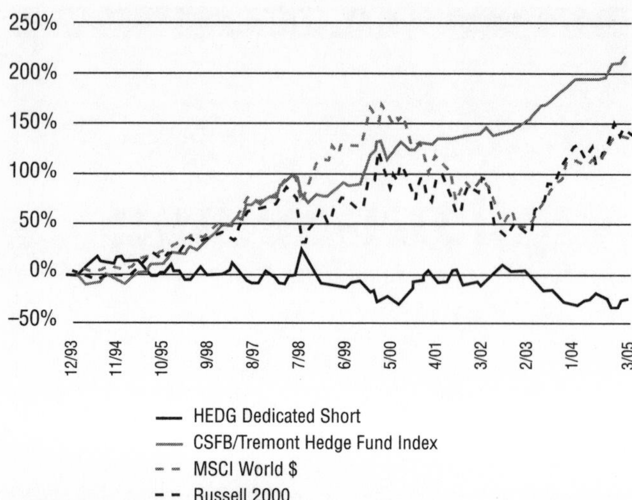

FIGURE 8.1 CSFB Tremont Dedicated Short Bias Index
Source: Courtesy of IASG.com.

was down –12 percent. That year we had the disaster of 9/11, which sent shock waves into the market, as well as the Enron bankruptcy, the ramifications of which were felt well into 2002. So in a year like that we would expect an index made up of fund managers who spend 24 hours a day trying to find companies to short, to be positive, or at least to have provided the hedge we needed.

It turns out that the index for these superb short-sellers was actually –3.58 percent in 2001 with 7 out of 12 months that year negative against the index. There were a couple of reasons this occurred:

1. The surprise rate cut in January 2001 took everyone by surprise and might have forced some short-sellers to liquidate positions. With a long position one can ride the beast a little bit, but with short-selling you can't take the chance of a triple-digit loss, so funds might have cut their losses and not have been fully invested when things started to go down further.
2. Severe moves to the downside tend to be met by even more severe moves on the upside. A great example is in the latter stages of 2001. The 9/11 incident crushed the market so fast and severely it was breathtaking. From the close on September 10, 2001, to the low on September 21, 2001, just five trading days later, the market was down 18 percent, a move rivaling the October 1987 crash. Pressing a trade at that point (under the guise of "the trend is your friend") would have

been disaster because from that low on September 21 to the end of the year, the S&P 500 returned 22 percent and the NASDAQ 100 returned 43 percent. Not pleasant if you were short.

So shorting the NASDAQ 100, through either the exchange-traded fund QQQQ or NASDAQ futures, both of which represent the index, is a dangerous game, bull or bear market. The volatility is two to three times that of the S&P 500 and, depending on the rumor, one can get whipsawed several percentage points within seconds.

The beauty of that volatility is that it is one of the few asset classes where shorting for extremely short periods can provide acceptable returns. The liquidity on both the NASDAQ 100 index (QQQQ) and NASDAQ futures (represented by the symbol NQ) is enough that getting in and out results in fairly low slippage, and transaction costs on futures amount to about five basis points round-trip per trade. There are other advantages to sticking with either QQQQ or NQ when shorting, the most important being that there is no uptick rule when shorting either an exchange-traded fund (ETF) or a futures contract.

PITFALLS OF SHORT-SELLING

As we saw in the example of the CSFB Dedicated Short Bias Index, there are some pitfalls to avoid.

Pitfall 1

Many market analysts talk about P/E ratios. The price over earnings ratio of the market is usually calculated by taking the average price of every company in the S&P 500 and dividing it by the average earnings per share of every company. A P/E ratio lower than 10 usually means that stocks are too cheap. Earnings above 20 are considered too expensive and many market analysts suggest that the market should be sold. To some extent, the analysts are correct. Buying the market when it was at P/Es below 10 presented enormous buying opportunities: If you had bought in July 1974 when P/Es dipped below 10 and held until P/Es hit 20 in July 1987, you would have had a 636 percent gain. The last time P/Es had dipped below 10 before that was October 1947, when buying then and holding until P/Es eclipsed 20 would have allowed you to ride the entire post–WWII bull market. You would have sold in April 1961 and made a 724 percent gain. However, doing the reverse—shorting when P/E ratios were supposedly too high and covering when they got back down to 15 (or even 10)—

would have resulted in five losing trades over the past century. Each trade would have wiped out the short-seller.

Pitfall 2

How about the January barometer? Supposedly, when the January market is up, good things are coming for the rest of the year. And when January is down, as many market pundits warn, this bodes poorly for the remainder of the year. However, since 1950, January has been down on 20 different occasions. On 10 of those occasions, the markets were up that year, and on 10 the markets were down. Shorting from February 1 to December 31 on each of those 20 occasions would have resulted in a small overall loss—not really a short-selling fantasy come true. Table 8.1 provides summary results of the worst post–WWII Januarys on the S&P 500 and the result for the remainder of those years.

TABLE 8.1 The January Effect

Percent January Change	Entry Date	Entry Price	Exit Date	Exit Price	Percent Change Rest of Year
-3.65	02/1956	$ 43.82	12/31/1956	$ 46.67	6.5
-4.18	02/1957	44.72	12/31/1957	39.99	-10.58
-7.15	02/1960	55.61	12/31/1960	58.11	4.5
-3.79	02/1962	68.84	12/31/1962	63.1	-8.34
-4.38	02/1968	92.24	12/31/1968	103.86	12.6
-7.65	02/1970	85.02	12/31/1970	92.15	8.39
-5.05	02/1977	102.03	12/31/1977	95.1	-6.79
-6.15	02/1978	89.25	12/31/1978	96.11	7.69
-4.57	02/1981	129.55	12/31/1981	122.55	-5.4
-6.88	02/1990	329.08	12/31/1990	330.22	0.35
-5.09	02/2000	1,394.46	12/31/2000	1,320.28	-5.32
-2.74	02/2003	855.7	12/31/2003	1,111.92	29.94
-3.63	02/2005	1,167.87	Open	Open	0

Pitfall 3

One also has to be careful when shorting fast moves up in the market. For instance, shorting the volatile NASDAQ 100 index (QQQQ) when it is up 4 percent intraday (in the middle of the day) and holding until the close is a strategy many people try, but few survive. Table 8.2 depicts the

TABLE 8.2 Short Trades: Results on QQQQ for 4 Percent Up System, March 13, 1999 to January 2, 2005

All Trades	125
Average Profit/Loss	–0.52%
Average Bars Held	1
Winning Trades	49 (39.20%)
Average Profit	1.53%
Maximum Consecutive Winning Trades	4
Losing Trades	76 (60.80%)
Average Loss	–1.84%
Maximum Consecutive Losing Trades	9

results of this short-selling approach—not that good. Even when the market is 4 percent higher than the prior day's close, shorting at that point is worse than gambling, with only a 39 percent success rate and an average return of 0.52 percent. In fact, I would recommend the reverse system. If the QQQQ is 4 percent up in the middle of the day, then the best thing to do is go long and squeeze all the people who feel smart enough to short at that point.

The key with the NASDAQ 100 is to leave the extremes alone. When investors are very excited or when they are throwing out the baby with the bathwater, it's best to step aside (or maybe even go long). But when the excitement is more tepid and the sadness is more of a melancholy than a full-scale depressive panic, then it is more appropriate to step in and take the chance that things are going to go down.

For instance, in the morning, many people attempt to fade a big gap. This entails shorting NASDAQ futures at 9:30 A.M. if QQQQ is up more than 1 percent from the prior days close, and covering at the close if the profit target is never hit. However, the bigger the gap, the more people are excited and the more that gap is likely to continue. As Table 8.3 demonstrates, there is not a high enough success rate or average profit to justify doing this in practice.

The worst mistake a short-seller can make is to say "This is ridiculous! The market is so overvalued here it can't possibly go further" or "The market has gone up for five straight days. It *has* to go down." It's exactly this psychology that propels the market even further, as everyone who is attempting to be right ultimately has to cover in order to prevent devastation, as we saw previously with the "four percent up" system. Similarly, a strategy of shorting the market the day after it has had four up days in a

TABLE 8.3 Short Only: Results for "Fading the Large Gap" System—Data on QQQQ from February 2000 to May 2005

Number of Trades	185
Average Profit/Loss	0.18%
Average Bars Held	1
Winning Trades	96
Winning Percentage	52%
Average Profit	2.19%
Average Bars Held	1
Maximum Consecutive Winning Trades	8
Losing Trades	89
Losing Percentage	48%
Average Loss	−2.02%
Maximum Consecutive Losing Trades	5

row has proven equally miserable, even when most of the data have occurred during a bear market. This is demonstrated in Table 8.4.

As long as things are going up, people refuse to take profits, and weaker and weaker traders pile into the market. At the latter stages of euphoria it is dangerous to jump in front of a runaway train. Examples of this can be found all over the Internet where traders congregate. Despite the universal academic condemnation of Yahoo! Finance mes-

TABLE 8.4 Short Only: Results of Shorting the Market after Four Up Days—Data on QQQQ from March 10, 1999, to January 2, 2005

Number of Trades	65
Average Profit/Loss	−0.09%
Average Bars Held	1
Winning Trades	32
Winning Percentage	49.23%
Average Profit	1.55%
Maximum Consecutive Winning Trades	3
Losing Trades	33
Losing Percentage	50.77%
Average Loss	−1.67%
Maximum Consecutive Losing Trades	6

sage boards, they are actually a treasure chest of footnotes to the great bull and bear markets that we have experienced since the rise of the Internet.

In 1999, Freemarkets, Inc. (FMKT) had one of the biggest IPOs of the bull market, pricing at $48 but closing at $280 on the day it went public. Six days later it was down slightly to $265 when the following appeared on a Yahoo! message board:

> Many mistakes
> I have made with stocks.
> *This wont be one of them!*
> I was so fortunate to get 50 shares at IPO and I will hold. Too many times I sold too early, too many times I regretted my mistake.
> Selling ICGE at 83 was one of them.

FMKT right now is $7 and change, having gone as low as $4 in 2002.

The Internet is an archive of the mania that occurred. However, shorting (and holding) this mania would definitely have been unhealthy, even in the case of FMKT. Anyone who had shorted the close on December 16, 1999, at $265 would have been sweating bullets 20 percent higher *the next day* when FMKT touched $317, or 40 percent higher when FMKT hit $370 two weeks later on January 3, 2000.

WHEN SHORT-SELLING WORKS

However, sometimes one can find fairly predictable systems where shorting has worked.

There's a saying that the "dumb money enters the market at the beginning of the week and the smart money comes in at the end of the week." In fact, looking at gap ups on Friday produces generally positive results on Fridays as opposed to any other day of the week.

The "fade the gap on Friday" system entails shorting the open on a Friday if QQQQ is gapping up between 0 and 1 percent (a small to moderate size gap up since we've already seen that shorting on a large gap might not be so productive). Cover at the end of the day. Table 8.5 demonstrates the results.

Another approach is to fade the gap on Friday if QQQQ is up from Monday to Thursday more than 2 percent. This works the same as the previous method except we are at the tail end of a nice up week. Short the open and cover at the end of the day. See Table 8.6 for the results of this system.

TABLE 8.5 Short Trades: Results for "Fade the Gap on Friday" System—Data on QQQQ from February 2000 to May 2005

All Trades	93
Average Profit/Loss	0.71%
Average Bars Held	1
Winning Trades	63 (67%)
Average Profit	1.55%
Maximum Consecutive Winning Trades	11
Losing Trades	30 (33%)
Average Loss %	–0.91%
Maximum Consecutive Losing Trades	6

TABLE 8.6 Short Trades: Results for Fading the Gap on Friday If QQQQ Is Up Prior Four Days by More Than 2 Percent

All Trades	18
Average Profit/Loss	1.29%
Winning Trades	13 (72%)
Average Profit	2.0%
Maximum Consecutive Winning Trades	5
Losing Trades	5 (28%)
Average Loss %	–0.5%
Maximum Consecutive Losing Trades	3

Look at the example in Figure 8.2. After three down years in a row, the market was riding the train safely into the station in the final quarter of a huge up year. October, November, and December were all up months, with most weeks up as well. Both the weeks prior to October 31, 2003, and November 7, 2003, were up greater than 2 percent on QQQQ. In both cases Friday was a gap up. Shorting that gap and holding for the day resulted in profits of 0.73 percent and 1.25 percent respectively.

One other method of short-selling that I'd like to mention is Option Expiration Friday. In general, shorting any gap up on an option's expiration day has been a successful strategy. Short any gap up on the morning of option expiration day, on QQQQ, and cover at 0.5 percent profit target or cover at the close if the target is never hit. See Table 8.7 for results.

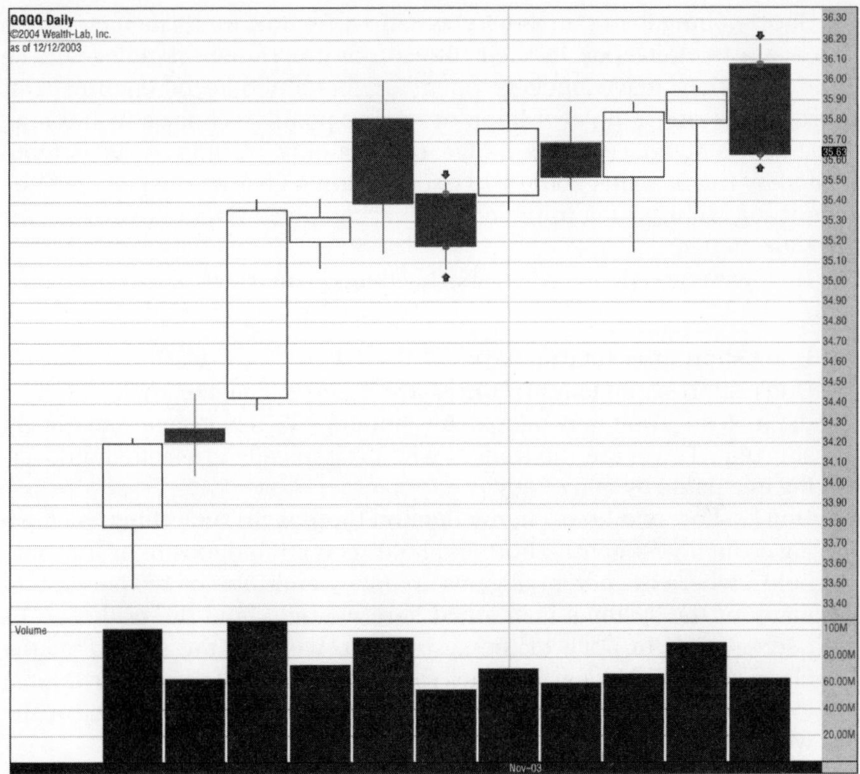

FIGURE 8.2 Shorting the Gap Up on QQQQ, October 31 and November 7, 2003
Source: Fidelity Investments. Charts created by using Wealth-Lab Developer software. The statements and opinions expressed in this book are those of the author. Fidelity Investments is not responsible for the accuracy or completeness of any statements or data contained in this book. Fidelity Investments has not examined, nor does it endorse, any trading strategy discussed in this publication.

TABLE 8.7 Results of Shorting Gap Up on Option Expiration Day—Data from February 2000 to May 2005

All Trades	30
Average Profit/Loss	0.47%
Winning Trades	29 (97%)
Average Profit	0.5%
Losing Trades	1 (3%)
Average Loss	–0.55%

Short-selling is not an asset class. Most fund of funds managers like to leave a bucket open in their allocations for the short-sellers in the same way they leave buckets open for fixed-income or equities. But short-selling offers no real hope of having positive returns in the long haul, nor is it an effective hedge of long-only managers, as demonstrated by the fact that 2001, a 12 percent down year where it seems like everything went wrong in the equity markets, was also a down year for the short-sellers.

Here are some don'ts when short-selling the market:

- Don't short after four up days.
- Don't short at midday if futures are 4 percent higher than the prior day's close. Too many people are thinking "This is insane!" and begin shorting. Those are the traders who are typically crushed and covering in a panic by end of day.
- Don't "short and hold." In my opinion there is no such thing as shorting as an investment. "Short and hold" is not the opposite of "buy and hold," where the potential gains are many multiples of 100 percent. In many of the systems mentioned here we only hold the trade for 0.5 percent, and in none of the systems do we hold the short past the close. As John Maynard Keynes said, "The markets can stay irrational longer than you can stay solvent," so it is best to just get out of the way when things are looking too crazy.

That said, there are several pockets of inefficiency in the market where short-selling opportunities can be found.

I must also add that short-sellers can occasionally have a sense of humor. In mid-2005 I wrote an article for the *Financial Times* about short-selling. The article was appearing at the same time as a favorite short-sellers conference. In particular, I wrote the following:

> *Last week was the annual "Bears in Hibernation" conference, an invitation-only meeting sponsored by Jim Chanos, founder of Kynikos hedge fund and dean of the short-sellers.*
>
> *He invites other hedge fund managers and analysts to swap short ideas and, presumably, engage in bearish rituals that optimists and bulls such as me cannot fathom. At the 2001 conference, Mr. Chanos revealed his bearish thesis on Enron which, as we know, turned out remarkably well.*

After my article appeared Chanos wrote me an e-mail, stating:

Dear Sir:

Your concern about our conference participants engaging "in bearish rituals" is misplaced. For example, we no longer sacrifice virgins, owing of course to our Miami Beach venue.

Respectfully,
James Chanos

So, when all the short-sellers are swapping stories by the campfire, I'm happy to know they are keeping themselves amused.

CHAPTER 9

The Finer Things in Life

When Picasso's *Boy with a Pipe* was sold for $104 million at Sotheby's in May 2004, nobody knew who the buyer was. Sotheby's announced that the buyer wished to remain anonymous. Speculation instantly turned toward the hedge fund managers who have devoted substantial parts of their wealth toward creating art collections: Stevie Cohen of SAC, Paul Tudor Jones, Henry Kravis, and others. Is the painting worth $100 million plus? Certainly to the buyer it was. And certainly the seller is probably pleased with his return on investment. And, like any asset class, there are periods where prices exceed value, depending on how you define value, and there are periods where prices tend to languish.

When people tire of one asset class, the dollars being pulled out of that asset class ultimately find a home elsewhere. When people tired of stocks in 2000, the money quickly found a welcome home in both real estate and bonds. With people now more cautious on real estate and bonds, dollars have flown into gold, oil, and other commodities. Things cycle, and one thing that has withstood the test of time is that ultimately money cycles back into the finer things in life: art, collectibles, music, and so on, that people will always appreciate. Whether or not these are actually investment categories remains unclear. Nevertheless, an argument can be made for art as an alternative asset class. Hedge funds and companies are out there now participating with collectors and artists in these burgeoning markets.

DON'T SPEND ALL YOUR RARE COINS IN ONE PLACE

Living the good life doesn't necessarily mean wining and dining, lying on the beach, and blowing all your money on roulette wheels in exotic casinos. Living large, enjoying life, and pursuing the finer pleasures can also go hand-in-hand with making more money—which, for many, is the ultimate joy in any case. Rare coins are often the currency of the rich and famous, whether historical biblical coins found at archaeological digs or the original silver dollars that launched our nation's currency.

There are collectors who, starting from humble beginnings, have amassed fortunes from buying and selling rare coins. John Jay Pittman, for instance, was an engineer at Kodak from 1947 to 1970, making between $10,000 and $15,000 per year. Each year he invested up to half his salary in rare gold and silver coins. Over the course of 20 years he probably made a total investment of about $100,000 in coins. Ultimately his collection was sold for over $30 million.

There are two ways you can get involved in coin collecting: Collect your own coins and master the subtleties of the different coins and grading mechanisms that are used to establish value for each coin, or invest alongside the masters.

I called on Silvano DiGenova, who made his first million when he was 21 trading rare coins. Silvano started out trading coins, then helped work out the process of grading rare coins, and more recently has been running Superior Galleries, a 75-year-old, California-based coin gallery, auction house, and public company. Silvano buys and trades everything from three-cent nickels to 1804-minted silver dollars and Saint-Gauden's gold coins from 1906. When he talks about coins and the value to be found he can't hide his excitement. If you take the 12-piece gold coin type set, which can be thought of as an index of the 12 most popularly traded coins, and if you had put $1,000 in that "index" in 1970 and held that basket of coins until now, your initial $1,000 would be worth $61,000 now. As Figure 9.1 shows, the same $1,000 put in the Dow Jones Industrial Average would only be worth $12,430 right now, despite the huge bull market in stocks from 1980 to 1999. (The 12-piece gold coin type set is described in the Appendix at the end of this chapter.)

"The history of money and the history of a country is usually found in its coins," DiGenova told me. "Coins are like holding history in your hands. Many of the best artists and sculptors of their times made coins. For instance, Augustus Saint-Gaudens was hired by Teddy Roosevelt to redesign America's coins. At the time he was America's top sculptor. In 1999, we bought and then resold a Saint-Gaudens 1907 $20 gold piece for $1.2 million, making a tidy profit on it. It's art and it's history and there are millions of collectors."

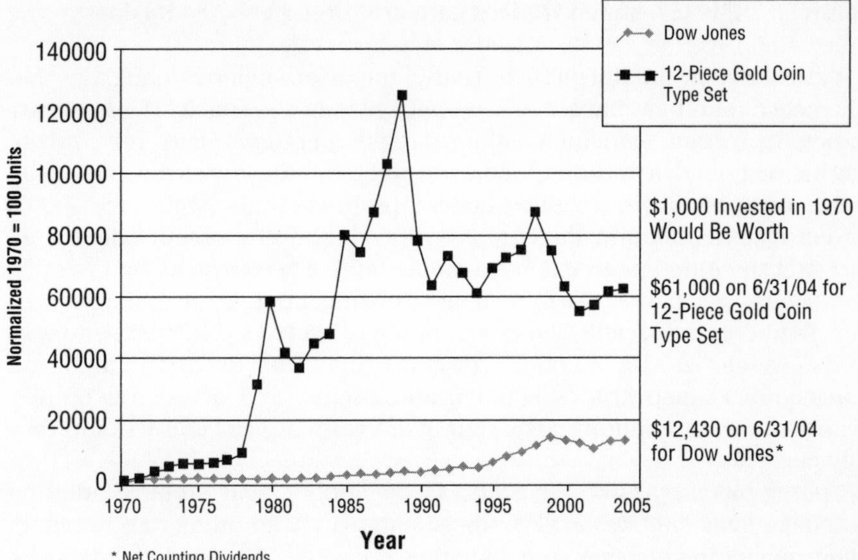

FIGURE 9.1 $1,000 Invested in 1970 12-Piece Gold Coin Type vs. Dow Jones (DJIA)
Source: Reproduced with permission of Superior Galleries. © 2005 by Superior Galleries.

Assessing the value of a rare coin does have similar characteristics to valuing a business. You use comparables and you make sure there is a significant margin of safety. The value of a coin depends in large part on its rarity, which is a function of both the particular time and place it was minted and its current condition. Depending on these two factors, there are various grading scales which will assign a grade based on the perceived rarity of the coin. Grades are between 1 and 70, with 60 to 70 being considered "rare." A coin that is graded 69 might be significantly more expensive than a coin graded 68.

The key to value investing in the coin space is to acquire coins that you think might have been graded too low or coins that are more rare than other similarly priced coins. For instance, a 1905 Liberty nickel with a 65 grade might cost $500 right now even though there might be only 157 other 1905 Liberty nickels with a 65 grade. This offers a better margin of safety than a Morgan silver dollar that might have a similar price but comes from a population of 3,000 to 7,000. In the long run, rarity is the best predictor of future price much in the same way that cash flows of a company are the best predictor of a company's stock price.

If you don't have the time or acumen to build and manage your own rare coin portfolio, there are other ways an investor can ride the potential returns of this investment style. There are three public companies in the space that together can be considered to be a "coin index."

The first company, publicly traded Superior Galleries, is run by Mr. DiGenova and is probably the only pure play in the space. The company generates income from coin auctions, retail operations (currently launching online coin stores through Amazon and Overstock), and also makes income from buying and selling coins ("proprietary trading") for its own inventory. Additionally, the company does high-yield, asset-backed lending, where coin collections are the collateral. The company had over 50 percent year-over-year (YoY) revenue growth in 2004.

While Superior sells the coins, publicly traded Collector's Universe is the premier grader of coins. Charging a $6 to $200 fee per item graded, the company also grades stamps, autographs, and other collectibles. Revenues were up 40 percent year-over-year last year and income rose 200 percent.

Greg Manning Auctions is also in the auction space and, in addition to coins, also sells baseball cards, stamps, art, and other rare items. In the past year revenues are up 22 percent year-over-year and income is up 96 percent.

Coins are here to stay and like any inflation investment, combined with artistry and precious metals, are likely to rise in value forever. That said, they aren't steady climbers and can often go years with slow or no growth, as seen in Figure 9.1.

BUT CAN I AFFORD A $100 MILLION PAINTING?

In late 2004, two friends of mine, both with hedge funds of $100 million or more in assets, dissolved their funds and returned all the money to their investors, though not because of poor returns—both funds were generating positive returns and beating the stock market indexes at the time of their shutdowns. One fund, a $300 million merger arbitrage fund that was up about 5 percent on the year, just simply decided it was too difficult to chase returns in this specialized field. With $1 trillion or more going into hedge funds and a large chunk of that going into the traditional alternatives of merger arbitrage, convertible arbitrage, and fixed income arbitrage, the spreads in every strategy were being reduced to nothing. For example, if two companies announce a $5 billion merger, and $10 billion or more is allocated across the alternative asset management world to merger arbitrage strategies, that $5 billion merger is going to have its spread reduced to zero very quickly. And then what happens, as was the case in the summer of 2004 in several instances, when a merger deal doesn't go through it's the proverbial "Fire!" in the movie theater. People are going to get hurt.

In the hunt for an asset class uncorrelated with the markets, I visited with Bruce Taub and Michael Plummer, who recently set up Fernwood Investments, an investment firm specializing in the "art economy." While every Wall Street bank has departments advising people on their art collections, it has been a recent phenomenon to look at art as an alternative asset class that has potential for returns equal to or greater than other asset classes while at the same time being relatively uncorrelated to the global markets. "Look at the recent $104 million purchase of Picasso's *Boy with a Pipe*," Taub says. "The painting was purchased for $30,000 in 1950. This represents a 16 percent annualized return commensurate with a good return on equities." Not every art purchase can boast a 16 percent return, but Taub points out that the British Railways Pension Fund has had an 11.3 percent annual return over the past 14 years primarily from a "buy and hold" art collection which they began selling in the 1990s. Similarly, the Mei/Moses Fine Art Index, formed by NYU professors Jianping Mei and Michael Moses, has demonstrated that art has returned 12.1 percent from 1953 to 2003, slightly higher than the equity markets during that period. (See Table 9.1 and Figure 9.2.)

TABLE 9.1 New Mei/Moses Fine Art Indexes versus Other Financial Assets, Compound Annual Returns

	Annual All Art	American Before 1950	Impressionist and Modern	Old Master	S&P 500 Total Return	U.S. Treasury 10-Year Notes Total Return	U.S. Treasury Bills Total Return
Past 50 Years	10.5%	10.0%	10.7%	10.0%	10.9%	6.6%	5.4%
Past 5 Years	7.3%	9.4%	6.3%	3.2%	−2.4%	7.5%	2.6%
Past Year	13.0%	25.2%	14.3%	1.8%	10.9%	5.1%	1.3%

Source: Beautifulassetadvisors.com, © 2005.

Fernwood attempts to improve on that result by adding value to their purchases in a variety of ways. They offer two funds. The first is a collection of sector funds that invests in art work in eight different categories of art: old masters, European, impressionists, American, modern, contemporary, postmodern, emerging. The idea is that the different categories are

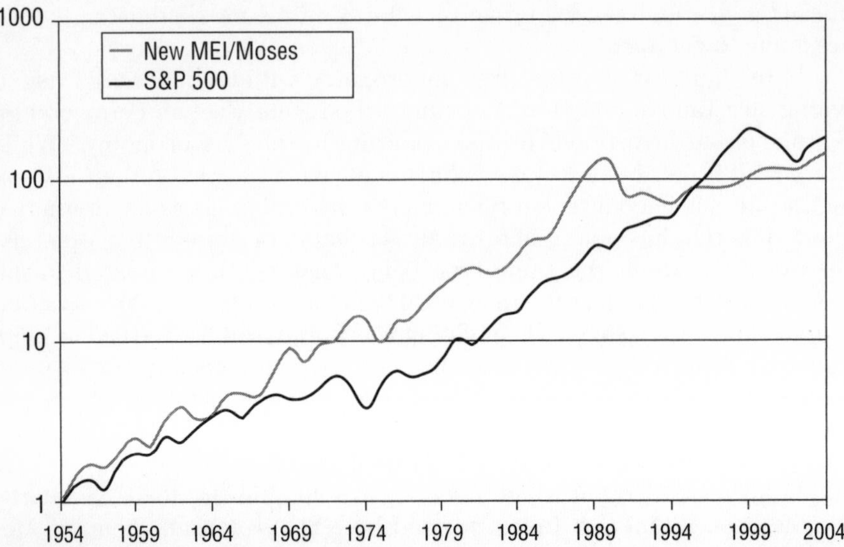

FIGURE 9.2 New MEI/Moses Annual All Art Index versus Total Return S&P 500
Source: Beautifulassetadvisors.com, © 2005.

not as correlated as one would suspect. In fact, just as in the equity markets, when one category dips, as tastes move in and out of favor, it is often the time to buy.

Fernwood's staff of expert art historians and curators not only attempt to find undervalued assets but also, in a similar vein to private equity and leveraged buyout funds, attempt to add value through active management. "We will put together collections; strategically loan out pieces to museums, which increases their value; and also promote research and critical analysis of the undervalued sectors where we have made purchases," says Bruce Taub.

The second fund Fernwood will roll out is an opportunistic fund. "Just like in the equity markets, there are often opportunities for arbitrage. For various reasons, art selling at one auction house might not attract the buyers that are currently available at other auction houses. Or there are cases where we can buy things for one price, knowing that there are buyers who are immediately willing to pay for the art at a higher price. This activity happens among dealers all the time but they are often too undercapitalized to take advantage of all of these arbitrage plays. Allying themselves with a fund such as ours will be to their advantage. Additionally, there are other types of financial transactions in the art economy, such as lending the art out for a fee, that we plan on participating in with this fund."

According to Taub, the art economy and the investment world will eventually converge—with the function of research, analysis, arbitrage, and investing playing larger roles for funds interested in art as an asset class. "A portion of wealth since antiquity has gone into art," says Taub. And now, with institutions looking for creative alternatives to the traditional asset classes, plus the increased interest in art and the availability of market data, Taub thinks that the barriers between the art economy and the investment world will erode, allowing investors to participate in the benefits of investing in fine art.

WHATEVER HAPPENED TO THE BOWIE BONDS?

I recently bought an iPod and have downloaded a special selection of "Fame," "Heroes," and "Rebel, Rebel" by David Bowie, as well as "I Feel Good" by James Brown, "Ain't No Mountain High Enough" by Ashford and Simpson, and "It's Your Thing" by the Isley Brothers. Why these songs? Because they are all assets that have been used to form Pullman Bonds, developed by David Pullman.

Pullman started these with the so-called Bowie Bonds, constructed in 1997, a $55 million deal securitized by the assets from David Bowie's extensive catalog of 25 gold albums and paying a 7.9 percent interest rate. The bonds are self-liquidating, meaning every year the remaining balance goes lower. Moody's has an investment-grade rating of BBB+ on the bonds. In the extreme case of a default, the bondholder would own the masters. In other words, the principal and 7.9 percent interest rate are backed by an asset that continues to generate more income each year than the year before, despite MP3, Napster, file sharing, peer to peer (P2P), and so on. Every time someone uses the song "Fame" in a ring tone, as a background (think of Dr. Dre's remake), or as background music in a movie, the ability of this asset to pay off its debt increases.

What I like about these assets is that they are completely uncorrelated to stocks and even to economic cycles. If you hear "Heroes" playing in the background in a department store, someone is getting paid a royalty even though you are hearing that music for free. After that initial Bowie deal, Pullman worked with artists such as James Brown, the Isley Brothers, Ashford and Simpson, and even the estate of John Steinbeck and the creators of cartoon character Casper the Friendly Ghost (hey, diversification).

I contacted Pullman to learn a little more.

How did it start, what's the next step, and how can investors get hold of the product you're putting out?
David Bowie was thinking of selling his masters and I was working with his business manager at the time, and we decided it would be in his better interest to securitize the cash flows instead. So now he still owns the masters, the income from the songs is better than ever, and the investors are happy since the principal has gone down every year because these are self-liquidating bonds, plus they got the 7.9 percent interest they signed up for.

What's involved in the due diligence on these assets?
I've looked at over 1,000 transactions and unlike when doing due diligence on a mortgage where you have to make sure the owner has the deed to the house, with these assets you have to deal with all the disparate parties that might have some claim on the cash flows—songwriter agreements, assignments, who owns the rights, the publishing, and so forth. Also, we analyze how consistent the cash flows are and we try to go over all the different things that can happen in the music world that could change those cash flows. A great example is MP3 and Napster. This was great for us. We got payments on the copyright litigation which the copyright holders won.

And what about peer to peer file sharing?
James Brown is making more money on "I Feel Good" than when it was a number-one hit in 1965, adjusted for inflation, despite MP3, Napster, file sharing, whatever. There's not just three broadcast networks now, there's close to 1,000 with a ton of music choices in them. His songs are used on TV, movies—anytime you hear "I Feel Good" on HBO, James Brown gets a royalty payment and the bond holders are happy. There's been a proliferation of outlets for music. That's never going to change. Apple sold 4 million iPods last year. That's an entire industry of people buying songs online now. The cash flows for the top-charted artists of all time are bigger than ever and that's who we like for these deals. When Moody's downgraded EMI to junk in March 2004 they only downgraded the Pullman Bonds we put together for David Bowie to BBB+, which is still investment grade. In other words, Bowie's cash flows are rated higher than the record label's cash flows.

Right now we are acting more like value investors and principals in these deals. We are looking for quality assets all over the entertainment world, pooling them together, and creating value out of the diversification. Then we are securitizing the cash flows on this pool and selling it to insurance companies, high net worth families, banks, anybody who wants diversification out of stocks, bonds, and other asset classes. Do I want to start a hedge fund? Not really. I don't want to deal with the administrative hassles, the overhead, and so on. However, we could potentially do joint ventures with institutions where we go in together as equity partners in a deal and they get a preferred return. But we'll see.

Another artist that has been heavily involved in the securitization of music assets is Michael Jackson. Michael Jackson bought the rights to 250 Beatles songs in 1985. Jackson then used the cash flows from this catalog of songs to secure a $200 million loan from Sony. When Jackson was going through his recent legal troubles it was rumored that Fortress, a New York City–based hedge fund, bought out this debt from Sony for an estimated $270 million.

APPENDIX: THE 12-PIECE UNITED STATES GOLD COIN TYPE SET

This description was written by Todd Imhof and Kathleen Duncan, Pinnacle Rarities, Inc.

In the 1970s and the 1980s, assembling a 12-piece U.S. gold coin type set was a popular challenge for most collectors. Countless 12-coin sets were sold to investors, and these dozen coins were often the starting point for in-depth specialized collections. As collecting habits became more focused in the late 1980s and the 1990s, the 12-coin set became less popular. But with the increasing difficulty of collecting by date, the type set is back and is becoming a very popular way to be introduced to numismatics.

The basic 12-piece United States gold coin type set consists of the following issues:

1. Type One gold dollar, 1849–1854
2. Type Two gold dollar, 1854–1856
3. Type Three gold dollar, 1856–1889
4. Liberty Head quarter eagle, 1840–1907
5. Indian Head quarter eagle, 1908–1929
6. Three Dollar gold piece, 1854–1889

7. Liberty Head half eagle, 1840–1908
8. Indian Head half eagle, 1908–1929
9. Liberty Head eagle, 1840–1907
10. Indian Head eagle, 1907–1933
11. Liberty Head double eagle, 1850–1907
12. Saint-Gaudens double eagle, 1908–1933

Generally speaking, a 12-coin type set features coins that grade Mint State-60 or better. The most common issues are typically represented by coins in the Mint State-63 to Mint State-65 range while the scarcer issues grade Mint State-60 to Mint State-63. Since this is a type set, most collectors choose the more common dates of each design. I have assembled a number of these sets over the years and would like to offer a few suggestions.

Type One Gold Dollar

This is an easy issue to locate in any Uncirculated grade up to Mint State-65. I would suggest purchasing at least a Mint State-64 (MS-64) example. A nice MS-64 is currently priced in the $1,500–$1,600 range while an MS-65 can be obtained for $4,000–$4,250. The best dates for type purposes are the 1849 and the 1851–1854 Philadelphia issues. Look for a coin that is well struck with clean surfaces and original color. Avoid coins that have spots or black streaks or those with naturally grainy surfaces. (See Figure 9.3.)

FIGURE 9.3 Type One Gold Dollar, 1851
Source: Courtesy of Pinnacle Rarities, Inc.

Type Two Gold Dollar

The Type Two gold dollar is the shortest-lived issue in the 12-coin type set. There are only two practical dates for type collectors: the 1854 and the 1855. These are equally rare and are priced similarly. Type Two gold dollars are moderately scarce in the lower Uncirculated grades, but are still costly due to their extreme popularity. A type collector on a limited budget should look for a piece that grades at least MS-61 to MS-62. Coins of this quality are available in the $3,500–$5,500 range. High-quality Type Two gold dollars are expensive but are seen in most major auctions or coin shows. A nice Mint State-64 is generally worth $16,000–$18,000 while a Mint State-65 is valued in the $30,000–$35,000+ range. When purchasing a Type Two gold dollar, eye appeal is crucial. Look for a coin with pretty original color and sharp detail at the centers. Pieces with excellent frosty luster are sometimes available and these are preferable to the typical dull, grainy example. (See Figure 9.4.)

FIGURE 9.4 Type Two Gold Dollar, 1855
Source: Courtesy of Pinnacle Rarities, Inc.

Type Three Gold Dollar

This is a readily obtainable issue with a variety of dates available to the type collector. A high-end Mint State-64 is currently available for around $1,000 while an MS-65 can be obtained for $1,950 or so. Unlike the other two gold dollar types, this design is sometimes seen in extremely high grades. A common date from the 1880s can be found in MS-66 for $2,000–$2,500 and MS-67s are currently priced at $3,500–$4,250. The best Type Three gold dollar issues for type purposes are the lower mintage issues from the 1880s. These are typically well made and are often found with superb coloration and luster. I personally prefer pieces that have rich frosty luster as opposed to the prooflike examples that are often seen. (See Figure 9.5.)

FIGURE 9.5 Type Three Gold Dollar, 1864
Source: Courtesy of Pinnacle Rarities, Inc.

Liberty Head Quarter Eagle

With a duration of over 60 years, there are numerous dates (and price ranges) for the type collector to consider. Liberty Head quarter eagles are quite common in lower Uncirculated grades and a nice Mint State-64 is currently in the $1,000 range. A Mint State-65 can be easily located in the $2,000 range while a common date in MS-66 can be purchased for $2,500–$2,750. Most type collectors focus on the issues produced from 1900 to 1907 as these constitute the majority of surviving high-grade Liberty Head quarter eagles. They tend to be extremely well manufactured and the collector can expect a piece that is sharply struck with excellent luster. Coins that are heavily spotted or which are unnaturally bright should be avoided. (See Figure 9.6.)

FIGURE 9.6 Liberty Head Quarter Eagle, 1857
Source: Courtesy of Pinnacle Rarities, Inc.

Indian Head Quarter Eagle

This is an attractive and popular issue which is one of just two U.S. gold coins with an incuse design. There are a number of common date Indian Head quarter eagles and type collectors typically pursue such dates as the 1925, 1925-D, 1926, 1927, or 1928. Coins that grade Mint State-64 are currently valued in the $1,750 range while MS-65s can be located for $6,500+. This is a very hard type to find in grades higher than MS-65. Collectors should look for coins with nice, rich luster and color and avoid those that have obvious scratches or abrasions. (See Figure 9.7.)

FIGURE 9.7 Indian Head Quarter Eagle, 1927
Source: Courtesy of Pinnacle Rarities, Inc.

Three Dollar Gold Piece

In most 12-coin gold type sets, the Three Dollar gold is among the centerpieces. It is the second rarest issue and certainly among the most unusual. There are only three relatively common dates in this series: 1854, 1874, and 1878. Every other issue is quite hard to locate in higher grades, even though it may not sell for a high premium. For many collectors a Mint State-62 or Mint State-63 will prove suitable. These are currently valued at $5,000–$6,000 and $8,000–$9,000 respectively. Gems are hard to find although not impossible. A nice Mint State-65 is currently valued at $18,000+. The type collector should seek a coin that has very good luster, no major spots, and pleasing natural coloration. (See Figure 9.8.)

FIGURE 9.8 Three Dollar Gold Piece, 1855
Source: Courtesy of Pinnacle Rarities, Inc.

Liberty Head Half Eagle

This long-lived type offers the collector a variety of options. Pieces struck prior to 1866 are known as the No Motto type and are, for the most part, very hard to locate in higher grades. Type collectors generally focus on the With Motto issues, especially those produced from 1880 onwards. A common date Liberty Head half eagle in Mint State-63 is worth only $700–$750 while an MS-64 is $1,450–$1,600. Gems are not very hard to locate. An MS-65 costs $3,250–$3,750 while an MS-66 will run in the $5,000–$6,000 range. The "perfect" type coin will be one with above-average luster, choice surfaces, and a sharp, even strike. (See Figure 9.9.)

FIGURE 9.9 Liberty Head Half Eagle, 1860
Source: Courtesy of Pinnacle Rarities, Inc.

Indian Head Half Eagle

This uniquely designed issue is the third hardest gold type coin in this set to find in high grades, trailing only the Type Two gold dollar and the Three Dollar gold piece. It was struck from 1908 to 1929 and at three mints: Philadelphia, Denver, and San Francisco. For type purposes, collectors tend to focus on issues such as the 1908, 1909-D, 1910, 1911, and 1912. A Mint State-63 Indian Head half eagle is easily located and generally sells for around $2,000. Mint State-64s are a bit harder to find and are valued at $3,850–$4,250. Mint State-65s can prove quite hard to find and are priced in the $17,500–$19,000 range. Collectors should pay close attention to the appearance of this type as eye appeal is crucial when evaluating an Indian Head half eagle. Coins should be selected for originality and those with excessive friction on the Indian's cheek should be avoided, as should examples with unnaturally bright color or deep, detracting abrasions. (See Figure 9.10.)

FIGURE 9.10 Indian Head Half Eagle, 1911
Source: Courtesy of Pinnacle Rarities, Inc.

Liberty Head Eagles

As with the half eagle of this design, there are two major types: the No Motto (1839–1866) and the With Motto (1866–1907). All No Motto issues are hard to locate in Uncirculated and are very rare in Mint State-63 or above. For type purposes, the post-1879 With Motto coins are more suitable. For the collector on a limited budget, a Mint State-64 is a good option with a number of dates available for around $1,800–$2,000. A Mint State-65 Liberty Head eagle can be located for approximately $4,500. The most common Liberty Head eagle in higher grades is the 1901-S, and this date will be included in many type sets. The collector might want to consider spending a little more money and purchasing a pre-1900 date to add a little pizzazz to his set. Coins with excessive spots or with marks on prime focal points such as Liberty's cheek should be avoided. (See Figure 9.11.)

Indian Head Eagle

Augustus Saint-Gaudens designed this issue and many collectors consider it to be among the most beautiful gold coins ever issued by this country. Two important types exist: the No Motto issues of 1907–1908 and the With Motto coins struck from 1908 through 1933. There are a number of dates that are available for type collectors seeking an affordable coin in the

FIGURE 9.11 Liberty Head Eagle, 1901
Source: Courtesy of Pinnacle Rarities, Inc.

Mint State-63 to Mint State-64 grade range. These include the 1910, 1910-D, 1911, 1912, 1913, and 1915. But most type collectors will purchase either a 1926 or a 1932 as these are, by far, the most common dates of this type. A Mint State-64 example of either of these two dates is valued at $2,000 or so, while an MS-65 is worth around $4,500. Most Indian Head eagles exhibit heavy marks on the surfaces and the collector should seek a coin that does not have these marks in readily visible locations. (See Figure 9.12.)

FIGURE 9.12 Indian Head Eagle, 1914
Source: Courtesy of Pinnacle Rarities, Inc.

Liberty Head Double Eagles

The Liberty Head double eagle was produced from 1850 until 1907. There are actually three distinct types but most type collectors focus on the most common: the Type Three that was struck from 1877 through 1907. It is almost a certainty that a type set will include a 1904 as its Liberty Head double eagle selection. This is the only Liberty Head double eagle that is common in higher grades. Mint State-64 examples are priced at $1,350–$1,450 while Mint State-65 coins trade for $4,250–$4,750. For the collector on a somewhat limited budget, a slightly scarcer pre-1900 issue in Mint State-63 (as opposed to a common 1904 in Mint State-64) might be a good alternative. Many examples of this type are seen with heavily abraded surfaces, and the type collector should seek a coin that has reasonably clean fields. It is also important to seek a coin with above-average luster and nice coloration. (See Figure 9.13.)

FIGURE 9.13 Liberty Head Double Eagle, 1904
Source: Courtesy of Pinnacle Rarities, Inc.

Saint-Gaudens Double Eagles

Known to most collectors as "the Saint," this is probably the single most popular United States gold type coin. There are two distinct types known: the No Motto (produced in 1907 and 1908) and the With Motto (made from 1908 until 1933). Most type collectors purchase a common With Motto issue such as a 1924, 1925, 1926, 1927, or 1928. These are very common in Mint State-64 and are typically priced around $800 while MS-65s are valued at $1,350. In Mint State-66, Saint-Gaudens double eagles are easily located and cost $2,400 or so. This is a type that will always be available, so the collector can be picky when deciding which coin to purchase. It is advisable to seek a Saint-Gaudens double eagle that has attractive coloration and no major marks in the obverse fields. (See Figure 9.14.)

FIGURE 9.14 Saint-Gaudens Double Eagle, 1913
Source: Courtesy of Pinnacle Rarities, Inc.

Assembling a 12-coin set is an excellent introduction to collecting United States gold coins. For more information on assembling a 12-coin set of United States gold coins please contact us at expectmore@pinnacle-rarities.com. Prices quoted here are for coins certified by third-party grading companies PCGS or NGC. We recommend only buying coins certified by one of these two firms.

CHAPTER 10

Trend versus Countertrend

There's a battle waging among investor and trader message boards across the Internet. Is the trend your friend, or your enemy? For instance, a search for "the trend is your friend" yielded 440 results on Yahoo! Message Boards one second before I wrote this.

On the one hand you have Boston Red Sox owner, John Henry, who has built a successful 20-year career out of studying the statistics behind trend following the markets. Henry's original fund has returned an annualized 8.94 percent since its inception in 1982. Table 10.1 shows the monthly results of his original program (as reported by Institutional Advisory Services Group).

In the description of the program courtesy of the Institutional Advisory Services Group (www.iasg.com), Henry states: "The Original Program seeks to capitalize on long-term trends in a broad spectrum of worldwide financial and nonfinancial futures markets. This broadly diversified program always maintains a position—long or short—in every market traded (two-phase investment style)."

Another example of a trend follower is Abraham Trading Company, started by Salem Abraham. The description of Abraham Trading states: "Abraham Trading Co.'s trading methodology is a systematic long-term trend-following approach implementing filtering techniques that avoid trends with adverse risk/reward characteristics. . . .

"ATC's portfolio contains 51 markets covering the grain, soft, meat, energy, metal, currency, and interest rate sectors. The markets are weighted so that their overall exposure is 60 percent commodity-based and 40 percent financial-based."

Abraham's results since inception are shown in Table 10.2. Its

TABLE 10.1 John Henry Original Fund, Monthly Performance 1982–2005

	JAN	FEB	MAR	APR	MAY	JUN	JUL	AUG	SEP	OCT	NOV	DEC	YEAR
2005	(19.00)	0.59	3.88	(25.11)E									(36.61)
2004	8.01	14.11	(2.94)	(9.24)	(7.85)	(15.05)	(1.29)	(0.10)	10.22	22.25	5.25	(16.09)	(0.26)
2003	22.39	8.21	(9.27)	0.53	0.83	(14.08)	4.36	5.63	(14.56)	(15.69)	8.60	4.71	(5.50)
2002	(0.04)	0.02	(9.20)	1.81	5.11	14.73	10.74	6.30	11.08	(7.82)	(8.10)	(1.59)	21.50
2001	(3.18)	(4.41)	17.44	(14.34)	0.69	(9.23)	(3.31)	3.69	6.35	2.49	(12.36)	2.10	(16.79)
2000	5.96	1.44	(4.90)	(6.68)	(5.13)	(2.73)	(3.31)	5.37	(10.15)	1.57	17.29	7.74	3.43
1999	(3.88)	5.11	(2.22)	5.98	(2.84)	2.14	(2.27)	0.59	(3.78)	(11.36)	4.63	(2.06)	(10.73)
1998	(1.30)	2.22	(4.10)	(0.52)	4.41	1.68	(3.97)	3.96	2.65	5.21	(12.82)	15.37	10.81
1997	3.42	0.21	1.63	0.50	1.10	(4.43)	2.05	(0.80)	(5.99)	3.59	0.00	4.86	5.73
1996	5.28	(7.35)	1.02	3.84	(6.48)	7.99	(4.36)	(2.33)	8.24	10.37	5.19	1.11	22.65
1995	2.16	17.87	16.58	9.09	(4.43)	1.65	(0.03)	(3.89)	(3.93)	3.25	1.15	6.84	53.23
1994	(2.95)	1.53	4.36	0.21	5.53	6.64	(7.15)	(4.73)	(2.83)	(14.11)	10.21	(0.04)	(5.68)
1993	(0.75)	9.54	(3.50)	10.36	0.12	(4.05)	14.92	(3.65)	0.63	(1.53)	3.45	11.40	40.64
1992	(6.12)	(8.79)	0.72	(0.84)	(4.46)	8.27	9.09	9.12	(2.75)	2.24	3.61	2.19	10.86
1991	(0.48)	0.30	(2.07)	(5.76)	4.40	(0.73)	(7.38)	(3.60)	10.74	(3.91)	(1.26)	17.71	5.43
1990	7.12	(2.04)	18.42	12.37	(10.93)	7.17	10.94	19.11	(2.12)	(1.90)	0.98	(2.32)	66.82
1989	0.80	(19.91)	11.70	(5.09)	28.97	(3.86)	8.08	(13.66)	(13.25)	(11.97)	7.35	9.82	(10.85)
1988	(6.90)	4.65	(16.05)	(5.10)	3.60	13.90	(19.80)	(4.30)	6.35	(2.45)	1.64	(12.53)	(35.16)
1987	8.99	3.65	2.66	21.91	0.75	(3.54)	8.84	(3.13)	(10.40)	35.80	16.48	11.93	129.81
1986	(4.39)	22.22	15.44	(5.83)	(2.78)	(2.13)	11.51	7.19	(2.86)	(10.25)	(1.94)	(2.98)	19.83
1985	2.43	0.88	(8.81)	(17.11)	11.00	4.37	16.80	1.74	(15.51)	9.57	7.36	18.62	26.77
1984	5.53	(4.81)	(7.54)	(2.09)	16.55	(10.30)	28.69	(9.03)	15.98	(5.24)	(2.18)	12.54	34.66
1983	14.36	(28.56)	1.63	4.86	8.27	(9.61)	10.91	13.41	(7.31)	(3.28)	(6.40)	(2.54)	(12.35)
1982										7.11	(16.85)	2.71	(8.52)

E = Estimated

Source: Courtesy of IASG.com.

TABLE 10.2 Abraham Trading Company, Monthly Performance 1988–2004

	JAN	FEB	MAR	APR	MAY	JUN	JUL	AUG	SEP	OCT	NOV	DEC	YEAR
2004	0.47	8.38	0.88	(6.22)	2.53	1.37	6.74	(12.25)	7.84	4.32	2.79	(0.51)	15.38
2003	24.18	13.18	(4.73)	2.02	5.59	(7.06)	(4.86)	(3.54)	7.02	22.09	(0.03)	8.69	74.66
2002	(1.73)	1.33	(6.62)	4.99	1.51	7.75	(3.97)	9.86	3.29	(10.19)	(1.80)	18.41	21.51
2001	2.28	2.99	15.17	(10.20)	5.13	4.47	(2.85)	4.89	9.28	4.13	(13.68)	(0.50)	19.16
2000	8.02	(9.05)	(4.16)	5.48	(2.58)	(2.19)	(5.26)	11.76	(4.53)	9.51	8.58	(0.18)	13.54
1999	(11.56)	13.35	(9.43)	7.52	(6.09)	(0.68)	(0.83)	3.12	0.99	(9.57)	13.64	8.41	4.76
1998	(0.90)	4.09	(4.45)	(4.45)	2.61	(2.34)	(0.83)	23.24	(3.33)	(11.39)	0.94	4.67	4.39
1997	5.28	9.15	(1.50)	(5.16)	(1.32)	0.38	4.11	(8.08)	4.95	(5.37)	2.10	7.46	10.88
1996	(6.85)	(13.78)	9.66	14.27	(9.41)	1.52	(6.30)	(3.34)E	6.03	16.84	2.45	(6.41)	(0.42)
1995	(7.91)	1.24	6.63	4.73	8.22	0.11	(8.75)	(5.34)	(1.84)	(6.67)	(0.19)	19.11	6.12
1994	(1.45)	(4.16)	2.87	(8.39)	15.01	1.47	0.98	(7.38)	5.05	5.43	14.24	1.06	24.22
1993	(4.21)	6.10	4.57	9.24	4.88	(1.22)	6.60	(5.28)	1.16	(6.59)	3.71	12.83	34.29
1992	(12.60)	(6.00)	(5.47)	0.31	(5.71)	6.58	16.52	1.92	(0.34)	(3.31)	4.65	(4.54)	(10.50)
1991	(15.94)	1.30	2.43	(13.70)	2.94	2.11	(1.52)	(6.33)	11.61	16.61	(2.09)	33.75	24.39
1990	3.65	1.81	9.45	12.90	(7.90)	2.49	20.08	18.54	8.57	(0.36)	0.31	(0.09)	89.95
1989	(8.05)	(12.64)	13.91	(20.08)	38.65	(4.40)	16.08	(13.84)	(7.75)	(14.40)	10.30	39.52	17.81
1988	4.17	(2.59)	(8.78)	(12.35)	32.34	71.99	(2.82)	3.45	(1.98)	8.01	17.83	4.51	142.04

E = Estimated

Source: Courtesy of IASG.com.

performance against the S&P 500 can be seen in Figure 10.1. The S&P 500 is the darker, flat line along the bottom of the graph.

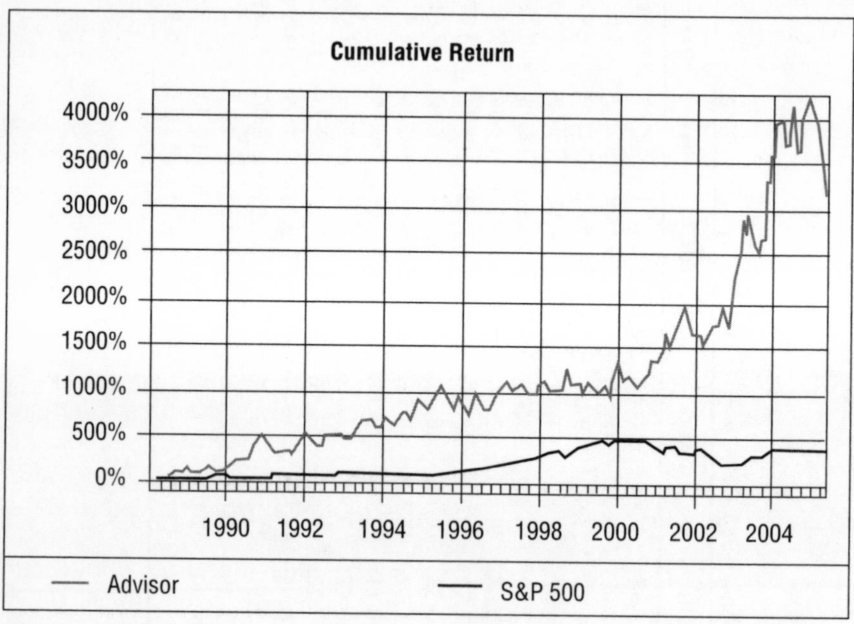

FIGURE 10.1 Comparison of Returns between Abraham Trading and S&P
Source: Courtesy of IASG.com.

The basic idea is that somewhere around the world, in any of the world's stock, commodity, currency, or bond markets, there are trends occurring. In choppy, trendless markets, get out as fast as possible. In the trending markets, get in, double down, and double down again. Using various statistical methodologies, the trend followers attempt to determine when a trending market is occurring, and then they use various methods to determine position size. A typical method for identifying trend-following markets is to use a moving average.

A moving average is simply the average price of the last X days/weeks/months (or whatever time period one is interested in). For instance, the 10-day moving average of stock XYZ is the simply the average closing price of the last 10 days of XYZ. A possible trend-following system (not necessarily the one followed by Henry or Abraham) is to buy (or add to) a position when the 10-day moving average crosses over the 50-day moving average. This could indicate that a market is quickly moving up.

Another possible trend-following method is to buy a market that is reaching a 50-day high. Add to it when it reaches a 100-day high.

I'm not a big fan of trend following, for the following reasons:

- Drawdowns could be immense. While it's true that one needs to take risks to make money, I think a potential 30–50 percent drawdown is too much for most investors to comfortably withstand.
- When markets reverse there is a mad rush to the door. Since the bear market of 2000–2002 (which trend followers survived quite nicely), an immense amount of money has been thrown at these funds. In fact, funds of funds just made up of trend followers sprang up to spread institutional money across the board at these funds. Given that these funds all use leverage to average into their positions as the positions move in their favor, it is no wonder that starting in mid-2004 and continuing into 2005 these funds would have double-digit losses in a month where key markets, such as oil or the dollar, reversed themselves, leaving the trend followers scrambling over each other to get out.

My guess is, within the next 10 years, the trend-following funds will all but disappear.

As far as systematic trading goes, I am a much bigger fan of the countertrend approach. The premise is that if a market goes straight down, then eventually it mean reverts and pops back up. The next few sections detail some of my favorite countertrend systems.

QQQQ CRASH REVISITED

At the time that I first wrote about this system—on June 2003, on www.thestreet.com—the system had been successful in 40 out of 40 prior occurrences. Now it is up to 55 out of 55 with the most recent occurrence being April 15, 2005, when QQQQ opened at 35.24. On April 21 it cruised up several percent, closing at 35.62, a gain of 1.08 percent.

The idea is that when the volatile NASDAQ 100 ETF, QQQQ (called "the Qs" by traders—this ETF represents the collective movement of the top 100 stocks in the NASDAQ) suffers a sharp dip down, chances are the dip is irrational and it is worth buying at least until there is an uptick. This system has worked well in bear markets. In fact, as will be seen in this section, it has worked better in bear markets than bull markets.

With this system, you buy when the price of QQQQ closes 1.5 standard deviations below the 10-day moving average of the low price of each day. To calculate this you can use the lower Bollinger band using a 10-day moving average, 1.5 standard deviations, and the price series of the lows of each day. You sell either at a loss after 20 days or if, on any day, QQQQ closes higher than the entry.

Table 10.3 shows all the recent occurrences for 2004–2005. Note that the gains have not been that great for each occurrence. Only two of them, on August 9, 2004, and April 15, 2005, were greater than 1 percent. And some of these occurrences would probably not have beaten commissions, particularly September 28, 2004.

TABLE 10.3 QQQQ Crash Recent Occurrences

Date	Entry	Exit Date	Exit	Percent Gain
1/29/2004	36.89	2/11/2004	37.22	0.89
3/9/2004	35.47	3/30/2004	35.57	0.29
5/3/2004	34.67	5/3/2004	34.77	0.29
8/9/2004	32.5	8/10/2004	32.89	1.2
9/28/2004	34.22	9/28/2004	34.24	0.06
1/5/2005	38.68	1/18/2005	38.72	0.1
1/21/2005	37.48	2/1/2005	37.52	0.11
3/17/2005	36.61	3/17/2005	36.71	0.27
4/15/2005	35.24	4/21/2005	35.62	1.08

I think there are a variety of ways to improve the system. One way is once it triggers, wait for a further selloff before entering the position. For instance, wait for 2 percent more.

Perhaps even better is the idea to apply the QQQQ crash to the individual components of the QQQQs. In other words, whenever a stock in the NASDAQ 100 closes lower than 1.5 standard deviations below the 10-day moving average of its lows, then buy the next morning and hold either until a profitable close or until 20 days are up.

I tested this on the NASDAQ 100 stocks and backtested from January 1, 1999, through December 31, 2004. There were 3,715 occurrences. Of those occurrences, 3,518 resulted in successful trades (94.7 percent). The average gain per trade on all 3,715 occurrences was 1.82 percent. Table 10.4 gives the annual returns, using 5 percent of equity per trade.

It is interesting to note that in the bear market years of 2000, 2001, and 2002, the system performed well despite its being a long-only system: 109 percent, 27 percent, and 35 percent respectively. Again, a choppy, aimless year like 2004 only turned in a 1.24 percent return and was also the year with the smallest number of entries. The equity curve of the system is shown in Figure 10.2.

TABLE 10.4 NASDAQ/QQQQ Crash Annual Returns

Period Starting Date	Percent Return	Percent Max DD[1]	Entries
1/4/1999	74.52	−7.58	461
1/3/2000	109.41	−11.92	548
1/2/2001	27.11	−25.07	429
1/2/2002	35.65	−13.55	536
1/2/2003	42.1	−6.19	423
1/2/2004	1.24	−14.03	379

[1]Maximum drawdown during the period.

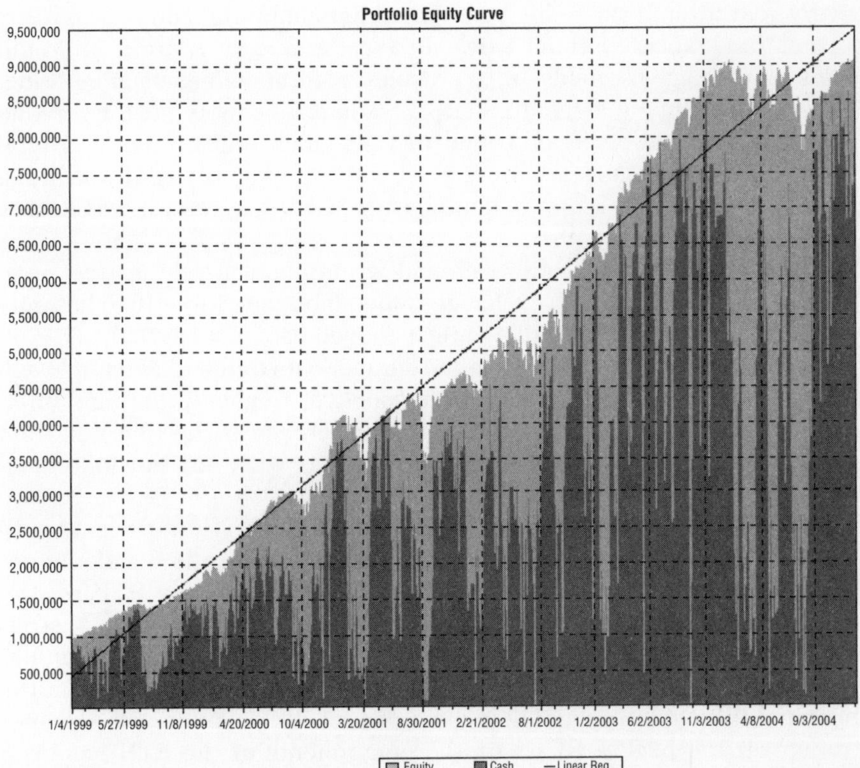

FIGURE 10.2 Portfolio Equity Curve

While I'm still unhappy with the results in a 2004-like period, I'm happy with the fact that the system continued to perform, albeit not as well; at least it didn't fall apart and lose money. I also feel that this family of systems is a good weapon for dealing with bear market years like 2000–2002 and bull market years like 1999 and 2003, while at least treading water in aimless markets. But it's back to the drawing board if one is looking for a holy grail.

THE CHRISTMAS SYSTEM

Every year around the holidays, news outlets jump the gun by reporting slower-than-expected retail sales. In fact, a Google search on "retail sales look sluggish" yields 10,100 results, with headlines such as "Sluggish Holiday Buying Leads to Sharp Discounts" being typical. Everyone becomes a would-be Peter Lynch in December, and normally erudite stock market analysts start coming out with statements like "I was in the parking lot at Home Depot in southeastern Kentucky, and it was empty. Not a good sign!"

In 2004 I tested this approach and wrote about it on thestreet.com. The Retail HOLDRs (RTH) exchange-traded fund (see Table 10.5) has only been around since 2001, so there aren't enough data to analyze the ETF on its own. However, I took a look at the components of the RTH dating back 20 years. In the tests, I ignored the respective weights in the fund (Wal-Mart and Home Depot alone made up 40 percent at the time) and did every simulated trade equal-weighted, which is what any portfolio manager, other than an index manager, would do.

So what happens if you buy each stock in the RTH on December 15 and hold for three weeks? The average weekly return is decidedly not bad: 1.16 percent. This makes the strategy of buying the RTH on December 15 and holding it for the holiday season a decent seasonal strategy. However, a slightly better twist is as follows: Between December 15 and 31, if a component of RTH falls 2 percent or more, buy it at the open the following day and hold it for one week. The average return per trade over the past 20 years on the components of the RTH has been 2.51 percent, a significant improvement over buying and holding every RTH component on December 15. I think the reason for this is that people panic unreasonably when they think that retail sales are going to be bad for a particular company. People tend to overestimate the effect, for instance, of cold weather on retail sales. They realize their mistake (or better, investors realize the mistake) within days, and the stock goes up accordingly.

TABLE 10.5 Retail HOLDR Components

Stock	Ticker	Share Amount	Current Weighting
Albertsons	ABS	8.00	1.91%
Amazon.com	AMZN	7.00	2.84%
Best Buy	BBY	6.00	3.49%
Costco	COST	8.00	3.95%
CVS	CVS	7.00	3.25%
Federated Department Stores	FD	4.00	2.28%
The Gap	GPS	16.00	3.46%
Home Depot	HD	40.00	17.24%
Kroger	KR	15.00	2.47%
Kohl's	KSS	6.00	2.97%
Lowe's	LOW	14.00	8.26%
Limited Brands	LTD	8.00	1.99%
The May Department Stores (Delaware)	MAY	6.00	1.76%
RadioShack	RSH	3.00	0.95%
Sears, Roebuck	S	6.00	3.30%
Safeway	SWY	9.00	1.75%
Target	TGT	16.00	8.47%
The TJX Companies	TJX	10.00	2.52%
Walgreen	WAG	19.00	7.61%
Wal-Mart	WMT	36.00	19.53%

Source: Reproduced with permission of Yahoo! Inc. © 2005 by Yahoo! Inc. YAHOO! and the YAHOO! logo are trademarks of Yahoo! Inc.

As a check to make sure this is a phenomenon peculiar to the holiday season, a test of the same strategy at any other time during the year (rather than limiting activity to December 15 to 31) over the past 20 years has resulted in an average return per trade of 0.50 percent. This lags the holiday period by 2 percent.

I would definitely be a buyer the day after any of the components of the RTH fell 2 percent on any day between December 15 and the end of the year, and I would buy the stock that fell 2 percent and hold for one week.

The results of the strategy in 2004: On December 17 Best Buy shares slipped 2.5 percent after Circuit City announced that sales were less than expected. Buying the open on Monday, December 20, at $56.89 resulted in a 1.76 percent profit, selling one week later at $57.89 (see Figure 10.3). The trades that were triggered according to the system in 2004, and their results, are shown in Table 10.6. Following the system resulted in an average return of 2.9 percent per trade, with six up trades and two negative ones.

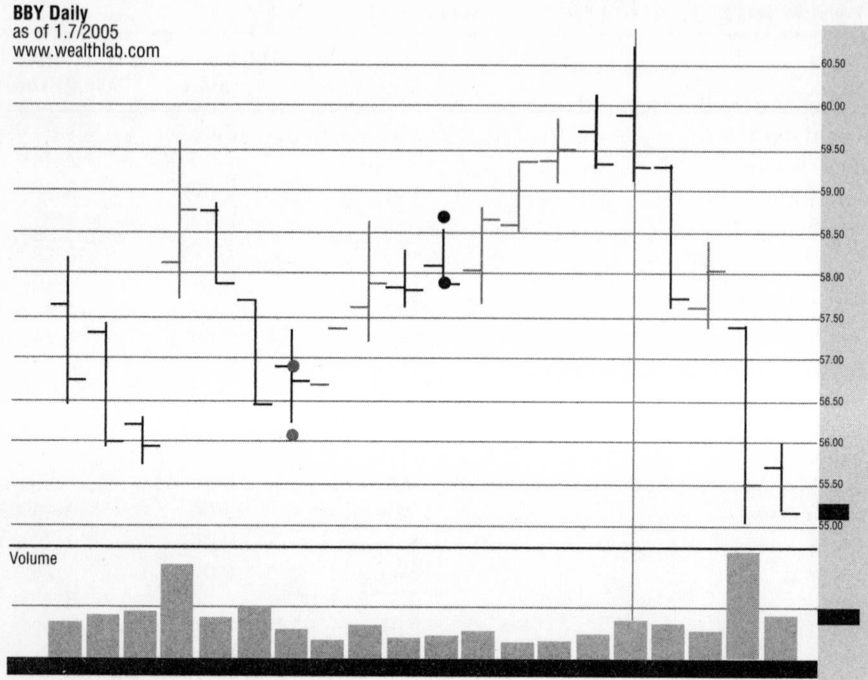

FIGURE 10.3 Best Buy
Source: Fidelity Investments. Charts created by using Wealth-Lab Developer software. The statements and opinions expressed in this book are those of the author. Fidelity Investments is not responsible for the accuracy or completeness of any statements or data contained in this book. Fidelity Investments has not examined, nor does it endorse, any trading strategy discussed in this publication.

TABLE 10.6 Eight Retail Trades, December 2004

Symbol	Entry Date	Entry Price	Exit Date	Exit Price	Percent Change
KSS	12/16/2004	$46.68	12/22/2004	$46.92	0.51
AMZN	12/17/2004	40.16	12/23/2004	38.93	−3.06
BBY	12/20/2004	56.89	12/27/2004	57.89	1.76
RSH	12/20/2004	31.35	12/27/2004	32.06	2.26
AMZN	12/21/2004	38.84	12/28/2004	44.63	14.91
ABS	12/21/2004	22.77	12/28/2004	23.47	3.07
LTD	12/21/2004	22.5	12/28/2004	22.41	−0.4
FD	12/27/2004	55.49	12/31/2004	57.79	4.14

FADING UNEMPLOYMENT

Most black-box system traders look at price only. In other words, when trying to make a buy and sell decision, the only inputs into their software might be the open, high, low, and close prices and possibly the volume data for whatever market they are looking at. A countertrend trader, on the other hand, when prices are steadily going in one direction will determine whether that movement represents a statistically significant extreme, and then make a trade in the opposite direction, betting on a reversion to the mean.

However, one can fade economic data as well. Typically, people overreact to negative economic data. Many of the "trend is your friend" adherents feel that as soon as things start to go bad, another depression is right around the corner. In other words, the bet they make when things are getting bad is that things are going to get a lot worse.

The typical attitude is reflected in the following quote:

> *Much of the American wealth is an illusion which is being secretly gnawed away and much of it will be completely wiped out in the near future. . . . So what is the rest of your future? A grisly list of unpleasant events—exploding inflation, price controls, erosion of your savings (eventually to nothing), a collapse of private as well as government pension programs, and eventually an international monetary holocaust which will sweep all paper currencies down the drain and turn the world upside down.*

This was written by Howard Ruff in 1979 in the book *How to Prosper During the Coming Bad Years*. One of the insightful blurbs on the cover was "Sound advice to help an inflation-weary investor and an eloquent plea for fiscal sanity"—a quote from George Bush.

So what happened to Mr. Ruff? From a recent talk he gave:

> *I lost my subscribers at the rate of 25 percent a year, by far the lowest attrition rate in the industry, but the sure road to failure, given the inexorable math and the nature of time, while some of my tougher and more savvy competitors are still in business with varying degrees of success, and some of them are very rich now. My wealth became barely a shadow of what it once was. As the list of followers shrank, so did the sales of the other products and services I offered them that I was counting on, until in the year 2002, my list had shrunk to only about 3,000 faithful followers. And how about my glorious Mapleton mansion? I lost it to foreclosure, as I became*

unable to pay the $8,000-a-month mortgage and the $2,000-a-month maintenance and utilities costs. Yielding to my fears had destroyed my business and my personal finances. As I relate this story, I can't even begin to tell you how stupid I feel.

So it is interesting to see what happens if you fade bad economic data. In other words, let's say that the economy is going down the toilet, and buy the S&P 500. For each month, buy the S&P 500 index at the close of the month if the unemployment rate that month crosses over from 5 to 6 percent. Sell one year later. This strategy would yield 17 occurrences, 17 successful trades, the first in February 1958 and the two most recent in December 2002 and April 2003. Average return per trade: 16.16 percent.

Next test: For each month, buy S&P 500 index at the close of the month if that month was the fourth consecutive month with the unemployment rate going higher. Sell one year later. Result: 33 occurrences, 28 successful trades, average return 20.76 percent.

CHAPTER 11

The Myth of the Index, or ETFs: Active or Passive?

"You can't beat the market," is a common refrain made by money managers while they encourage their clients to invest in passively managed ETFs like the QQQQ or SPY (an index fund tracking the S&P 500), the idea being that these ETFs represent the broader market, seldom change, and require minimal commissions, especially when compared with mutual funds and hedge funds.

However, these ETFs are more actively managed than people realize. The QQQQ, which mimics the NASDAQ 100 index, often has up to 20–50 deletions and additions per year. That's active trading if you ask me.

The year 2006 will be the sixth anniversary since the NASDAQ hit its all-time peak. Many articles appeared in 2005 about the fifth anniversary of the peak of the market in March 2000, and the subsequent crash in April 2000. It's interesting to see now how the "Class of 1999," the additions and deletions into the NASDAQ 100 index, have subsequently fared. Thirty stocks were added to the NASDAQ 100 index in 1999. The index makers are always attracted to the hottest new topics. It is no surprise that CMGI, now trading for $1.98, was included in the index in 1999. At the time CMGI seemed like it had all the answers, their CEO's picture was plastered on the cover of *BusinessWeek*. CMGI was like a public venture capital (VC) company and had invested in the likes of Lycos, which later went public; Geocities, which went public and was then bought by Yahoo!; Half.com (bought by eBay); even Snapfish (which was just scooped up by Hewlett-Packard); and finally, Vaultus (my old company, which is still living and breathing but not yet bought by anyone). CMGI was heavily covered by analysts and media. One time I had to speak at a CMGI analyst meeting about CMGI's prospects in the wireless world. There were hundreds of analysts there and I am sure I contributed to at least a 0.1 percent uptick in CMGI's price that day (see Figure 11.1). Nevertheless, the stock is now down 98 percent since January 1, 2000. Looking at the 30 other 1999 additions to the NASDAQ 100, if on January 1, 2000, you had bought all 30 you would have had 29 out of 30 losing trades, with eBay (up 150 percent since then) the only winner. Overall you would now be down 73 percent. Several of the stocks—Global Crossing, Adelphia, AtHome, and Metromedia—have gone bankrupt. Buying the entire NASDAQ 100 index on January 1, 2000, would have led to only slightly better returns, down not quite as much—only 62 percent. (See Figure 11.2.)

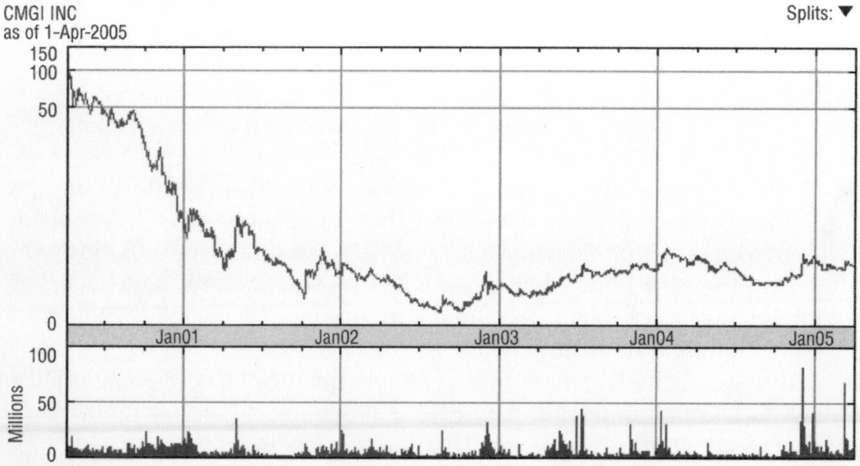

FIGURE 11.1 Five-Year Chart of CMGI, Inc.
Source: http://finance.yahoo.com/. Reproduced with permission of Yahoo! Inc. © 2005 by Yahoo! Inc. YAHOO! and the YAHOO! logo are trademarks of Yahoo! Inc.

Meanwhile, what happened to the poor, miserable stocks that were not good enough to be included in the NASDAQ 100 and so were kicked out in 1999? Less sexy names like AutoDesk, Lincare, Ross Stores (which sells clothes to people in their 50s—how did that ever get into the NASDAQ 100?), Stewart Enterprises (a funeral home no less!), and others were removed from the NASDAQ 100 in 1999.

At least five of the deletions are up over 100 percent since January 1, 2000. Ross Stores (serving an even hotter demographic than the tech trend, for instance, is up 255 percent since January 1, 2000. Cracker Barrel Old Country Stores (CBRL, the last company that would come to mind when thinking of the NASDAQ 100), turned in a +357 percent return since being

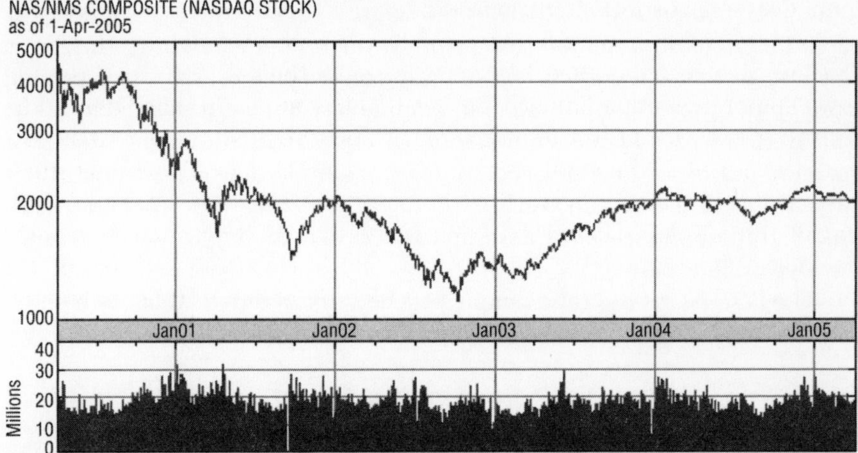

FIGURE 11.2 Five-Year Chart of NASDAQ
Source: http://finance.yahoo.com/. Reproduced with permission of Yahoo! Inc. © 2005 by Yahoo! Inc. YAHOO! and the YAHOO! logo are trademarks of Yahoo! Inc.

deleted from the NASDAQ 100 index in 1999 (see Figure 11.3). Even a tech stock, Tech Data Corporation (it's hard to find a name of a company more tech related than that), is up 52 percent since being deleted from the index in 1999.

Another classic example of a stock that gets into trouble when it is added to an index is JDS Uniphase Corporation (JDSU). This was added

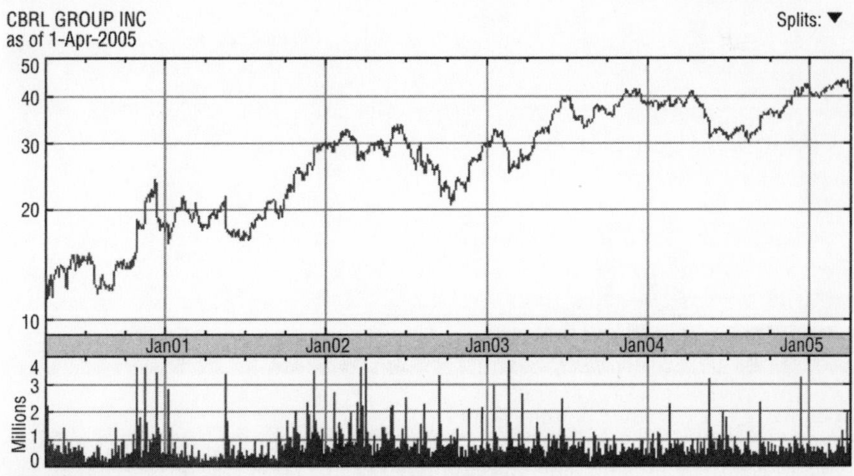

FIGURE 11.3 Five-Year Chart of CBRL Group, Inc.
Source: http://finance.yahoo.com/. Reproduced with permission of Yahoo! Inc. © 2005 by Yahoo! Inc. YAHOO! and the YAHOO! logo are trademarks of Yahoo! Inc.

to the S&P 500 on July 26, 2000. Although the peak of the market had just passed, many still assumed that video through fiber straight to the home was just around the corner, without any competitive pressures on pricing to equipment providers or telecom companies. So, naturally, the sages at S&P decided to add the granddaddy of equipment providers—JDSU, a conglomeration of profitless equipment makers that was now one of the largest companies in the world. The day it was added it reached its all-time high (see Figure 11.4) and then proceeded to dive to where it is today, below $2 a share.

The S&P 600 is a great example of when to buy stocks that are deleted from an index and the corresponding ETFs that represent that index. Over

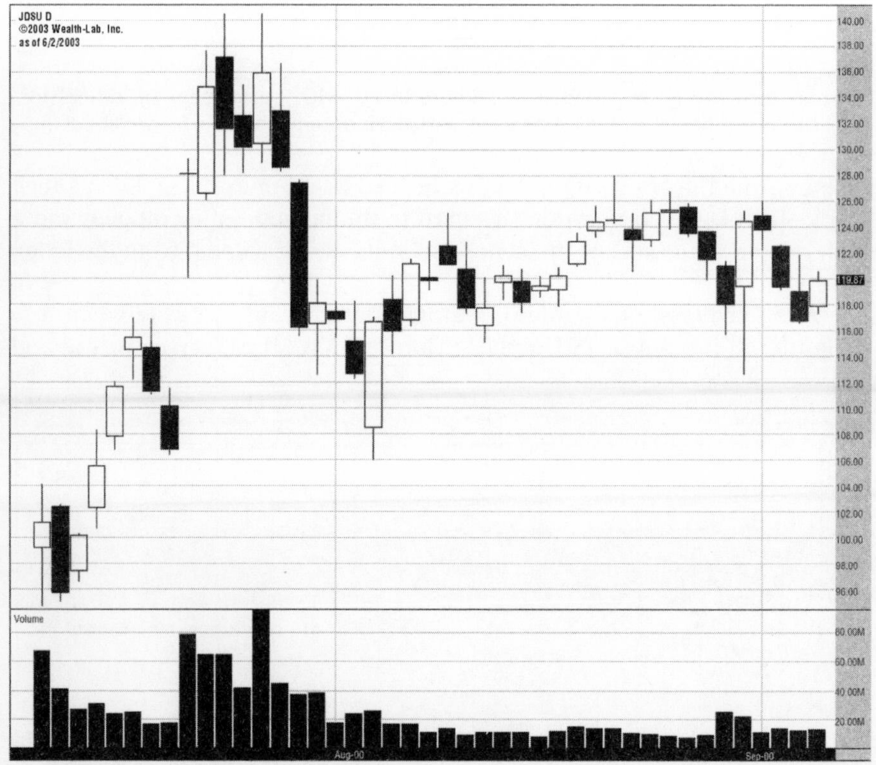

FIGURE 11.4 JDSU's Fall from Grace
Source: Fidelity Investments. Charts created by using Wealth-Lab Developer software. The statements and opinions expressed in this book are those of the author. Fidelity Investments is not responsible for the accuracy or completeness of any statements or data contained in this book. Fidelity Investments has not examined, nor does it endorse, any trading strategy discussed in this publication.

the past 10 years, buying an S&P 600 stock the day it is deleted and holding for the month after the deletion has resulted in an average return of 10 percent per trade, as opposed to an average return of 1 percent per month of buying random stocks in the ETFs for the S&P 600 index. For any index with more than its share of speculative stocks (NASDAQ 100, Russell 2000, etc.) the results are going to be similar.

Take for example, Salton (SFP), the maker of the Foreman Grill. First off, I love the Foreman Grill. My wife does wonders with a salmon steak on this thing. But I have no idea whether the company is going to last. Clearly, S&P figured it would not last, and deleted the stock from the index on May 13, 2004, when it was trading at 2.77, and replaced it with World Acceptance Corporation. One month later, on June 10, 2004, the stock closed at 6.80, 150 percent higher (See Figure 11.5).

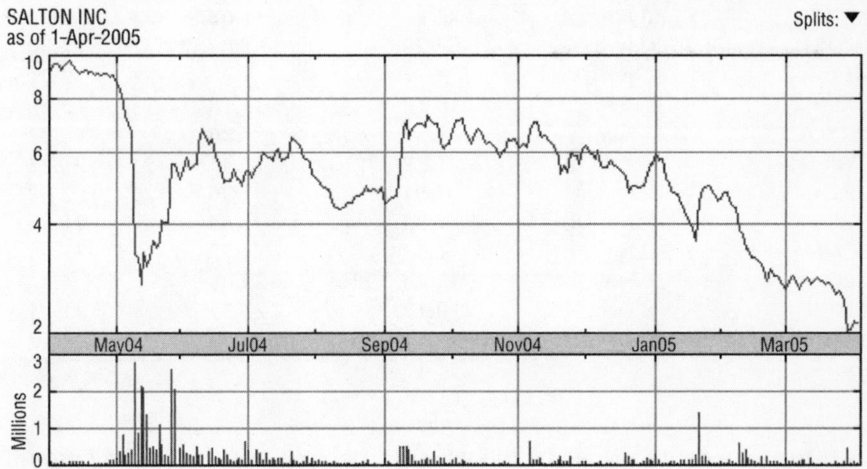

FIGURE 11.5 Salton, Inc.
Source: http://finance.yahoo.com/. Reproduced with permission of Yahoo! Inc. © 2005 by Yahoo! Inc. YAHOO! and the YAHOO! logo are trademarks of Yahoo! Inc.

Admittedly, the stock at this time is now trading near its lows, but the chart in Figure 11.5 still demonstrates that once the selling pressure abated after the actual deletion from the index, the snapback was ferocious enough to produce a nice gain, as is often the case with deletions.

Table 11.1 is a list of all the deletions from the S&P 600 during 2004. I include the stock symbol, the day the stock is deleted, the price the day before deletion, and the price one month later.

TABLE 11.1 S&P 600 Deletions, 2004

Stock Symbol	Day Deleted	Price when Deleted	Price 30 Days Later	Percent Difference
ESI	21 Jan	$51.62	$59.03	14.35
HAR	26 Feb	76.07	75.18	–1.17
JEF	26 Feb	36.36	34.17	–6.02
CEPH	26 Feb	56.7	56.53	–0.30
RGS	26 Feb	43.08	43.83	1.74
ANN	26 Feb	30.23	27.8	–8.04
NFX	29 Mar	45.83	53.3	16.30
RYL	31 Mar	44.35	40.39	–8.93
THO	1 Apr	26.76	27.8	3.89
PSUN	22 Apr	22.96	21.3	–7.23
ATK	28 Apr	62.17	61.2	–1.56
RCI	11 May	32.71	33.01	0.92
SFP	17 May	2.77	6.8	145.49
MWY	30 Jun	12.2	11.06	–9.34
IMDC	30 Jun	62.79	51.8	–17.50
ATX	30 Jun	4.77	5.2	9.015
URBN	31 Aug	30.12	34.18	13.48
WTSLA	31 Aug	1.3	1.36	4.62
TWR	22 Oct	1.22	2.4	96.72
TFS	12 Nov	1.91	1.96	2.62
FLYI	12 Nov	1.52	1.84	21.05
SCMM	30 Nov	3.32	4.55	37.05
TECH	30 Nov	38.24	39.95	4.47
CMN	8 Dec	19.17	23.37	21.91
STLD	17 Dec	35.41	36.89	4.18

The average return per trade was 13.4 percent and the holding period for each trade was 20 trading days. The worst trade was Midway (MWY), with a –9 percent return one month later, and the best trade was Salton, with a 145 percent return.

In 2004, it's interesting to note that the mysterious men and women who decide on the makeup of the NASDAQ 100 are up to their usual tricks, buying stocks that can be easily talked about at cocktail parties. In 2004, XM Satellite Radio (which lost $651 million in 2004 and has over $1 billion in debt) was added. Stocks deleted that year include Gentex ($500 million in cash, $0 debt, and generated over $100 million cash from operations with year-over-year growth), and Compuware ($600 million in cash, $0 debt, and $227 million cash generated from operations). (See Figure 11.6.)

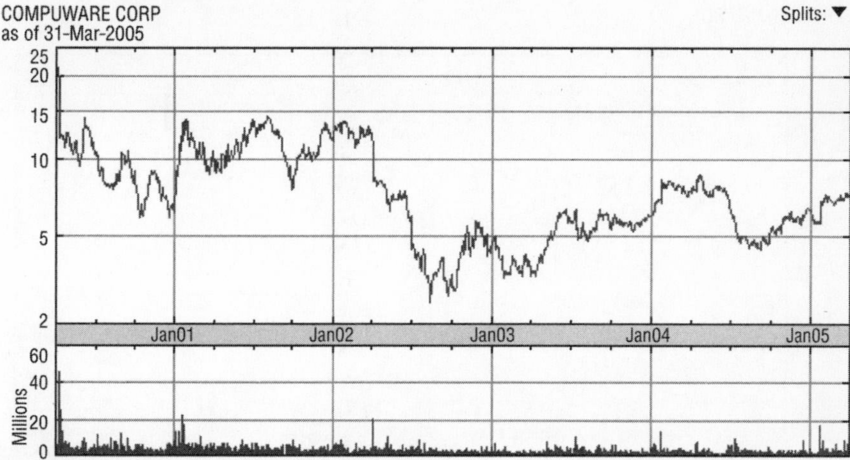

FIGURE 11.6 Compuware Corporation, Deleted from S&P 600 in 2004
Source: http://finance.yahoo.com/. Reproduced with permission of Yahoo! Inc. © 2005 by Yahoo! Inc. YAHOO! and the YAHOO! logo are trademarks of Yahoo! Inc.

WHATEVER HAPPENED TO THE ORIGINAL DOW JONES?

A look at the active nature of the so-called passive ETFs and their underlying indexes cannot be concluded without mentioning the granddaddy of all the indexes, the Dow Jones Industrial Average, and a look at the companies that still exist that were once part of the original Dow. Every once in a while, the managers of the Dow decide to do a shakeup, get rid of whatever is no longer the popular industry, and replace these with the more exciting industries. Only one component of the original Dow, General Electric, still exists today.

Seven of the original Dow components are still public in one form or other. Here's a brief review of the seven stalwart stocks.

1. Fortune Brands. American Tobacco became American Brands, which then became Fortune Brands (FO:NYSE). Fortune sells everything from Jim Beam liquor to golf shoes, has revenue of almost $7 billion, a market value of $10 billion, and its dividend yields 1.77 percent. (See Figure 11.7.)
2. People's Energy. Chicago Gas is now called People's Energy (PGL:NYSE), a utility company that primarily serves the Chicago area. People's has a $1.6 billion market cap, $2.14 billion in revenue, and a dividend yield above 5 percent. (See Figure 11.8.)

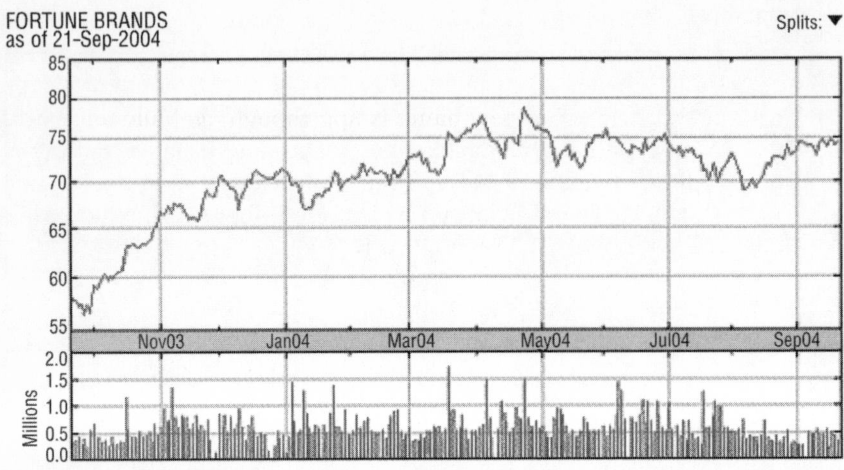

FIGURE 11.7 Fortune Brands
Source: http://finance.yahoo.com/. Reproduced with permission of Yahoo! Inc. © 2005 by Yahoo! Inc. YAHOO! and the YAHOO! logo are trademarks of Yahoo! Inc.

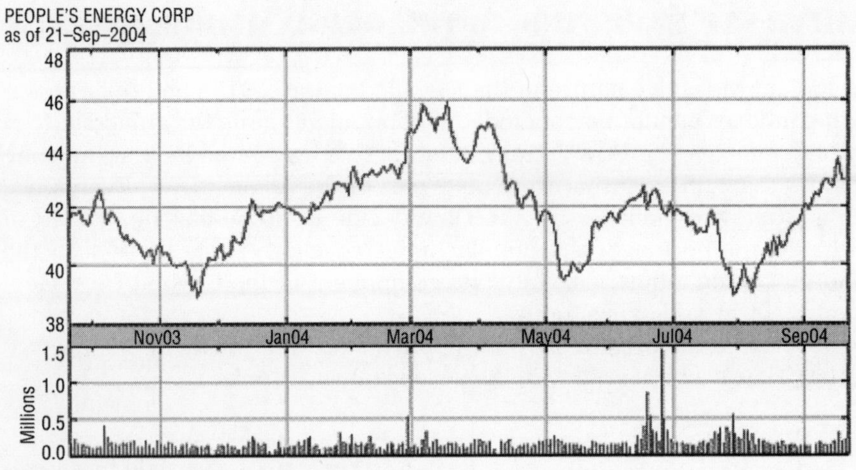

FIGURE 11.8 People's Energy Corporation
Source: http://finance.yahoo.com/. Reproduced with permission of Yahoo! Inc. © 2005 by Yahoo! Inc. YAHOO! and the YAHOO! logo are trademarks of Yahoo! Inc.

3. Millennium Chemicals. Distilling and Cattle Feeding changed a simply great name and now calls itself Millennium Chemicals (MCH:NYSE). (Imagine if a hedge fund were to call itself Cattle Feeding Trading Partners? Classic!) The new name is apt, though, as Millennium does what its name suggests—makes chemicals—and it has a market cap of $1.3 billion, revenue of $1.8 billion, and no dividend at the moment. (In late 2004, MCH was acquired by Lyondell Chemicals, which trades under the symbol LYO). (See Figure 11.9.)

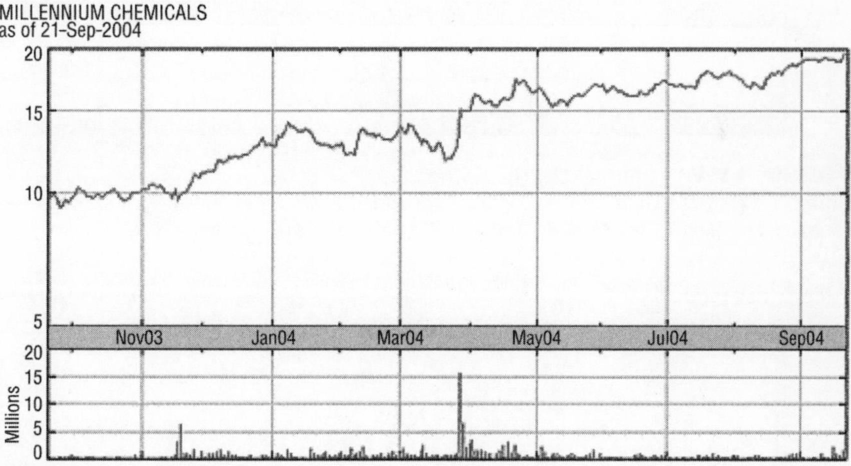

FIGURE 11.9 Millennium Chemicals
Source: http://finance.yahoo.com/. Reproduced with permission of Yahoo! Inc. © 2005 by Yahoo! Inc. YAHOO! and the YAHOO! logo are trademarks of Yahoo! Inc.

4. General Electric. General Electric (GE:NYSE) has basically been the success story of the original Dow. The giant has revenue of $140 billion, a market cap of $363 billion, and a dividend yield of 2.32 percent. (See Figure 11.10.)
5. Laclede Gas. Still called Laclede Gas (LG:NYSE), Laclede has a market cap of $611 million, revenue of $1.2 billion, and a dividend yield of 4.67 percent. (See Figure 11.11.)
6. NL Industries. National Lead decided to shorten its name and is now called NL Industries (NL:NYSE). Like our friends Distilling and Cattle Feeding, NL primarily manufactures titanium dioxide. So between the old National Lead and Distilling and Cattle Feeding, the primary ingredient for almost all sunscreens is produced. NL's role in that effort

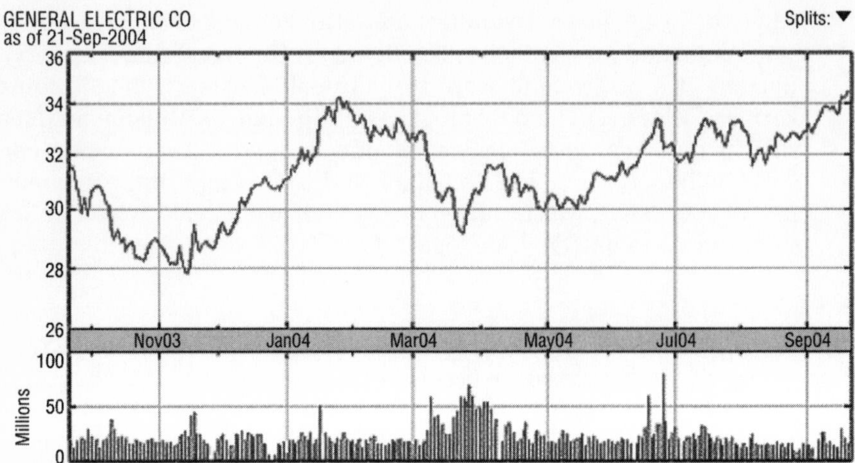

FIGURE 11.10 General Electric Company
Source: http://finance.yahoo.com/. Reproduced with permission of Yahoo! Inc. © 2005 by Yahoo! Inc. YAHOO! and the YAHOO! logo are trademarks of Yahoo! Inc.

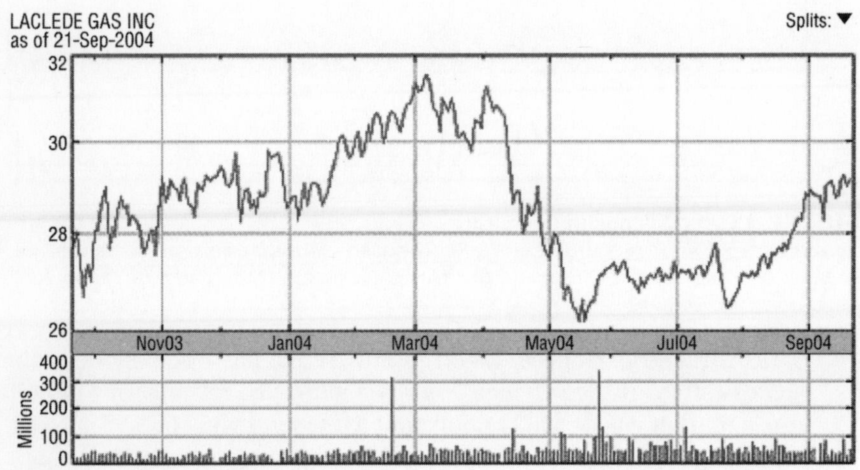

FIGURE 11.11 Laclede Gas, Inc.
Source: http://finance.yahoo.com/. Reproduced with permission of Yahoo! Inc. © 2005 by Yahoo! Inc. YAHOO! and the YAHOO! logo are trademarks of Yahoo! Inc.

produces revenues of $1 billion, a market cap of $825 million, and a dividend yield of 4.69 percent. (See Figure 11.12.)

7. Ameren. North American, a utility company, became Union Electric, which then became Ameren (AEE:NYSE), which operates primarily in Missouri and Illinois and generates revenue of $4.7 billion, a market cap of $9 billion, and a dividend yield of 5.43 percent. (See Figure 11.13.)

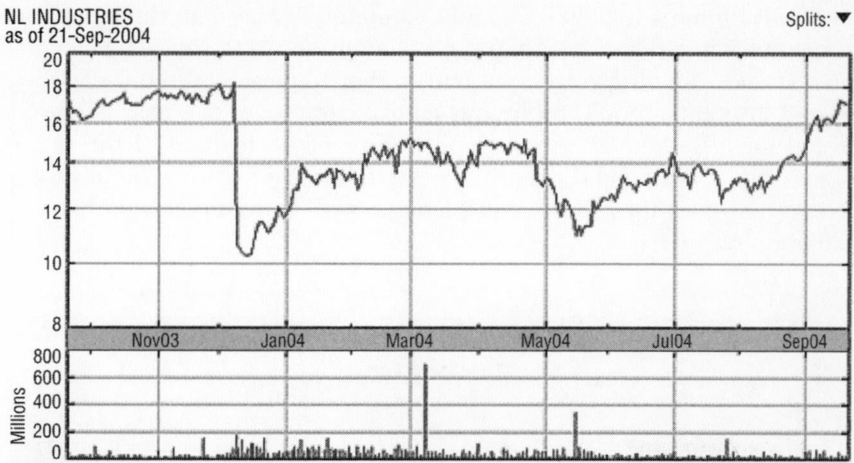

FIGURE 11.12 NL Industries
Source: http://finance.yahoo.com/. Reproduced with permission of Yahoo! Inc. © 2005 by Yahoo! Inc. YAHOO! and the YAHOO! logo are trademarks of Yahoo! Inc.

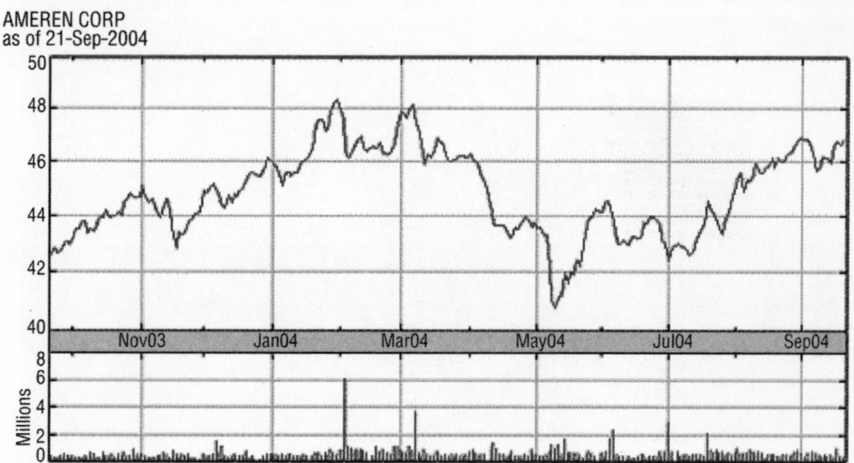

FIGURE 11.13 Ameren Corporation
Source: http://finance.yahoo.com/. Reproduced with permission of Yahoo! Inc. © 2005 by Yahoo! Inc. YAHOO! and the YAHOO! logo are trademarks of Yahoo! Inc.

If on January 1, 2000, you had completely ignored all the latest fads in the market and had simply put all of your money in the seven original Dow stocks, dividing your equity up so that 14 percent of your cash was placed into each stock, then your equity curve over the past five years would have looked like the one in Figure 11.14, instead of the one in Figure 11.15, which is the equity curve if you had put all of your money those five years into the current Dow Jones. You would have been up 120 percent.

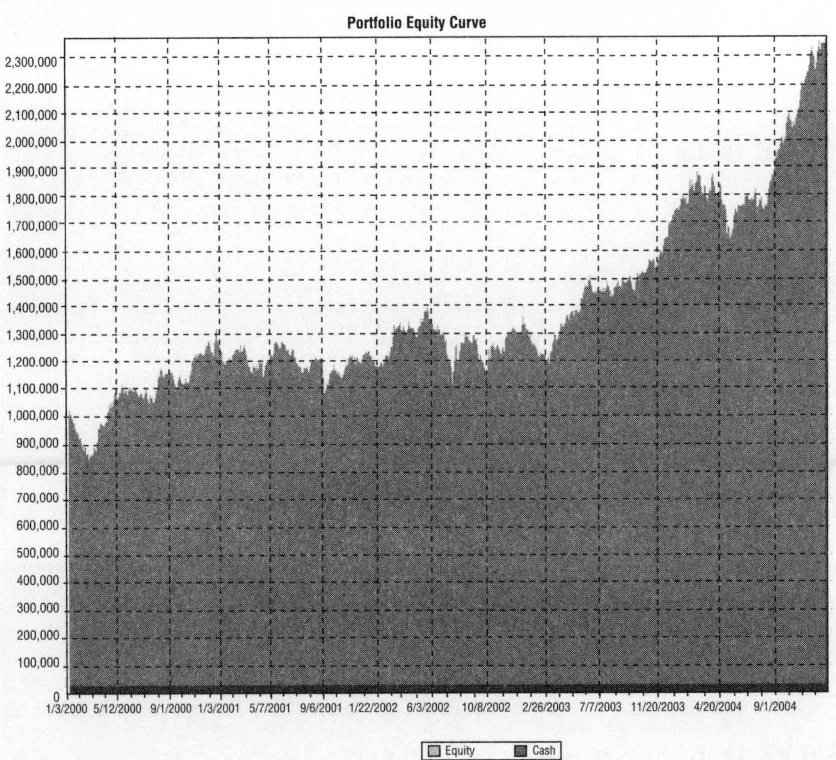

FIGURE 11.14 Portfolio Equity Curve for Seven Original Dow Stocks, 2000–2004

Source: Fidelity Investments. Charts created by using Wealth-Lab Developer software. The statements and opinions expressed in this book are those of the author. Fidelity Investments is not responsible for the accuracy or completeness of any statements or data contained in this book. Fidelity Investments has not examined, nor does it endorse, any trading strategy discussed in this publication.

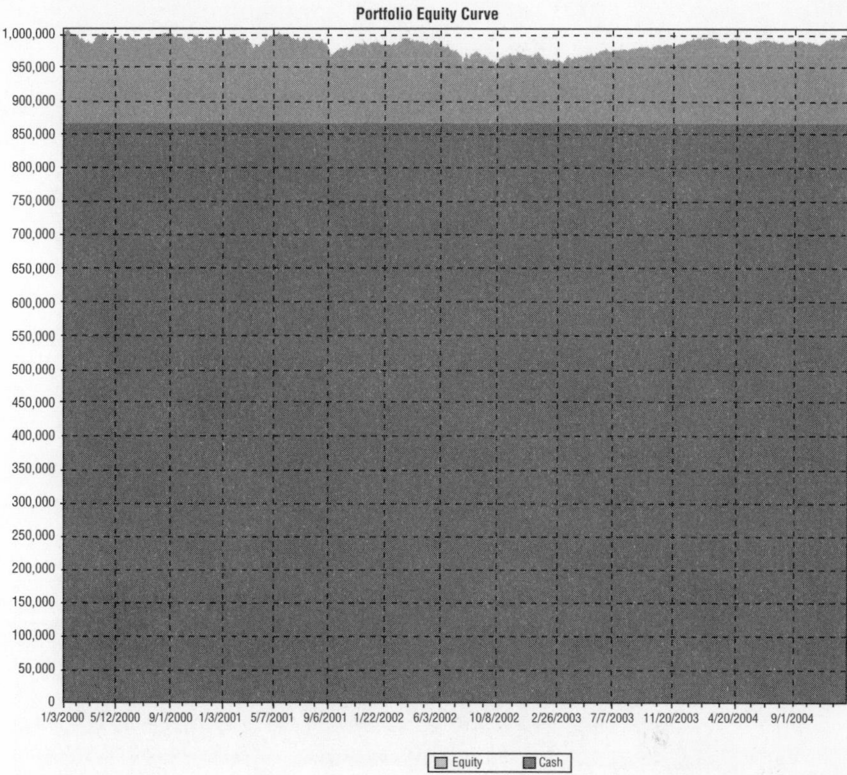

FIGURE 11.15 Portfolio Equity Curve for Dow Jones Industrial Average, 2000–2004
Source: Fidelity Investments. Charts created by using Wealth-Lab Developer software. The statements and opinions expressed in this book are those of the author. Fidelity Investments is not responsible for the accuracy or completeness of any statements or data contained in this book. Fidelity Investments has not examined, nor does it endorse, any trading strategy discussed in this publication.

Despite the $260 billion that is currently invested in ETFs, this aspect of investing remains a largely inefficient market. When dollars are chasing an investment concept without really digging under the fundamentals, it is inevitable that a large amount of the money can be labeled "dumb." Exploiting the desire for people to grab for safe returns rather than informed returns creates opportunity. Buying the stocks that are ignored, stepped on, and thrown out of the indexes has consistently outperformed the ETFs that represent the indexes.

CHAPTER 12

Watch Out!

Turning cash into supercash requires extra precautions. Suffice it to say, fraud is everywhere. It's a shame but when money is involved, particularly the trillions of dollars that go in and out of the financial markets every day, some people spend their every waking moment trying to figure out how to rip you and me off. Forget Enron for a second. What happened there was certainly a shame, but retail investors were given a million warnings that something funny was happening under the hood, particularly when Jeff Skilling left his job as CEO after only a few months on the case for the universal "family reasons." Everybody loves their family the day they get caught.

What worries me more are hedge fund scams. Throughout 2004 and 2005 we saw three hedge fund scams come to light where either the SEC or the Commodity Futures Trading Commission (CFTC) had to go in and seize assets. All three cases involved the hedge fund sending false audited returns to investors, claiming returns that weren't there. In one case a hedge fund that supposedly had $230 million actually had only about $10 million after it had amassed, in two months, $220 million in losses despite claiming positive returns for those months. Another fund sent out audited returns saying they were up 34 percent. In fact, they were down 21 percent. The next month they were down another 50 percent. Not good.

With a hedge fund you essentially wire money from your bank account into someone else's bank account and then, if all goes well, eventually you get back more than you put in. But who knows? It's someone's bank account you just sent the money to. Its not Goldman Sachs or Citibank with brokers and trillion-dollar banks that are audited by public accountants and overseen by regulators and who can get sued if and when there's fraud. Personally, I think the best strategy someone can follow if they have a lot of money is to leverage up and then diversify by investing in a couple dozen hedge funds that invest in uncorrelated and low-volatility strategies. Many of the strategies I mention in this book are ones that I like.

But I can't stress it enough: You're wiring money out of your bank account into someone else's, and if someone really wants to steal your money there's almost nothing you can do about it.

In March 2004 I helped a family office allocate some money to hedge funds. I took a brief look at a fund of funds called CSA simply because they had a very attractive feature: They never had a down month. Ultimately, we decided not to invest for various reasons that have nothing to do with stunning due diligence: They were located in Hong Kong and I hate to travel. I like to visit a fund before investing, and I also always assume that if there's ever a problem I may potentially have to spend a lot of time on location. Also, I had no idea what the laws were in Hong Kong. In other words, if there were a problem, would I be last in line to get my money back? So I decided to pass. In June 2004, scandal erupted.

On June 15, 2004, Jennifer Carver, COO of CSA Absolute Return Fund, sent an e-mail to CSA's investors stating that "irregularities" were suspected in the way Charles Schmitt, the founder of CSA (which stood for "Charles Schmitt & Associates"), was handling CSA's funds. Schmitt is currently awaiting trial in Hong Kong and most of the assets of CSA have been recovered. The irregularities included allegedly setting up bank accounts with similar names to the funds he was planning on investing in, and then wiring the money into those accounts instead of the funds. For instance, instead of investing in the legitimate XYZ Fund LLC, Charles would set up a bank account for XYZ Partners LLC, owned by him, and wire the money there (again, allegedly).

Meanwhile, if I were Jennifer Carver, I don't know what I would have done. I think I would have had a heart attack. I can't imagine the anguish she must have gone through during this period. But she immediately picked herself up, dusted herself off, and with her other colleagues from CSA managed to start up a fund of funds group called Oria. Recently, I had the chance to talk with her about her experiences since that fateful day in June when her whole life became consumed by scandal.

How did you first find out about the scandal at CSA? What was your position there at the time? How did you get started there?

I was in the office on a Saturday and ran across some misfiled documents. I was COO at the time. I met Charles in 1993 when I was running my own investment advisory firm. I moved to San Francisco in 1994 and asked him to monitor the day-to-day management of my client portfolios. He did so until 1997 and it was fine. I then ran into him again in 2001 after having been with an Internet start-up that ran out of funding, and he asked me to join him to help manage the business, acquire other asset management firms, and manage the assets.

What was your first gut, emotional reaction when you found out? What did you do next?
I started shaking. I couldn't believe what it looked like I had found. The other principal of CSA, Brian MacDougall, entered the office about one hour later, so I showed him what I had found. He couldn't believe it either. We kept thinking that there must be some logical explanation for what we were seeing. He had to leave town for three days, so we agreed that I would keep snooping over that period to confirm whether or not our fears were well grounded. The more I looked, the worse it appeared. When Brian returned, we went to see a lawyer who advised us not to speak to Charles about it (which was what we thought we should do) as it would only make us accomplices. We then went directly to the Securities and Futures Commission (SFC). I spent two days with them. They then appeared in our offices on the following Tuesday and asked Charles some questions. They weren't happy with the answers, so they called in the Commercial Crimes Bureau and he was arrested.

What was the initial reaction of investors? Did any panic? How did you deal with all the investor concerns?
Most investors panicked. The Securities and Futures Commission called me at 6:30 the night that Charles was arrested and told me they were issuing a restriction notice on the company, so we were restricted from trading and they could freeze the bank accounts. They were also issuing a press release. That meant we had only a few hours to tell 1,600 clients before they read about it in the papers. Brian and I sent out e-mails to everyone on our distribution list immediately and then we got on the phone with investors in Europe and eventually the United States. We were up all night. And we spent the better part of the next week on the phone with panicked investors. We started sending out daily e-mails and eventually just started posting them on our web site. Because we were so forthcoming with updates, investors in the two funds that I was managing that were unaffected stuck with us. They were appreciative of the continual communication.

How much did investors eventually get back? What was the final outcome for CSA and its founder?
PricewaterhouseCoopers (PwC) has been appointed liquidator and will start returning money to investors in about June 2005. Because there were only 10 days between when I found the documents and Charles was arrested, 80 percent of the funds were located. PwC has been working on retrieving all the assets since last summer. Charles's court case will start in September 2005.

How did you get Oria started?
At CSA we had three main funds of hedge funds: the Absolute Return Fund that Charles was managing, which had $200 million in assets; the Absolute Return Fund Dublin (now the Oria Market Neutral Fund); and the Absolute Return Fund Plus (now the Oria Plus Fund) that I was managing. The latter two collectively had about $100 million in assets. One of our objectives was to limit the damage to the two good funds from the one that blew up. We set up a new company and worked closely with the SFC to get a new license. They transferred Brian's and my licenses within two weeks after establishing Oria—which was phenomenal for them. Once we got the new company established, the directors of the Oria Market Neutral Fund and the shareholders of the Oria Plus Fund appointed us as the managers. Then we had to have third party audits done for both funds before the SFC would allow us to begin trading again. All of this was accomplished by the end of September 2004. We then had to get new agreements signed with service providers and we were able to begin trading those two funds by the end of October.

Did investors in CSA switch over to Oria? Did people trust you?
Investors that were in these two funds at CSA have stuck with us at Oria. Brian and I have been tested and proven that we are honest people. Many people who were caught in the fund that blew up have been watching us and say they will invest with us when they get their money back. I think many people have just been watching to see if we would survive. It's been eight months and we're taking in new money, our performance is very good, so they can see now that we're not going anywhere.

How could the CSA scandal have been avoided? By authorities, by investors, by you?
This experience has taught us a lot about due diligence and about human nature. Basically, if someone wants to cheat the

system, they will and no amount of external due diligence will find it. However, someone who is trying to steal will generally not be as transparent as an honest person. We have also learned that you can't depend on third party professionals to do due diligence for you. Custodians, auditors, and administrators can only do so much. As an investor, you have to do your own due diligence and get as much transparency from the manager as physically possible. I could go on for pages about what that really means, but that's more detail than you probably want here. At Oria, we are completely transparent. Every one of our staff knows what's happening with our portfolios and at least four people are involved in the asset allocation and trading process. We also provide complete transparency to investors. After all, we feel that it's their money, and they should be able to see where it is going.

So how do we get a handle on the situation so we can invest in hedge funds? Is it hopeless? Note that it is unlikely that SEC registration would have stopped the CSA situation, even if CSA were an onshore hedge fund. Nor do I really think the SEC is going to have the resources to fully monitor hedge funds even if every hedge fund with $25 million in assets or more were required to register.

I also checked in with Keith Black, author of the book *Managing a Hedge Fund.* Keith is also a consultant to various funds and a professor at the Illinois Institute of Technology and has written on the topic of hedge fund registration. He gave me five reasons why he thinks the SEC might not really be capable of preventing corruption even if these funds are required to register.

1. There are loopholes in the registration requirements. For instance, many hedge funds are considering extending their lockup to two years, which (at least at the moment) would save them from registering.
2. Many hedge funds still would not be subject to registration. According to Van Hedge, 45 percent of hedge funds manage less than $45 million. Arguably, these are the funds that perhaps require more scrutiny than the more established larger funds that are the recipients of institutional money (and subject to institutional due diligence).
3. The SEC is already dangerously short of resources. Between the $7.5 trillion mutual fund industry and 10,000 public companies, many of which are playgrounds for fraud against the mom and pop investor, the SEC has its work cut out for it.

4. The instance of fraud in the hedge fund community is minuscule compared to fraud in the mutual fund and equity markets. The amount in fines that hedge funds paid in the past several years as compared with mutual funds and investment banks is minuscule.
5. Despite the fact that the mutual funds and equity markets have been heavily regulated, the SEC still has not been able to prevent fraud. The reality is, the SEC has shown immense improvement in its ability to work with enforcement groups and combat fraud. But it is an extremely difficult task and already requires the full limits of the SEC's powers.

It's a shame this registration matter is such an issue. Most start-up hedge funds I know are in a quandary since no $20 million hedge fund wants to fork over $400,000 a year to hire a compliance officer.

I spoke with Hartley Bernstein, who runs the web site www.stockpatrol.com, which is an excellent site for finding out the latest abuses and suspicious behavior among micro caps and the hedge funds that invest in them. I asked Hartley where he thought hedge funds could be more regulated. What follows here are his comments, interspersed with my notes.

> *Hedge funds lack transparency—which distinguishes them from most other securities. Regulators historically have taken the view that hedge fund investors are sophisticated and capable of absorbing losses, and therefore need less protection than other investors. That logic, however, is flawed because (1) the proliferation of hedge funds and massive levels of hedge fund investments means that today hedge fund activity can impact the greater market; and (2) more and more investors have sufficient funds to qualify as "accredited" but lack the necessary investment sophistication to make informed decisions.*
>
> *Consequently, regulators should focus on the following:*
>
> 1. *Increased disclosure by hedge funds. In particular, hedge funds should be required to disclose their investment strategy and allocation of assets. What percentage of the fund is committed to short sales? What percentage of the assets is allocated to over-the-counter stocks?*

My comment: Right now most hedge funds do annual audits. Although I am not in favor of increased SEC oversight because I think the SEC lacks the centralized resources to monitor all of these hedge funds, I do think monthly verification of results by third-party agencies (either an approved accounting firm or administrator) should be required. Not only should the monthly net asset value be verified by the third party but the written and consistent strategy as described by Hartley should be verified each month by the administrator. If the fund is doing a higher percentage of short sales than the fund manager has stated he will do, then the administrator will note that (with possible response from the manager) and distribute that in the monthly letter to all investors.

2. *Hedge fund managers should be required to disclose all fees and manner of compensation. What is the basis for those fees? Are they based upon fund performance or asset value? Is there potential for assets to be inflated in order to trigger fees?*

My comment: In addition to fees I'd like to see a breakdown of *all* soft dollars on a monthly basis, both accrued and actual. In an audit the soft dollars might be seen as one line item but I'd like to see a breakdown of every soft dollar. If a hedge fund manager is using a soft-dollar broker to hide expenses in the form of trading commissions then I'd like to see a look-through view of where all of those expenses are going. If a manager is taking a due diligence trip to Hawaii to look at the latest pineapple farm IPO and then plans to amortize that over 18 months, then I want to see every detail of this. I want to know if offices, employees, computers, research (and what kinds), databases, and so on are being soft-dollared. I might not have anything against any of these expenses. I just want to know what they are, and I think a manager will be less likely to expense certain items if he knows they are all being disclosed on a monthly basis to the third party administrator I described previously.

3. *Hedge funds should be required to disclose all potential conflicts of interest. Do hedge fund managers hold the same securities for personal accounts? Are there limitations on the ability of hedge fund managers to trade these same securities?*

My comment: Conflicts of interest can also include any advisory fees that hedge funds receive from the companies they invest in. Normally in a hedge fund offering memorandum the manager states that "the general partner may engage in advisory services or perform other services outside the scope of running the fund." Well, I want to know what all of these services are.

4. *Investors should be informed, in advance, of the hedge fund's valuation methodology. How are assets valued, particularly if they include restricted or illiquid securities?*

My comment: This is particularly important for funds such as PIPE funds, funds that trade mortgage-backed securities, or funds that trade illiquid securities such as long-dated futures contracts which are illiquid and often (in my opinion) manipulated. A written, consistent methodology is needed and third-party monthly verification should be required.

I also spoke with Jay Kaplowitz, of the law firm Gersten, Savage, Kaplowitz, which has represented over 400 hedge funds over the past 20 years. He said, "As more and more high net worth investors participate in hedge funds and more funds and strategies proliferate, the role of the third party marketer (TPM) becomes more important. Even very sophisticated investors, particularly non-institutional investors, may elect to rely on the expertise offered by a TPM. Investors rely on these firms to do due diligence, strategy checks, background checks, and so on. There should be a minimum standard which the requirements for a registered broker dealer begin to address." However, Kaplowitz concludes, "The benefits that hedge funds bestow on capital markets may be diminished if creativity is sacrificed to regulation."

DO-IT-YOURSELF DUE DILIGENCE

These are the steps to follow when performing your own due diligence.

Basic Background Checks

There are various online sites you can use to do basic background checks at minimal cost. Check out www.zabasearch.com for a basic background check, or www.privateeye.com for IRS liens, arrests, property search, marriage search, and so on.

A fund of funds manager told me recently he had a fund that was performing great for him. During his ongoing due diligence he uncovered the fact that the fund manager had been arrested for DWI and "possession" (I neglected to ask my friend what he was possessing but I'll assume now either a gun or marijuana). He asked the manager what the scoop was and the manager said, "Oh! That's not supposed to be in the public records." Wrong answer. Always be up front and you'll be surprised how many eyes are turned the other way if you are performing well. As it stands, my friend had to redeem his money.

NASD Violations

Check out the web site http://www.nasd.com/web/idcplg?IdcService=SS_GET_PAGE&nodeId=469 to see if the investment managers have ever been guilty of any National Association of Securities Dealers (NASD) violations. Note that a violation is certainly a red flag, but wait until you hear an explanation before making a judgment.

Review the Documents

The documents are your one chance to really examine up front the risks and the strategy (so you can later determine if drift occurred). Just as important: Get copies of all side letters. Side letters are a catastrophe waiting to happen in the hedge fund world. Basically, your documents say one thing but many large investors ask for special conditions. If a special condition is "material" (and this is certainly an ambiguous term) then it needs to be disclosed to all investors, but side letters are seldom disclosed.

Investments in hedge funds made without full knowledge of the side letters could result in an automatic "put" on your position. In other words, if an investor wasn't aware of a material note affecting his investment and the hedge fund then proceeds to lose money, that investor can get *all* his money back without suffering the loss. Check your side letters.

Employment/Education Verification

Employment and education verification is critical. I was once looking to invest in a fund that is rather well-known in one of the sectors. In fact, it has raised over $1 billion from institutional investors, so how bad could it be? I mean, one of those billion-dollar investors must have checked it out. The manager supposedly had a PhD in Chemistry from a university in Moscow. It turns out the school didn't even offer graduate degrees—and it was a nursing school. So go figure.

Search SEC Filings

Has the investment manager ever filed a 13D before, suggesting that this was a larger position? Or have they ever been in an 8K or SB-2 before, suggesting that they did a private placement? These little pieces of information, particularly if the fund does not offer transparency, can give a lot of clues into the makeups of their portfolios, their prior investment experiences, and what exactly happens to your money once you put it in.

One time I looked at another well-known fund that had raised about $300 million. I found a private placement they had made into a company with no assets. At the time they made the investment the public company, a penny stock, had no assets. Shortly after the investment, the public company bought an undisclosed amount of an "investment company." That investment in the investment company became their only asset. The investment company was the company that controlled the fund I was looking at. In other words, people invested in the fund, the fund invested in the micro cap, and the micro cap invested in the management company of the fund, putting the fund dollars right in the pockets of the managers—once you connect the dots. I asked a lawyer about this. "Perfectly legal," he told me, "but it begs the question." Not liking to beg, we elected not to invest.

Service Provider Checks

Your auditor/accountant/lawyer should sign off on the auditors/lawyers/administrators of the funds you invest in.

Reference Checks

It always helps to personally know people who are investors in the fund. Similarly, when possible, I like to talk to funds who have coinvested in deals with the funds I'm investing in. I also like to talk to the CEOs of companies my funds invest in.

Suffice it to say, this is not an exhaustive list. Due diligence is ultimately more art than science and no two people will necessarily do it the same way. The artist can keep on working, tweaking, adding a little here and there, and never finish. But ultimately you've got to take a step back from your work and say, "Yes, I did everything I could. This is ready to go." It never truly is done, but at some point you've got to take the plunge and trust that you did all you could.

APPENDIX: SAMPLE BACKGROUND CHECK REPORT

This sample report is provided by BackTrack Reports (www.backtrack reports.com).

Preface

The following is a mock sample of a fund manager investigative report prepared by BackTrack Reports, Inc. Many due diligence organizations are content to conduct searches of a boilerplate source list, copy the indexes, and present them as a report. In contrast, and as you will see in this sample, BackTrack's reports are thorough histories of the subjects, with emphasis on any areas that might cause you or your clients concern.

We begin by collecting the information your office has about the subject(s) (e.g., resume, known professional associations, birth date, Social Security number, etc.). These data, which can be forwarded via fax, e-mail, or discussed verbally, serves both as a guide in our initial searches and later as a tool of comparison against our own findings. A subject's candor frequently can be assessed in part by the accuracy and comprehensiveness of the information included in his biography. We welcome all information regarding any claims the subject(s) may have made about their background. Unlike many of our competitors, BackTrack compares and contrasts those assertions with the results of our investigation, and highlights any discrepancies.

Please note that while we request information such as resumes or biographies, we rarely make use of the references provided by the subject, as these typically are self-serving. We instead develop useful character insight by interviewing those sources developed during the course of our investigation, as elucidated below.

The client is apprised of the investigation's salient points via verbal briefing at approximately five business days. A second verbal update is provided at 10 business days, while the written report is submitted on or about the 15th business day.

Introduction

BackTrack's findings are presented as an analytic distillation of a fund manager's background. Organized chronologically, the report moves through the significant events of each subject's history, highlighting those achievements, issues, or events that can impact your future relationship.

We pride ourselves on the readability of BackTrack reports. Each report is a narrative account of what are often complicated matters, providing a clear understanding of the subject's pattern of behavior.

Distinguishing between information that pertains to the subject and information relating merely to unrelated parties with the same name is a key element of preparing a report with reliable conclusions. The information used by BackTrack to draw these conclusions is obtained from a variety of identification sources, independent interviews, and property records, as well as from the biographical information provided by the client. This is a critical evaluation but is not provided by many investigative firms.

The following sets out information developed regarding a typical fund and its two managers.

This investigation was initiated pursuant to your request and authorization to determine the background and reputation of CornerPoint Group, LLC. Your office is considering a business transaction with CornerPoint, and, therefore, wished to determine whether there is anything in its background or the backgrounds of Scott W. Prixi and Michael F. Dunhill that might influence this decision.

With your authorization, this investigation included research of non-intrusive records combined with interviews of independent sources identified and located by BackTrack. Non-intrusive records searched included court records, media, legal, identification, and corporate sources; regulatory agency records; internal reference materials; and other similar sources. Media sources researched included such nationally recognized publications as the *Wall Street Journal*, *Forbes*, *BusinessWeek*, and many others, as well as targeted regional and trade sources, including, among others, *Financial News*, the *London Times*, *London Finance*, *Smart Investing*, *Money Magazine*, *European Finance*, the *Pittsburgh Post-Gazette*, the *Plain Dealer* (Cleveland, Ohio), *Financial Times Transcript*, *The Record* (Bergen County, NJ), and *Financial News Europe*. (Note that many sources, including the *Wall Street Journal*, are not covered sufficiently on Nexis; BackTrack utilizes additional database sources to ensure that the crucial information contained in these publications is not missed.) Please see Exhibit A for copies of media references found.

The Business History section details BackTrack's research into corporate documents, the records of Secretaries of State, news reports, regulatory filings, court documents, interview sources, as well as a variety of other sources of information on the companies with which the subject has been involved. These include both those companies indicated in supplied resumes or biographies, and any others we may have discovered. BackTrack's unique research strategy frequently enables us to discover previously unidentified business entities connected to the subject. Once the subject's affiliation with these entities is determined, BackTrack investigators conduct further research to determine the companies' fate and, if possible, the reason(s) for their omission.

A significant amount of the "adverse" information developed in management investigations is found during the review of news media sources. To ensure a thorough search, our investigators review corporate and other information sources prior to conducting the search of media sources. To fill in the widely recognized gaps in Nexis' coverage (e.g., *Wall Street Journal*, *San Francisco Chronicle*, *Chicago Sun-Times*, and the *San Jose Mercury News*), BackTrack also searches other major media databases. We then conduct media research specific to these entities to find telling stories citing the entity but not the subject. As with litigation materials, the investigators then begin analyzing the raw documents, ascertaining whether they relate to the subject. Once this is determined, each matter is investigated and then summarized in the report narrative. Copies of relevant records are included in the Exhibits section, should you wish to refer to them.

During the course of the investigation, BackTrack identifies independent sources believed capable of adding valuable insight into the subject's history, candor, and character. BackTrack will suggest these targeted interviews when appropriate, then will conduct interviews with your authorization. Our investigators' honed interviewing skills enable them to elicit valuable information frequently unavailable from public records.

Scott W. Prixi

Identification/Education

Scott William Prixi was born December 20, 1964. BackTrack confirmed the 1986 B.S. in business administration from Fairfield University claimed in his biography (sent by your office and attached at Exhibit C); BackTrack learned he transferred here from Connecticut State College in 1985.

Business History

The first record of Mr. Prixi's employment is not reflected in the biography. In 1989, three years after the completion of his studies at Fairfield, Mr. Prixi signed on with Lowenstein Brothers, Inc., according to records on file with the National Association of Securities Dealers (NASD). These records indicate a disclosure event being held against Mr. Prixi, to wit, a September 1991 termination from Lowenstein resultant of his failure to meet clients while on a business trip.

BackTrack's review of Standard & Poor's directories revealed that Paul E. Burke was operations officer at Lowenstein during Mr. Prixi's employment. When contacted by BackTrack and queried regarding his professional relationship with Mr. Prixi, Mr. Burke said, "I'm surprised he even put Lowenstein on his resume, actually. It most likely wasn't his most prestigious effort."

Mr. Burke spoke willingly of his experiences with Mr. Prixi, saying that the subject's "attendance record"—both in the office and on the road meeting with clients—was problematic. Mr. Burke attributed this to Mr. Prixi's immaturity at the time. When pressed to elaborate, Mr. Burke said, "Let me just say again that I hold nothing against him personally. I think he was a very intelligent, insightful employee. He just had a lot of growing up to do, which, really, I'm sure he has by now. Basically he was still in college mode. I mean, we do a lot of wining and dining of clients, and quite frankly, that was the area where he was worst off, if you know what I mean. He drank too much, back then. But that is most likely different now."

BackTrack asked about the terms of Mr. Prixi's termination. "Now, I'm not happy saying this, but it wasn't the first time it had happened. We sent him on trips, he'd go out the night before, and not make a meeting with a client. His attendance record was not the best at the office either. He was often out Fridays or Mondays, which is something employers are wary of. But again, he had been backpacking through Europe since he graduated."

Mitigating these criticisms, Mr. Burke described Mr. Prixi as a "very intelligent, insightful employee." When asked if he would work with Mr. Prixi again, Mr. Burke answered, "Well, I tell you what. I always liked the guy myself. Everyone in the office did, on a personal level. I would have to see if he had grown up a bit, first. In fact, I'd be interested to know what he was up to. He did have some talent." He paused before adding, "I guess what I am sidestepping here is that he was a fun guy—you know, socially or whatever—but I would be somewhat nervous with him handling my money."

Mr. Prixi's NASD employment history next shows him to be at New York's **Immidinet Corporation**. He was there between January 1992 and July 1993 at a position unspecified. This is another entity not mentioned in his biography. Note that BackTrack spoke with Alicia Jackson in the company's verification department, who confirmed the above-referenced dates.

The first entity noted on Mr. Prixi's biography is **Levine Brunswick**, where he holds that he "started his career," though no exact date for this "start" is given. His NASD biography shows him to have started in August 1993 (seven years after his college graduation, the event he lists as previous to his employment at Levine Brunswick), and to have left by May 1994. The biography states that he was there "before joining R.W. Brown in 1994." Mr. Prixi fixes the dates of his employment at **R.W. Brown** as May 1994 to February 1995, but is again contradicted by his NASD records. These show him to have been at R.W. Brown from June 1995 to July 1996. R.W. Brown itself requires a signed release for verification of personnel records; according to Susan H. in Levine Brunswick's human resources department, the company was acquired in 1996 by Powell Samson Capital and personnel records predating the event are unavailable.

An interview with James Milhouse, former compliance officer at Levine Brunswick and now, BackTrack determined, with CitiFunds International, served to clear this discrepancy; he recalled that when Mr. Prixi ended his "under a year" tenure at Levine in 1994, "he gave the impression that he wanted to take a break . . . he mentioned taking a trip to Indonesia or something." Mr. Milhouse said he later "heard [that Mr. Prixi] . . . was working for R.W. Brown." Again, the time off was not cited on either of Mr. Prixi's biographies.

Mr. Milhouse's comments about the subject's performance at Levine were positive, calling him a "fairly talented trader" with "moments of keen insight that sometimes surprised me, given how young he was at the time." Mr. Prixi's short time at the company was blamed on the "bad management at the international desk," not Mr. Prixi himself. Upon being asked if he would work with Mr. Prixi again, Mr. Milhouse said, "Yeah, sure, as long as he hasn't lost that insight."

After R.W. Brown, Mr. Prixi's biography next shows him at **BCM, Inc.** acting as vice president and head of international equity trading. He maintains he held this position from March 1995 to December 1995. His NASD biography once again says otherwise, putting him there between December 1995 and January 1997. (More accurately, at BCM subsidiary Kaplan Michaels, Inc. from December 1995 to April 1996, and at BCM itself from May 1996 to January 1997.) Human resources officials at BCM confirmed these NASD-given dates for Mr. Prixi's tenure at Kaplan Michaels and BCM.

Philip Isaacs, identified by BackTrack's review as formerly head of BCM's international desk, told BackTrack in an interview that, although "not sure of the exact date," he was partial to the NASD's dates for Mr. Prixi's employment, saying that they jived more with his own recollections. "I know he was here at Kaplan Michaels to begin with, and then, uh, then he worked with me up here until the summer of 1997. I'm not sure of the exact date though, I admit."

Mr. Isaacs spoke well of the "five or six months" that he worked with Mr. Prixi, saying he was "very pleased" with Mr. Prixi's performance. Praising Mr. Prixi's "intuition" for the market, Mr. Isaacs said Mr. Prixi often "acted on trends before they occurred," and made BCM "a good deal of money. I was disappointed when he left. He would have done really well here."

When asked to discuss Mr. Prixi's weaknesses, if any, Mr. Isaacs said that Mr. Prixi had a penchant for being "a little abrupt, or blunt around the office." Citing the speed of the business, Mr. Isaacs characterized Mr. Prixi's bluntness as a "necessary trait" that "helped him, in fact." Mr. Isaacs would "certainly work with him again." He stated that Mr. Prixi left on good terms, and he wishes "him well in all he's up to now."

Although BackTrack's interviews cleared up many discrepancies between Mr. Prixi's self-given biography and the information set forth on his NASD records, BackTrack recommends speaking with Mr. Prixi himself about these issues—namely, to discover his reasons behind omitting numerous past employers in addition to obscuring employment dates. With your authorization, BackTrack will conduct this interview.

The biography contained within the CornerPoint memorandum engenders the impression that Mr. Prixi was at **Lehman Brothers** beginning December 1995. The biography available through the NASD shows a start date of February 1997, dovetailing his Lehman tenure with that of BCM, above. Lehman verified the NASD-given date, citing the end of his tenure as August 2000.

BackTrack's search of court documents yielded a 1999 civil case, *Rodriguez vs. Lehman Brothers and Scott W. Prixi*. The suit had it that Mr. Prixi encouraged the racial discrimination plaintiff Carl Rodriguez was alleged to have encountered, going so far as to mouth racist abuse and leave threatening messages on home answering machines. (At one point the suit alleges Mr. Prixi asked another employee "to ask of a male black visitor [to the company offices] how many bananas he was carrying.") After leaving the firm, Mr. Rodriguez filed suit for $115,000 in April 1999. The matter was handed over to arbitrators in December 1999, and dismissed with prejudice in January 2001. Dismissed "with prejudice" means the case has been decided, and cannot be brought again. A dismissal does not indicate the suit had no merit, and, as in this case, often is tied to a settlement.

BackTrack interviewed Mr. Rodriguez regarding this action. Though he was extremely reticent to discuss the details of the action's settlement or the content of the telephone messages that court documents state were left by Mr. Prixi, Mr. Rodriguez did characterize the events leading up to the suit. When asked if his discrimination claim resulted more from the actions of Mr. Prixi than of Lehman in general, Mr. Rodriguez said that "90 percent" of the claim was the result of Mr. Prixi's actions, saying, "The firm was included because they were unwilling to do anything about it." He continued: "I wasn't at the firm very long, only three months, if that gives you any idea how, uh, how harassed I felt."

BackTrack inquired about the nature of the messages that court documents allege Mr. Prixi left on his answering machine. "Well, I'd rather not get into that. I can say—safely I feel—that these messages were left between the time I spoke to his superiors and the time my attorney contacted him. I wish I'd saved half of them, but I didn't." Mr. Rodriguez refused to discuss the tapes further.

Mr. Rodriguez revealed that Mr. Prixi and Lehman both reached separate settlements outside of court, although he added, "I'm not going to talk amounts now, because those are still, well, the amounts haven't been completely paid. By either party."

"Suffice it to say that I'm not a big fan of Mr. Prixi. I would *not* work with him again, and I certainly wouldn't trust him in any position where there was some sort of client interaction." He did, however, add, "[Mr. Prixi] was always good at his job, I will say that. He's a very shrewd investor. But how they could have him doing international work, with different cultures, I mean, that boggles me."

Coinciding almost perfectly with this lawsuit's filing was Lehman Brothers' transfer of Mr. Prixi from its New York office, site of the alleged maltreatment, to its London quarters. A June 1999 issue of the *Financial*

Times contained an item noting his transfer from Lehman's New York ADR desk to the London office, where he would assume the head of trading role. Mr. Prixi's calling it a day at Lehman also registered in the papers. *London Finance* noted both his departure and his destination—the then-unnamed CornerPoint Group.

Current Venture

Reports on the foundation of CornerPoint Capital were in print by July 2000, and by August CornerPoint had completed registration with the Secretaries of State of both Delaware, the site of its initial incorporation, and New York, the site of its corporate offices. The *London Times* noted in late September 2000 Mr. Prixi's assumption of duties as director of trading at CornerPoint Capital, a date seconded by his biography.

Other Associations

BackTrack's independent research revealed Mr. Prixi's stake in the **Cleveland Indians Baseball Club**. News sources, including the *Cincinnati Enquirer* and the *Plain Dealer*, reported in May 1998 that Mr. Prixi purchased an additional 20,000 shares in the baseball club, upping his stake in the team to almost 5 percent.

Regulatory Associations

Searches of National Futures Association (NFA), NASD, and Securities and Exchange Commission (SEC) records revealed the above-referenced Lowenstein Brothers disclosure event but no other disciplinary history citing Mr. Prixi.

Legal Actions

Aside from the above action, BackTrack located a judgment, apparently for an unpaid debt to Citibank in 1991, for almost $20,000, against Mr. Prixi. No record of payment regarding this was shown, though it is noted that payment records are sometimes incomplete.

No matters naming CornerPoint were located.

Michael F. Dunhill

Identification/Education

Michael Fitzpatrick Dunhill was born in November 1966. According to the biography sent by your office, and also attached at Exhibit C, Mr. Dunhill was educated at New York University, where he earned a B.S. in business administration in 1989. BackTrack confirmed this degree with NYU.

Business History

Upon graduation, Mr. Dunhill was hired by **Glendale Martin Securities**, per the biography. Various news sources culled by BackTrack told of his lowly start at the company and his determined efforts at advancement. According to *Crain's New York Business*, "I picked up the bosses' dry cleaning. I ordered the stationery supplies and put together office furniture. My goal was to advance, and I did anything I could to get there." Mr. Dunhill's biography holds that by the time of the Holmdel, New Jersey–based **Camden Group**'s April 1997 acquisition of Glendale Martin Securities, he had made portfolio manager. His ascent continued through 1998, when a *Financial Times* transcript labeled him a "senior analyst."

The news record shows Mr. Dunhill as being on very good terms with his boss/mentor Stan Carroll, the renowned founder of the Camden Group. Mr. Dunhill is shown by an alternate biography filed with the National Association of Securities Dealers (NASD) as leaving the Camden Group in 1998 for a two-month stint at a capital management company, **StarCap, Inc.** The business press reported two years after the fact that his return was affected by Mr. Carroll's personal request that he do so. Mr. Dunhill's hiatus from the Camden Group did nothing to slow his rise, and in January 1999 *Finance News Europe* was reporting his nomination to the position of senior vice president, saying this occurred as a reward for his "deadly accurate analysis" in his delegated field of coverage.

When Mr. Dunhill finally left the Camden Group in early 2000, one business reporter speculated that it was the absence of founder Mr. Carroll, who had left the firm over a year earlier, that finally drove Mr. Dunhill out.

BackTrack interviewed Bob Friedman, whom a 1999 *PR Newswire* release named as a senior analyst at the Camden Group during Mr. Dunhill's employment. Mr. Friedman, explaining that he and Mr. Dunhill were on the same level as senior analysts, praised Mr. Dunhill as the "best investment analyst at the firm," saying that Mr. Dunhill was "consistently number one" in Fidelity's industry rankings, among "about twenty credible competitors." Mr. Dunhill's success, according to Mr. Friedman, was attributable to two factors: "extremely strong skills in the financial industry" and a "very thorough understanding of clients' needs." Added Mr. Friedman, "It is hard to find people that do understand your needs and listen to your remarks."

When BackTrack asked Mr. Friedman if Mr. Dunhill had any weaknesses, Mr. Friedman replied: "One weakness might be that I've never understood how this guy could find time for non-work-related projects." Mr. Friedman cautioned that his remarks should only be taken in the context of the financial industry.

Mr. Friedman concurred with news accounts stating that Mr. Dunhill had a close relationship with Mr. Carroll, and that Mr. Dunhill was urged to return to the Camden Group after his two-month hiatus by his mentor. "When Mr. Carroll left, we feared losing Mr. Dunhill. I guess we were right."

Mr. Friedman concluded his interview by recommending that BackTrack speak with Allen Winters, who remains at the Camden Group. Mr. Winters told BackTrack that he worked with Mr. Dunhill from 1997 to 2000, saying that Mr. Dunhill was his line manager in the Camden Group's international group. Calling Mr. Dunhill an "excellent" supervisor, Mr. Winter described Mr. Dunhill as "very responsible, responsive, open to suggestions, good listener, super-focused, incredibly smart." Mr. Winters concluded by averring that Mr. Dunhill was his "mentor" within the industry.

Current Venture

Business media widely reported Mr. Dunhill's summer 2000 foundation of **CornerPoint Group**, LLC. Backed by $90 million, much of it supplied by Swedish entrepreneur Johann Steigg, Mr. Dunhill began the company as a management device for his new global hedge fund, a July 27, 2000, *Money Magazine* article said. By August, as noted above, CornerPoint had registered itself with the Secretaries of State of Delaware, where it was incorporated, and New York, where it maintained its principal offices.

CornerPoint continued its presence in the news in the following months as it staffed a variety of positions. Mr. Dunhill's most recent appearance in the business press came in January 2001 when *Money Magazine* tapped the CornerPoint head for a quote on the European growth slowdown.

CornerPoint Group is listed with the National Futures Association (NFA) as a registered commodity pool operator and commodity trading adviser, and is an approved NFA member as of September 17, 2000.

Legal Actions/Regulatory Matters

BackTrack conducted an extensive court search of specific, targeted jurisdictions where Mr. Dunhill has lived, and a broader search of areas further afield, for lawsuits naming him or companies with which he has been associated. No such matters were found, nor were any disciplinary actions filed against him by the NFA, NASD, or SEC, according to representatives of the respective agencies.

Please see the Litigation section that follows for a description of the courts and jurisdictions covered in BackTrack's legal review.

Litigation Summary

One of the most important management investigation functions is litigation research. BackTrack begins by researching court records in those jurisdictions where the subject has been reported to have lived or worked in the past. Unlike our competitors, BackTrack endeavors to identify any additional areas where a subject may have been active.

Experience has shown that to ensure a comprehensive reporting of lawsuits, judicial opinions, liens, judgments, and UCC filings involving the subject, it is necessary to search the actual court records in each identified jurisdiction. Popular online search services are insufficient. Lexis, for example, may provide a wealth of information, but its records primarily are drawn from actions that have been appealed, a small minority of those filed.

While traditional due diligence reports are often mere reprints of indices, BackTrack recognizes the importance of placing each suit in its proper context. Upon identification, BackTrack retrieves copies of the various matters of litigation involving the subject(s) and/or the subject company. This often-voluminous collection of court documents is then reviewed and analyzed. We first ascertain whether the suits relate to the subject or unrelated parties with the same name. Once this is determined, each matter is reviewed and its salient points summarized for the report narrative. Copies of all relevant court documents also are included in the Exhibits section for easy reference.

Rather than focusing merely on the work and home areas your office provided for the subjects, BackTrack compiled address histories for them by reviewing identification sources, their employment and education records, archived news items, and the biographical information provided by your office. Courts having jurisdiction over the addresses attached to Messrs. Prixi, Dunhill, and CornerPoint Group, LLC were then searched for matters naming them. Note that cases can be and often are filed outside of these jurisdictions and/or at branch locations of a company. For that reason, BackTrack suggests asking all subjects for a complete listing of present and past litigation involving them and/or their company(ies). The following courts were searched for the parties indicated:

NEW YORK—Messrs. Prixi, Dunhill and/or CornerPoint Group, LLC

U.S. District Court, Southern District of New York

U.S. Bankruptcy Court, Southern District of New York

State Supreme Court, New York City boroughs and surrounding counties, civil index

New York County Supreme Court, criminal

The following matter was located:

NAME OF COURT: U.S. District Court, Southern District of New York

CASE NAME: **Carl A. Rodriguez**
vs.
Lehman Brothers and Scott W. Prixi

DATE FILED: April 9, 1999

CASE NUMBER: 99-CV-0000

DESCRIPTION/STATUS: Mr. Rodriguez filed this job discrimination suit against Lehman Brothers and his boss there, vice president Scott Prixi, alleging mistreatment on the basis of race. Mr. Rodriguez, a Hispanic, claimed to have been subjected to racist ridicule and general discriminatory treatment that thwarted his advancement in the organization. He was handled in such a manner from mid-November 1998 until his early March 1999 resignation. After quitting, Mr. Rodriguez was denied his non-discretionary bonus and Mr. Prixi was said to have left threatening messages on Mr. Rodriguez's home answering machine. He sought $115,000 in compensatory damages.

The matter was submitted for arbitration in December 1999, and dismissed with prejudice on January 23, 2001. Note that the term "dismissed" indicates that the case has been closed. Dismissed "with prejudice" means the case has been decided, and cannot be brought again. Dismissed "without prejudice" is the opposite, that is, the case can be brought again. Recognize that a dismissal does not indicate the suit had no merit, and frequently is tied to a settlement executed between the parties.

Please see Exhibit B for copies of documents pertaining to this suit.

NEW JERSEY—Messrs. Prixi and Dunhill

U.S. District Court, District of New Jersey

U.S. Bankruptcy Court, District of New Jersey

State Superior Courts, statewide civil defendant index

Essex County Superior Court criminal records

Monmouth County Superior Court criminal records

No matters were found.

NEW MEXICO—Mr. Prixi

U.S. District Court, District of New Mexico

U.S. Bankruptcy Court, District of New Mexico

Lincoln County District Court, civil and criminal

Again, no actions were located. Note that Mr. Prixi likely resided in this state between the completion of his college degree and the beginning of his first recorded place of employment, Lowenstein Brothers, between 1986 and 1989.

Interviews

During the course of the investigation, BackTrack identifies independent sources believed capable of adding valuable insight into the subject's history, candor, and character. (As indicated, it is our policy not to conduct any interviews without the client's express authorization.) Our trained investigators' honed interviewing skills enable them to elicit valuable information frequently unavailable from public records. Pertinent information gained from these interviews is integrated into the body of a standard report, and furnished more completely here.

BackTrack's research revealed that the following parties were familiar with the subjects' business careers. With your authorization, BackTrack located and interviewed the following parties, beginning with four connected to Scott Prixi.

Carl Rodriguez

Mr. Rodriguez filed a lawsuit against Mr. Prixi and Lehman Brothers after claiming to have been the victim of racial discrimination. BackTrack contacted Mr. Rodriguez to learn more about this case. He agreed to offer commentary on his experiences with Mr. Prixi after viewing BackTrack's web site, although he was reticent at first. He additionally was assured that BackTrack's contract forbids subjects from viewing the written report. Even still, he stated, "I really don't know how much I should say, since it was a recent matter, and well, I'm going to stop when I'm not comfortable."

BackTrack asked about Mr. Prixi's personal level of involvement in the aforesaid matter, as compared with, for example, Lehman in general. "This was, mostly, I'd say 90 percent about Mr. Prixi's actions. The firm was included because they were unwilling to do anything about it. I spoke to some people in higher positions and found that no one was going to do anything without legal recourse." He continued: "I wasn't at the firm very long, only three months, if that gives you any idea how, uh, how harassed I felt."

BackTrack inquired about the nature of the messages that court documents allege Mr. Prixi left on his answering machine. "Well, I'd rather not get into that. I can say—safely I feel—that these messages were left between the time I spoke to his superiors and the time my attorney contacted him. I wish I'd saved half of them, but I didn't. I was able to bring what I had into evidence." Mr. Rodriguez did not wish to discuss the tapes further.

"You know how places like that used to be, an old boy network of sorts. I just assumed that professionally, stuff like that couldn't go on anymore. At least, not so overtly."

Mr. Rodriguez revealed that Mr. Prixi and Lehman both reached separate settlements outside of court, although he added, "I'm not going to talk amounts now, because those are still, well, the amounts haven't been completely paid. By either party."

"Suffice it to say that I'm not a big fan of Mr. Prixi. I would *not* work with him again, and I certainly wouldn't trust him in any position where there was some sort of client interaction. I guess I wasn't even a client. Even after it all, I feel like he doesn't really get it." He did, however, add, "[Mr. Prixi] was always good at his job, I will say that. He's a very shrewd investor. But how they could have him doing international work, with different cultures, I mean, that boggles me."

Philip Isaacs

Mr. Isaacs worked with Mr. Prixi at BCM, Inc. while he was vice president and head of international equity trading. An issue as to his dates of employment was found: The dates in his biography vary from the dates provided in his NASD biography. Mr. Isaacs believed that the NASD dates were more accurate. "I know he was here at Kaplan Michaels to begin with, and then, uh, then he worked with me up here until the summer of 1997. I'm not sure of the exact date though, I admit."

Mr. Isaacs enjoyed working with Mr. Prixi. "He worked for me for about, I'd say five or six months, directly. At that time, I was very pleased with his performance. I have no complaints. He headed up my equity trading department." Mr. Isaacs later clarified, "We worked the international accounts."

Mr. Isaacs stated that "intuition" was one of Mr. Prixi's strengths: "He had a good eye for the market. He acted on trends before they occurred, really, and well, he made us a good deal of money." Mr. Isaacs laughed. "I was disappointed when he left. He would have done really well here."

Mr. Isaacs was less firm about Mr. Prixi's weaknesses. "I guess, if I had to name one, it would be his interpersonal skills. He always took care of business, but he could be a little abrupt, or blunt around the office. It wasn't really a problem though, because, I mean, we work quick here. It was almost a necessary trait. I'd say it helped him, in fact." Mr. Isaacs would "certainly work with him again." He stated that Mr. Prixi left on good terms, and he wishes "him well in all he's up to now."

James Milhouse

BackTrack contacted Mr. Milhouse, who worked with the subject at Levine Brunswick in 1993/1994, at his current employer, CitiFunds International. He recalled "vaguely" his experiences with Mr. Prixi, saying, "I don't think he was with Levine for long, though, under a year, in . . . let me think . . . 1994." He qualified this statement, saying that the company "had a pretty high turnover back then, because of some bad management at the international desk." Mr. Milhouse stressed that the subject was not a part of the management department.

Mr. Milhouse offered his personal opinion of Mr. Prixi, calling him a "fairly talented trader . . . he had a few moments of keen insight that sometimes surprised me, given how young he was at the time." BackTrack noted that the subject would have been about 29 or 30 at the time of his employment—not an age generally considered to be altogether "young." Mr. Milhouse responded, "That may have been true, but he didn't have a wife or family, and definitely lived the bachelor lifestyle, as I recall. He went to Mardi Gras down in New Orleans, went to one of those beach spots in Mexico with his buddies, things like that." Mr. Milhouse stated that these activities "didn't seem to affect his work—I probably only remember it because I was envious of him at the time."

Given the inconsistencies and omissions in Mr. Prixi's biography, as discussed at length above, BackTrack asked Mr. Milhouse if he recollected where the subject worked both before and after his time with Levine Brunswick. Recall that while Mr. Prixi intimated on his biography that he began at R.W. Brown Markets in May 1994, just after his tenure with Levine, the NASD places him there in June 1995, leaving about thirteen months unaccounted for. Mr. Milhouse could not remember where Mr. Prixi had worked prior to Levine, but averred that at the time the subject left the company, "he gave the impression that he wanted to take a break from the grind, I think he mentioned taking a trip to Indonesia or something. I heard later that he was working for R.W. Brown, but it wasn't until a while afterwards." Upon being asked if he would work with Mr. Prixi again, Mr. Milhouse said, "Yeah, sure, as long as he hasn't lost that insight."

Paul E. Burke

Recall that Mr. Prixi was let go from Lowenstein Brothers, ostensibly for standing up clients on a business trip. BackTrack located and contacted Paul Burke, Lowenstein's operations officer at the time, to learn more about this. "Oh yes, I remember [Mr. Prixi]." Mr. Burke at first was under the impression that he was contacted by BackTrack as a reference given by Mr. Prixi; upon learning that he was developed independently as a source familiar with the subject, he said, "That makes more sense. I'm surprised he even put Lowenstein on his resume, actually. It most likely wasn't his most prestigious, uh, effort. I hope."

He continued, "I have no gripe with him really. We were his first hire out of college. I think he was still a little too immature for the position we gave him. He was a junior account executive, so we really threw him in there to learn the ropes. He had a lot of potential . . . a really bright boy. But, uh, I don't think he was up for it."

When pressed to elaborate, Mr. Burke said, "Let me just say again, that I hold nothing against him personally. I think he was a very intelligent, insightful employee. He just had a lot of growing up to do, which, really I'm sure he has by now. Basically he was still in college mode. I mean, we do a lot of wining and dining of clients, and quite frankly, that was the area where he was worst off, if you know what I mean. He drank too much, back then. But that is most likely different now."

BackTrack asked about the terms of Mr. Prixi's termination. "Now, I'm only saying this because it is confidential, but it wasn't the first time it had happened. We sent him on trips, he'd go out the night before, and not make a meeting with a client. His attendance record was not the best at the office either. He was often out Fridays or Mondays, which is something employers are wary of. But again, he had been backpacking through Europe since he graduated."

Recall that Mr. Prixi did not begin working at Lowenstein until three years after his graduation. When asked if he ever confirmed that, Mr. Burke answered, "Of course not. We had no reason not to trust him. And quite frankly he behaved like he had been staying in hostels and living out of a bag."

When asked if he would work with Mr. Prixi again, Mr. Burke answered, "Well, I tell you what. I always liked the guy myself. Everyone in the office did, on a personal level. I would have to see if he had grown up a bit, first. In fact, I'd be interested to know what he was up to. He did have some talent." He paused before adding, "I guess what I am sidestepping here is that he was a fun guy—you know, socially or whatever—but I would be somewhat nervous with him handling my money."

The following interview was conducted concerning Michael Dunhill.

Bob Friedman, Allen Winters

BackTrack was able to speak with both Mr. Friedman and Mr. Winters, identified as colleagues of Mr. Dunhill at the Camden Group. "Sure, I remember him. Great guy," Mr. Friedman began. When asked about Mr. Dunhill's position, Mr. Friedman answered, "Technically, Mike [Dunhill] and I were on the same level. We were both senior analysts." (Mr. Friedman also directed BackTrack to speak with Mr. Winters, who also worked with Mr. Dunhill.)

Mr. Friedman described his experience with Mr. Dunhill as "extremely positive." Mr. Dunhill was "the best investment analyst at the firm," he continued. Mr. Friedman told BackTrack that his positive perception of Mr. Dunhill's conduct was based on two factors: Mr. Dunhill's "extremely strong skills in the financial industry," and his "very thorough understanding of clients' needs." Added Mr. Friedman, "It is hard to find people that do understand your needs and listen to your remarks."

When BackTrack asked Mr. Friedman if Mr. Dunhill had any weaknesses, Mr. Friedman replied: "One weakness might be that I've never understood how this guy could find time for non-work-related projects." Mr. Friedman cautioned that his remarks should only be taken in the context of the financial industry.

In sum, Mr. Friedman indicated that he would "definitely" work with Mr. Dunhill again, given the opportunity. "It was very frustrating for me when [Mr. Dunhill] left the Camden Group," said Mr. Friedman, continuing that Mr. Dunhill was "systematically" and "consistently number one" in international trading. When asked to elaborate, Mr. Friedman explained that Fidelity had a system of ranking the "sell-side" brokers every three months; here, Mr. Friedman indicated that Mr. Dunhill was top among "about twenty credible competitors."

Mr. Friedman concurred with news accounts stating that Mr. Dunhill had a close relationship with Mr. Carroll, and that Mr. Dunhill was urged to return to the Camden Group after his two-month hiatus by his mentor. "When Mr. Carroll left, we feared losing Mr. Dunhill. I guess we were right."

As noted above, Mr. Friedman also recommended contacting Allen Winters, who works at the Camden Group. Mr. Winters said he worked with Mr. Dunhill from 1997 until Mr. Dunhill left the Camden Group in 2000. Mr. Winters told BackTrack that he reported directly to Mr. Dunhill in the international group; Mr. Winters was an analyst, and Mr. Dunhill was his "line manager," he indicated.

Mr. Winters told BackTrack that Mr. Dunhill was "excellent" to work for. When asked to expand, Mr. Winters said Mr. Dunhill possessed the following strengths: "very responsible, responsive, open to suggestions, good listener, super-focused, incredibly smart." Mr. Winters added that Mr. Dunhill was his "mentor" within the industry.

The preceding is a typical example of the information uncovered in a BackTrack report. As is manifest, this insight both allows you to meet critical fiduciary responsibilities, while also providing a qualitative measure of the risk in placing funds with a potential manager. When combined with your analysis of the fund and manager's strategy, consistency, and performance record, BackTrack's reports complete your standard fund evaluation process.

Exhibits

The Exhibits section of a BackTrack report includes an organized collection of materials recovered in the course of the investigation, including various media articles, court documents, and other similar records, and, if provided, the subjects' biographies or resumes. These have not been included in this sample report.

CHAPTER 13

So You Want to Start a Hedge Fund?

MISTAKES START-UP HEDGE FUND MANAGERS MAKE

The magazine *Trader's Monthly* puts out an annual list of the top-paid traders, most of whom are hedge fund managers who have had more than $100 million in cash going into their pockets over the past year. It's no wonder then, with more than 8,000 hedge funds to choose from, that many people want a piece of this pie. And a day doesn't go by that someone doesn't tell me he wants to start a hedge fund.

And I don't think it's necessarily a bad idea. Just as in the early 1980s, when some people claimed that there were too many mutual funds (and I'm sure, if the word was popular then, people would have been talking about the "mutual fund bubble") and now there are $8 trillion in mutual funds, people are now saying there is a "hedge fund bubble" and collapse is imminent. Considering that mutual funds primarily invest in only one asset class, long U.S. stocks, and hedge funds invest in hundreds of asset classes, suggesting that capacity for hedge funds is much greater than the ultimate capacity of mutual funds (which doesn't seem near its peak anyway), this argument is just ridiculous.

However, I think before someone jumps into the hedge fund fray they need to be aware of many of the common mistakes that start-up hedge funds make. Many talented (and many untalented) traders and investors have the misconception that if they have a decent trading idea, or a good track record, that is enough to start a hedge fund. Few take into account that starting a hedge fund is like starting any other business and that there are many business-related pitfalls along the way, other than simply having a good idea sketched out on a napkin. Some of the pitfalls I list here are operational, some are related to branding and strategy, and some are related to psychology and life choices, all of which come into play when making the decision to start a fund.

Several things can go wrong in the first stages of starting up a fund, some of which can't really be planned for in advance. Some of these possible roadblocks include:

- Your investment idea might work well on paper but not in practice. You won't really know until you start. Anyone investing in you at your inception is taking "seeding risk" since they also don't really know in advance how your strategy will work in practice.
- You might not be able to handle the psychology of risk and loss. A friend called recently to tell me he was about to launch a fund. I told him, "Welcome to hell," and he didn't really understand. "You mean," he said, "will it be tough to deal with investors and fundraising?" and my response was that it will be tough to deal with losing money if you've never done it before.
- As with any business, don't underestimate the expenses it will take to get to maturity as a business, and don't underestimate the importance of standard entrepreneurial concepts such as branding, marketing, customer relations, legal matters, accounting, and so on.

Some of the psychology can be dealt with by a careful reading of the previous chapters in this book. In other words, when starting a hedge fund, think carefully who your customers are. Your customers are not really your investors. Rather, your customers are the market participants who are paying you money for the service you provide. The question is, what is that service? Is it in the form of supposed liquidity that you are providing the market? Is it because you are lending into situations the traditional banks are avoiding?

Assuming you get through and understand the basic psychology of hedge fund management and the concepts behind (at least, my theories on) having customers within the capitalist markets that are willing to pay you, there are then several basic mistakes that start-up managers tend to make.

Mistake 1: Offering Monthly Liquidity

In order to attract initial investors, many people feel they have to bend over backwards and make sacrifices. On the surface this makes sense. If someone is taking "seeding risk" by putting money with you before you have a real business and track record, then they are going to want special conditions, including an ability to pull money out of the fund at a second's notice. However, this is the easiest way to guarantee your business will fail even before you open up on day one.

To build your business you are going to have to outlay money for office, legal, accounting, and other expenses. If your largest investor (assuming your seed investors are your largest) can pull out at the end of any month, then the one time you really need that investor to stay in (you are fighting a market dip, for instance) will be the month they pull. Note that they might pull for reasons that have nothing to do with your track record. You could be having a great year but they might not be and might need the cash for other reasons that have nothing to do with you (maybe they are getting redemptions if they are a fund of funds, maybe they need cash for a house or a tax bill, etc.), and suddenly you are out of business.

Mistake 2: Not Charging a Management Fee

Warren Buffett, in the hedge fund he started in 1957, had no management fee, just an incentive fee of 25 percent, so he would only get paid if his investors did well. This is a great model if you can do it. But not everyone is Warren Buffett—and I'll also note that Buffett worked out of his living room for the first couple of years of his business. People get what they pay for, and when they pay nothing they are essentially treating your services as if you are worthless. That said, again, there are circumstances where you just have to make accommodation, but avoid this if you can.

Mistake 3: Having One Investor Too Large

In the past few months a multi-strategy firm I'm familiar with had to close down shop when a combination of mistake 1 and mistake 3 came back to haunt him. Assets under his management went from almost \$150 million to less than \$100 million when one investor had to pull, setting off a death spiral when liquidating assets to meet the monthly liquidity requirement caused losses, which caused other redemptions.

Mistake 4: Not Having Living Expenses Set Aside

Set aside enough for at least a year, and preferably two or three, in the bank before launching your business. The last thing you want to be thinking about on a down day is how you are going to be paying your mortgage that month.

Also, it's going to take longer than you think to raise money and build a viable entity. A very good hedge fund that I know of has had only one down month in the past three years, great audited returns, great backgrounds of the managers, and has only just in the past three months made the leap from $10 million in assets to $40 million in assets, and its founder is now able to pay his living expenses. Repeat: That was three years of great returns.

GETTING BY ON $600,000 A YEAR

Further underlining the perils of starting a hedge fund, I was recently having breakfast with a friend who runs a successful long/short hedge fund with about $60 million in assets. He seemed stressed. "It's hard to make ends meet in this business," he told me.

"What do you mean? Your business has been doing great," I said. "You've beaten the market every year. Your business is growing."

"Listen," he said, "let's go through the breakdown. Let's say you have $60 million in assets and you charge two and twenty." He's referring to his 2 percent management fee (a fee taken as a percentage of all assets) and his 20 percent performance fee (a fee taken as a percentage of profits). "So that's $1.2 million in definite cash flow for the year. Plus another $1.2 million if I return 10 percent on the year, so $2.4 million. About half of the money I've raised was through a third party marketer. The deal is I give the third party marketing firm 20 percent of the fees I make. So that's $500,000 out the door. I'm down to $1.9 million. I have three professionals working for me. One does admin, client relations, and so on. That's a full-time job. Two help with stock picking, trading, risk management, due diligence, and so on. They average out at $150,000 each plus insurance, so that's about $500,000 out. By the way, don't print my name. I don't want them to know what the average salary is between them. So now we're down to $1.4 million.

"I have to have a good office. I bring clients up here, show them around, everyone hard at work, nice views, and so on. Fifth Avenue address. That's $10,000 a month. Then a secretary, office supplies, and so on, somehow or other adds up to about $80,000. Let's round it to $100,000 after including travel expenses, and so now I'm down to $1.2 million. Well, I have a partner—the guy who helped bring in the initial $15 million to get us started—and he meets all potential clients that the third-party firm sets up and he also finds new clients. He's on the road all the time trying to raise more money, going to conferences, and so on. So my partner and I split fifty-fifty. Now I'm down to $600,000 for me."

"You realize, of course, that this puts you in the top 99.9 percent of income for the global population," I gently reminded him.

"Well, let's go through it. First off, taxes take out about $250,000 for me. So now I'm down to $350,000. Mortgage payments on my 2,200-square-foot apartment are about $8,000 a month, property taxes another $2,000. That's $120,000. Two kids going to private school plus all the expenses that entails—supplies, piano lessons, religious stuff, and so on—that's about $50,000, bringing us to $170,000. Where am I going to stay in the summer? All my kids' and wife's friends are in the Hamptons. A Hamptons house is going to cost me another $50,000 at least. I'm being generous here. Camp for kids—let's say another $15,000. Now we're at $235,000. Let's add up basic household staff: nanny for kids plus housekeeper adds up to about $60,000. Now I'm at $295,000. Well, now between my wife and me we probably average about $1,000 a week on everything else: food, entertainment, furniture, HBO, travel—two vacations a year are going to cost me about $10,000 each one—and so on. Again, I'm being very generous. I don't even think I'm counting clothing or dry cleaning costs here. But this takes me to right about $350,000.

"And let's not forget," he adds, "this assumes I'm up 10 percent this year. Right now the S&P is down about 0.5 percent and all the hedge fund indexes are hanging out around flat. I'm up 4.8 percent on the year so I'm killing all of them. But here we are eight months into the year and I'm on track to do 6 or 7 percent. Being up 7 percent instead of 10 percent would lop about $90,000 off my yearly take. So in a year where I am totally killing it I'm not even doing as well as in the scenarios I just described where I can't even make ends meet.

"And further. What happens when this SEC regulation kicks in? I have to hire a compliance officer. Right now, today, as we sit here, compliance officers are making between $200,000 and $500,000 a year. What happens when funds are required to hire a compliance officer? There's about 3,000 funds that are going to have to hire one. Do you think there are 3,000 unemployed compliance officers out there? What's this going to cost?" My friend threw up his hands and I just didn't have any answers for him.

This conversation reminded me of the excellent 1980 book by Andrew Tobias, *Getting By on $100,000 a Year*, which I highly recommend, which details similar scenarios, albeit in pre-hedge fund days. All of this is to say, I think the hedge fund business, just like the Internet business, is quickly becoming institutionalized, and ultimately only the big players will survive, with the rest either disappearing or getting acquired through rollups of funds. Personally, other than starting a hedge fund, I think one of the better business models out there is to raise money to buy stakes in the management companies of smaller hedge funds that may need help on the financing side once they realize the money doesn't fall like manna from heaven.

Mistake 5: Going for Home Runs

There's a saying, "If you can return 1 percent a month you'll raise $1 billion." This statement is true. The largest allocators of money are institutions that have as their goals a modest 8 to 10 percent a year with low volatility. Anybody returning 12 percent a year is a dream come true for these allocators. Aiming for 50 percent a year can cause you to quickly go out of business if you miss. And even getting your goal of 50 percent could make you too volatile for an allocator.

Mistake 6: Starting a Hedge Fund in the First Place

This is a tough business with a lot of competition. One of the mistakes I've made in trying to survive in this business is starting off with no pedigree. I never worked at Goldman Sachs, or Morgan Stanley, or any of the big hedge funds. The recent Deutsche Bank Asset Management survey discusses how pedigree is the most important characteristic (behind performance) for an allocator. It's the difference between launching with $300 million as opposed to $3 million. My background is that I had a software business in the 1990s, sold it, started another software business (which still exists), and then began trading, investing, and writing about investing. I didn't come up through the traditional ranks, and every step of the way has been excruciatingly difficult.

In retrospect, I wish I had focused my efforts on somehow ending up at a bank or at a large hedge fund, even taking entry-level jobs just to learn the ins and outs and rise up through the ranks before going out on my own. For one thing, you avoid all the start-up costs and headaches. Second, you can focus on the investing rather than the business aspects. And third, the payout might be greater: guaranteed salary in most cases, plus a performance-based bonus that might be greater than what you would have made starting your own fund. Similarly, there are shops such as proprietary trading firms that give up to a 90 percent performance bonus rather than the 20 percent one would get (hopefully) starting one's own fund.

That said, I'm ultimately happy with my choices, and regrets come and go every day in this business.

CHAPTER 14

Classic Investment Reading and New Media Resources

BOOKS ABOUT INVESTMENT

A few times in the past I've reviewed recently published books, and on those occasions I've been asked about what I felt were the best investment books ever. Everybody has their own investment style and what is great for one investor might not be relevant for the style of another. However, I can list my favorite investment books and why.

The first is *Supermoney*, by Adam Smith. Published in 1973, this book has perhaps been overshadowed by Smith's other more popular book, *The Money Game*. Both books underline the idea that the markets are difficult and even the professionals often end up right where they started, back at zero, or perhaps even in jail if they try to overstep the obstacles the market put in their way. I like *Supermoney* not only for the author's style and intelligence but, in retrospect, for its prescience. For instance, in one chapter, the author goes up to Omaha to drive around town with then-unknown investor Warren Buffett. He wrote this chapter shortly after Buffett had wound down his hedge fund and was trying to figure out what to do with the rest of his life now that he had achieved the princely sum of about $40 million in net worth. One of the best moments in the chapter is when they drive by the Nebraska Furniture Mart—Buffett points it out and says one day he'd like to own it.

Another chapter in the book features Paul Erdmann, who ran a Swiss bank that Smith had invested in until Erdmann ran it into the ground and went to jail for it. While in jail he passed the time away by writing fiction. Little did Smith know when he wrote *Supermoney* that Erdmann would become the best-selling financial thriller author ever, leaving behind his troubled past. Right now I'm reading *The Wheeler Dealers*, Adam Smith's first book (although he used his real name, George Goodman), written in 1959.

My next pick is *The Funny Money Game*, written in 1973 by Andrew Tobias. Tobias later wrote the best-seller *How to Get By on $100,000 a Year* and the personal finance best-seller *The Only Investment Guide You'll Ever Need* (recently re-released for the 2005 Christmas season). But his first book is his best. *The Funny Money Game* is about the rise and fall of National Student Marketing. Tobias had front-row seats, being a vice president at the company while the stock rose up to frothy levels in the late 1960s despite little or no earnings and an executive team of recent college grads—very similar to the late 1990s start-ups that rose and fell. *The Funny Money Game* is an excellent demonstration of how the dot-coms were not the first example of this kind of exuberance, nor will they be the last.

The Billion Dollar Sure Thing, *The Panic of '89*, and *The Silver Bears* are three books by Paul Erdmann. Although these books are all works of fiction, Erdmann does an excellent job of bringing complex economic and financial issues into the realm of the layman while he looks at fantastic what-if scenarios and their effect on the markets. *The Silver Bears* is an excellent exposition on silver, and *The Panic of '89* and *The Billion Dollar Sure Thing* (as well as *The Set-Up*) are practically textbooks on the Fed, interest rates, bonds, and Swiss banks, all topics Erdmann is expert in. Pick up these books before reading recent financial thriller writers Stephen Frey and Christopher Reich.

I also recommend *My Story*, by Bernard Baruch. Never the richest and never the most powerful, Baruch was somehow always in the mix and lived to tell the tale. It is fascinating to read about the birth of his career and how he dealt with initial frustrations and loss before really hitting his stride. The development of his discipline and the ways in which he averted future loss because of it is a must-read. Stuff like this is inspirational for me. I definitely suffered loss and subsequent depression after the dot-com bubble and bust, and reading the stories of people who went through their own rise and fall a couple of times before dominating their field helps me to persevere.

The Essential Drucker is essential reading. The late Peter Drucker was the 90-plus management consultant whose texts on the art and philosophy of management have inspired probably thousands of executives. Why should a text on management philosophy be considered an important book for investing? Because, as stated repeatedly in this book, investing needs to be treated like any other business. Before you outlay cash in an investment you must figure out what product or service your cash will be creating, who the customer is, and why that customer should pay you as opposed to anyone else for the service you are offering. Drucker's primary focus was in helping managers determine what the purpose of their business is. I love classic quotes from his book like the following: "It is the customer who determines what a business is. It is the customer alone whose willingness to pay for a good or for a service converts economy resources into wealth, things into goods. What the customer buys and considers value is never just a product. It is always a utility, that is, what a product or service does for him."

A very interesting book is *Wiped Out: How I Lost a Fortune in the Stock Market While the Averages Were Making New Highs*, by Anonymous Investor. I recently spoke at the Las Vegas Trader's Expo conference. The conference had about 9,000 attendees. Everyone was convinced that they could somehow beat the markets, make a living, get rich, and so on. This book, written in 1966, is a classic reminder of how everything remains the same. First off, the dedication: "Dedicated to my brokers, each and every one, whose capacity for self-delusion is commensurate with my own." To open Chapter 4, the author has this quote: "I was now on my own, and though slightly nervous about my commitment, confident of great prospects. A goal of a 15 percent accretion in capital in a given year I now considered contemptible; I would aim to double my money annually, as advised to do in the book I had recently read. . . . Clearly great wealth was imminent."

Then, a few chapters later: "I found it hard to believe that I had only $8,000 left. I went over and over the figures, balancing them in different columns, just to drum into my head how disastrous the last year—a banner year for the market as a whole—had been. What could I possibly do now to regain all those tens of thousands of dollars that I had lost?"

While it's a shame that I get such pleasure out of reading about the failings of what seems like an otherwise intelligent and pleasant guy, it does remind me that discipline, persistence, and perseverance are the names of the game in this business. There are so many frustrations on the path to building a career either as a trader, an analyst, a hedge fund manager, or a portfolio manager, that one must keep in mind the history, both the successes and failures, of those who trod this way before.

BLOGS FOR HEDGE FUNDS

With the Dean Scream echoing out of the blogosphere and Dan Rather's career being burned in effigy by random blogs connected only by the passionate obsessions of their writers, 2004 was clearly the Year of the Blog. With 4 million blogs and counting (a blog is being created every second, according to one of those statistics that appear out of nowhere and have no source to attribute), the only question I can ask is, what use is this to me?

On a daily basis I like to look at several blogs written by other hedge fund managers, analysts, venture capitalists, and researchers for the latest analysis and other news that might not be hitting my radar screen from the traditional sources. Here are my top seven: If you have other suggestions, please e-mail me with them.

1. **Seeking Alpha (www.seekingalpha.com)**, written by David Jackson, who runs a long-short portfolio and was previously a research analyst with Morgan Stanley covering communications equipment stocks. Seeking Alpha is usually updated daily and contains posts on the state of the hedge fund world as well as updates of his blog about Internet stocks.
2. **The J Curve (jurvetson.blogspot.com)**. Steve Jurvetson of venture capital firm Draper Fisher Jurvetson (famous for its initial investment in Hotmail) updates this blog with commentary on what's going on at the cutting edge of technology. In particular, he explores the intersection between computation, biotech, and nanotechnology and tries to piece together this puzzle in real time when determining where the next great investment boom might come from. Sometimes he's so over the top it's funny, like in his most recent post, which he starts: "While reading Jeff Hawkins' book *On Intelligence*, I was struck by the resonant coherence of his memory-prediction framework for how the cortex works. It was like my first exposure to complexity theory at the Santa Fe Institute—providing a perceptual prism for the seeing of the consilience across various scientific conundrums." Go for it, J!
3. **Securities Litigation Watch (http://slw.issproxy.com/)**. Basically, finding investment returns largely consists of two tasks: finding value and avoiding corruption. Both are extremely difficult. Securities Litigation Watch, run by Bruce Carton, executive director of ISS Securities Class Action Services and a former corporate lawyer, provides a constant update into the latest scandals and investigations. Another useful blog in this arena that he often links to

is http://www.the10b-5daily.com/, run by Wilson Sonsini lawyer Lyle Roberts. And for all CEOs out there, check out his latest entry, which begins: "Don't you hate it when your wife ignores your specific 'entreaties' that she not share inside information about your publicly traded company with her brother, and gets herself sued by the SEC?"

4. **Footnoted.org,** run by Michelle Leder, author of *Financial Fine Print,* does what it says—it reads the footnotes of SEC filings, press releases, and so on, and asks the right questions about what's going on in the fine print. I really like it when a post starts off, "Does anyone really believe it when a CEO says he wants to spend more time with his family?" and then goes from there. A great site for finding either shorting opportunities or at least stocks to avoid.
5. **Infectious Greed (www.paul.kedrosky.com)**. I've been following ex–hedge fund manager and now Professor Paul Kedrosky's stuff on www.thestreet.com for almost three years, so it has been a pleasure to read his almost daily commentary at his blog where he comments on topics ranging from iPods to bird flu, the failure of Transmeta, analysis of Sequoia's distribution of Google shares, and a host of other topics that may or may not come in useful but adds to my general understanding of the world.
6. **Blog Maverick (www.blogmaverick.com)**. Mark Cuban, founder of Broadcast.com, which sold to Yahoo! for billions, publishes this blog where he writes about anything from the Dallas Mavericks basketball team, which he owns, to thoughts on his own idea for a hedge fund focused on gambling, which isn't as bad an idea as it seems once you read his argument. Blog Maverick is hosted by Jason Calcanis's company, Weblogs, Inc., which hosts a variety of blogs useful to the investor on topics throughout finance and technology.
7. **Random Roger's Big Picture (http://randomroger.blogspot.com/).** Roger Nusbaum is a portfolio manager living in Prescott, Arizona, writing on topics such as closed-end fund arbitrage, whether dividend-paying stocks are good investments (he says yes, Seeking Alpha's David Jackson says no), energy trusts/MLPs (some of my favorite investments), and ETFs. Like all good bloggers, he's opinionated. For instance, his take on mutual funds: "For the life of me I can't fathom how a professional can use open-end funds to build a portfolio around."

The question is, reading all the news, the press releases, the SEC filings, the earnings reports, and the rest is hard enough. Why waste further time reading the blogs that I'm mentioning? I like to get the perspective of guys in the business who are putting their thoughts straight down, completely unedited, not afraid to make mistakes and admit it (the good ones). With 8,000 hedge funds and countless other investors, there is almost no way to get an edge or an understanding of the investment universe by just looking at the traditional sources. What Phil Fisher called "scuttlebut" in his investment classic, *Common Stocks and Uncommon Profits*, is more likely to be found now in the blogosphere than anywhere else.

There are two more blogs I recommend. The first is Jeff Mathews Is Not Making This Up (jeffmathewsisnotmakingthisup.com). Jeff and I used to both write on the same web site, StreetInsight.com, before I went off to RealMoney.com and he went off to write primarily for his blog. I like the title of that blog since every post does have the reader thinking out loud, "What!? He's got to be making this up." But he isn't. A recent series of posts about Overstock.com and Jeff's views on the value of the stock prompted Overstock.com CEO Patrick Byrne to hold a press conference accusing Jeff and others of conspiring to bring down the stock and backed by a "Sith Lord" from the 1980s (a long, long, time ago). Blogs definitely inspire passion in their readers, in part because they are admittedly biased and free from the pseudo-neutral editorial concerns of most mainstream media.

The other is John Rutledge's Blog at www.rutledgeblog.com. John is Dr. FeelGood, and I mean this in the best possible way. Whenever I am worried about the economy I check out the Rutledge blog because sooner or later he's going to take the worries constructed by the media and filter them through what I call "the capitalist massage." One of my favorite recent posts from John is this one from August 2005, when he is commenting on the effect oil prices have on inflation:

> *Oil prices, inflation, interest rates. Lots of folks today saying oil prices could hit $75 in the next few weeks. Truth is, over short periods, oil prices could do almost anything; they may be right. You will be hearing people say this is the end of the world, that it will throw the United States into recession, that it will increase inflation and push rates higher. Not so. Over longer periods people adapt to oil prices. That's why we use about half as much oil per dollar of GDP than we did when oil was cheap. And all the growth of the U.S. economy is in the service sector where the only thing you need oil for is the dressing on your Caesar salad. Not saying oil doesn't matter (double negative? No it's not.). Just saying we need to take a deep breath before biting down on our cyanide capsules. Loose credit markets dominate high oil prices for growth.*

Regarding inflation, a spike in oil prices causes a spike in prices, not an increase in sustainable inflation. It pushes output down, not up. They know this at the Fed too. High oil prices are more likely to cause the Fed to back away from raising the Fed funds rate target than to push it higher. And bond yields (10-year Treasury is 4.26 percent today) will ignore the whole thing.

CHAPTER 15

Where to Find the Data

Most of the time I really hate turning on the news and watching people spit at each other while blabbering stuff like, "The Dow broke below its 200-day moving average and this is a bearish sign." Is this true? Should traders short? Or should they fade the pundit and go long? (Answer: yes.) But only by examining the data, and testing the question, "What has happened every time the Dow has broken below its 200-day moving average?" can one determine what the average result has been, what the standard deviation of results has been, and whether the result is statistically significant (and, if so, is the average result worthy of a trade after commissions and slippage?).

Over the years I have tested everything from the above statement to "What happens after the Fed hikes rates six times in a row" to "What happens when there is more than three inches of snow falling on Central Park?" Every strategy, every idea, including those written about in this book, should be tested as much as possible, and for most tests, you need data. As a rule, I like to get my data fast and cheap, and I pull them from a variety of sources. Here are some of those sources:

- Daily market data: For questions like "What happens when the S&P closes up 1 percent for three days in a row?" I like to use free data source Yahoo! Finance, which provides open, high, low, close, and volume daily data. QCharts at quote.com is slightly more expensive but slightly cleaner data. I use the software Wealth-Lab, from www.wealth-lab.com and owned by Fidelity, to process and test the data.

- Intraday market data: For one-minute, five-minute, or one-hour data, I use QCharts. Many data sources provide one-minute data but only for the most recent three to six months. QCharts can get you data for at least the last five years. QCharts also has data on various indicators such as the Tick, the Arms Indicator, new highs/new lows data, and so on.
- Economic data: The Fred II database at the St. Louis Federal Reserve site (www.stlouisfed.org) has GDP data going back five decades, population data, employment data, consumer spending data, inflation data, and so on. I can't stress enough how valuable this is when people start talking about a "soft patch" or saying, "The economy is overheating." Looking at the past and seeing where we are relative to various other soft patches or overheated moments is immensely revealing.
- Hedge fund data: For a fund of funds manager it is important to be able to quickly go through hundreds of potential managers, examine and compare track records and styles, peruse manager biographies, and compare fees. I have found www.iasg.com to be a great site to compare the various CTAs, including John Henry and Quadriga's superfund. Two of my favorite hedge fund sites are www.hedgefund.net and www.cogenthedge.com.
- Market heuristics: For P/E ratios (not just in the United States but in every country), market dividend yields, capitalization of the entire market, index data back to 1871, and even stock price data for the South Sea Company in the 1700s, check out Global Financial Data at www.globalfindata.com. Additionally, various yield rates ranging from the Fed funds rate (from 1914 on) to the 30-year yields can be found at Global Financial Data.
- Business cycles: Check out the National Bureau of Economic Research at www.nber.org/cycles.html for dates and durations of all the business cycles and expansions over the past century. This is useful to see average duration and depth or strength of the cycle, which can be used to help determine where we might fit into the picture now.
- IPO data: Ivo Welch, a professor at Yale, keeps track of a lot of interesting data on IPOs at his IPO resources page, www.iporesources.org. Additionally, ipodata.com allows me to keep track of the IPO pipeline and quickly go through data on the various planned offerings as well as look through lists of the top 25 underwriters, top performers year-to-date, and so on.
- Futures data: In addition to Qcharts, data for some contracts can be found at www.turtletrader.com. Global Financial Data also has data for futures contracts and spot data for various U.S. and international commodities markets.

- Index changes: It's good to keep track of index changes (1) to avoid survivorship bias in testing and (2) to perhaps develop systems based on the change of index, such as Russell 2000 changes or S&P 600 deletions. For NASDAQ 100 changes check out www.nasdaq.com/reference/nasdaq_100_changes.xls. For S&P additions/deletions look at http://www2.standardandpoors.com/servlet/Satellite?pagename=sp/Page/IndicesIndexChangesPg&r=3&b=4&s=&ig=&i=". For an interesting study on S&P 500 additions/deletions, check out http://www.cob.vt.edu/finance/quotes/articles/priceresponse.pdf. The Russell 2000 rebalances annually in June. For a list of additions/deletions to that index go to www.russell.com/US/Indexes/US/reconstitution/default.asp.
- Bankruptcies: For data on recent bankruptcies go to www.bankruptcydata.com/recearchcenter2.htm, and for trading halts (which tend to happen when a company declares bankruptcy) go to www.nasdaqtrader.com/asp/TradeHaltShowPage.asp.

And finally, if you ever get tired of staring at the quote screen and just want to know how you should price the original Picasso hanging on your wall, check out www.artprice.com for the latest prices.

Index

Abraham, Salem, 131
Abraham Trading Company, 131, 133
Accountability, 162–163
Activism:
  Chapman on, 44–46
  Cutter & Buck example, 41–42
  Gencorp example, 42, 43–44
  mimicking, 46
  modus operandi of, 22–23
  National Wireless Holdings (NWH) example, 28–35
  overview of, 4, 22
  Shamrock Holdings example, 24, 25–27
  Star Gas Partners example, 36–41
  typical demands and, 23
Aldabra, 73–74
Ameren, 152, 153
Apollo, 91
Arbitrage. *See* Closed-end fund arbitrage
Arbitrage strategies and liquidity, 91–92
Arons, Rick, 47, 48
Art collections, 111, 114–117
Artprice.com web site, 203
Asia Tigers Fund, 97
Asset classes, 111
Asset Investors, 53–54
Auto finance, subprime, 10–11

Background checks:
  conducting, 164
  report example, 166–183
BackTrack Reports, 166–183
Bank:
  activities uninteresting to, 49
  starting, 19
Bankruptcy data, 203
Barbeques Galore, 85, 86
Baruch, Bernard, *My Story*, 194
Berkshire Hathaway, 78
Bernstein, Hartley, 162–164
Best Buy, 139, 140
Biggs, Barton, 47, 48
Biggs, Wende, 47, 48
Billionaire, trading like:
  The Billion Dollar Sure Thing (Erdmann), 194
  Cuban, 80–81
  Dell, 81–82
  B. Gates, 81
  Icahn, 87–89
  Kellog, 87
  Kovner, 82–84
  Lynch, 84–86
  overview of, 79–80
  Soros, 87
Black, Keith, 161–162
Blockbuster Video, 78, 87
Blog Maverick, 197
Blogs, 196–199
Books about investment, 193–195
Bowie, David, 5–6, 117, 118
Bowie Bonds, 5–6, 117
Briazz, 76
British Railways Pension Fund, 115
Brookdale Global Opportunity Fund, 97
Brown, James, 118

Buffett, Warren, 3, 78, 187, 193
Business cycle data, 202
Byrne, Patrick, 198

Cadence Resources Corporation, 60–61
Camelot Capital Management, 96–97
Carton, Bruce, 196
Carver, Jennifer, 158–161
Cash and liquidity, 1
Cassidy, Terrence, 27, 29, 30, 31, 32
Caxton Associates, 82, 84
Cefa.com web site, 96
Centrix Financial, 10–11
Chanos, Jim, 108–109
Chap-Cap Partners, 27, 44–46
Chapman, Bob, 22, 27–36, 44–46
Chen, Richard, 18
Christmas system, 138–140
Closed-end fund arbitrage:
  discounting mechanisms, 92–93
  do-it-yourself, 93–98
  overview of, 5, 91–92
Closed-end funds, 91
CMGI, 143–144
Cohen, Stevie, 111
Coin collecting, 112–114, 119–129
Coinmach Corp., 72
Collector's Universe, 114
CollegeCard business, 47
Common stock and PIPEs, 60–61, 66, 68–69
Common Stocks and Uncommon Profits (Fisher), 198
Compuware, 148–149
Conflicts of interest, 163
Consolidated Energy, Inc., 62–63
Convertible debentures and PIPEs, 61–64, 66–67
Countertrend trader, 141
Cracker Barrel Old Country Stores, 144–145
Credit card debt:
  Asset Investors and, 53–54
  charged-off, 48–49
  CollegeCard business and, 47–48
  household debt service payments as percentage of disposable personal income, 49–50
  overview of, 4
  statistics on, 50–51
  students and, 50
  Talisman Partners and, 51–53
CSA, 158–161
CSFB Tremont Dedicated Short Bias Index, 99–100
Cuban, Mark, 80–81, 197
Cutter & Buck, 41–42

Daily market data, 201
Data dump, 7
Data resources, 201–203
Death spirals and PIPEs, 58–59
Dell, Michael, 81–82
DFAN14 filings, 46
DiBenedetto, Thomas, 33
DiGenova, Silvano, 112, 114
Discounting mechanisms, 92–93
Disney, Roy, 23–24
Document review, 165
Donaldson, Lufkin & Jenrette Inc., 55
Dow Jones Industrial Average, 149–155
Draper Fisher Jurvetson, 196
Drucker, Peter, 194–195
Druckman, Michael, 11, 12–14, 51, 52–53
Due diligence, 164–166
Dumauld, Ted, 53–54
Duncan, Kathleen, 119
Dutch auction IPOs, 75–76

Economic data, 202
Efficient market theory, 2
8K filings, 46
Eisner, Michael, 23
Elxsi Corp., 87
Employment and education verification, 165
Equity Income Partners fund, 11–14
Erdmann, Paul, 193–194
The Essential Drucker (Drucker), 194–195

Etfconnect.com web site, 93–94
ETFs (exchange-traded funds):
  belief in investing in, 6
  as inefficient market, 155–156
  NASDAQ 100, 135–138
  passively managed, 143
  Retail HOLDRs, 138–139
  shorting, 101

“Fade the gap on Friday” system, 105–106, 107
Fairchild Corp., 78
Fernwood Investments, 115–117
Fisher, Phil, *Common Stocks and Uncommon Profits*, 198
Floating convertible, 63, 67
Flynn, Sean Masaki, 93
Footnoted.org blog, 197
Form 4 filings, 46, 80
Fortune Brands, 149, 150
Fraud, watching out for, 6, 157
Fred II database, 202
Freemarkets, Inc., 105
The Funny Money Game (Tobias), 194
Futures data, 202

Gasbarro, Dominic, 93
Gates, Bill, 81
Gates, Clark, 11
Gencorp, 42, 43–44
General Electric, 151, 152
Genitope, 56, 57
Gentex, 148
Gersten, Savage, Kaplowitz, 164
Getting By on $100,000 a Year (Tobias), 189–190
Gillette, 3
Global Financial Data, 202
Global Sources LTD, 78
Gold, Stanley, 23–24
Gold coin type set:
  description of, 119–120
  Indian Head Eagle, 126–127
  Indian Head Half Eagle, 125–126
  Indian Head Quarter Eagle, 123
  Liberty Head Double Eagles, 128
  Liberty Head Eagles, 126, 127
  Liberty Head Half Eagle, 124–125
  Liberty Head Quarter Eagle, 122–123
  St. Gaudens Double Eagles, 128–129
  Three Dollar Gold Piece, 124
  Type One Gold Dollar, 120
  Type Three Gold Dollar, 121–122
  Type Two Gold Dollar, 121
Google, 76
GPStrategies, 82–83, 84
Greenspan, Alan, 9
Greg Manning Auctions, 114
GTCR, 72
GVI Securities Solutions, 78

Hambrecht, Bill, 75–76
Hambrecht & Quist, 55, 75
Hammer, Armand, 77
Hard-money real estate lending, 11–14
Harvard Management Corporation, 97
Hedge funds:
  Greenspan on, 9
  as new banks, 4, 9–10, 49
  registration of, 161–162
  starting, 6, 185–188, 190–191
Henry, John, 131, 132
Hewlett-Packard, 89
Hollywood Entertainment, 87
Home run, going for, 190
HouseRaising Inc, 65
How to Prosper During the Coming Bad Years (Ruff), 141
Hudson, Tom, 41

Iasg.com web site, 202
Icahn, Carl, 87–89
IIG Trade Opportunities Fund, 11
Imhof, Todd, 119
Income, 188–190
Index, myth of, 6
Index change data, 203
Infectious Greed blog, 197
Initial public offerings. *See* IPOs (initial public offerings)
Institutional Shareholder Services (ISS), 23
Integramed, 87

Interest rates:
  credit card debt portfolios and, 54
  hard-money real estate lending and, 13
Intermix, 78
Intraday market data, 202
Intrado, 24–27
IPass, 24, 25
IPOs (initial public offerings):
  banks and, 71–72
  data on, 202
  Dutch auction, 75–76
  new approach with, 5
  reverse merger and, 76–78
  specialty acquisition corporations and, 72–74
Isonics Corporation, 67–68

Jackson, David, 196
Jackson, Michael, 119
January effect, 102
The J Curve blog, 196
JDS Uniphase Corporation, 145–146
Jeff Mathews Is Not Making This Up blog, 198
Jones, Paul Tudor, 111
Jurvetson, Steve, 196

Kaplowitz, Jay, 74, 164
Katzenberg, Jeffrey, 23
Kedrosky, Paul, 197
Kellog, Peter, 87
Kohlberg Kravis Roberts, 91
Korean Equity Fund, 97, 98
Kovner, Bruce, 82–84
Kravis, Henry, 111

Laclede Gas, 151, 152
Larson, Jeffrey, 97
Leder, Michelle, 197
Leight, Nathan, 73
Lichtenstein, Warren, 42–43
Life insurance premium financing, 14–16
Liquidity:
  arbitrage strategies and, 91–92
  cash and, 1
  hedge funds and, 9
  starting hedge fund and, 186–187
Living expenses, 187–188
Lloyd, Louis, 33
Loeb, Dan, 27, 36–41
Lynch, Peter, 84–86

MacDougall, Brian, 159, 160
Management fees, 187
Market heuristics, 202
Mathews, Jeff, 198
McManus, Michael, Jr., 32–33, 34
MD Sass, 18
Mei, Jianping, 115
Mei/Moses Fine Art Index, 115, 116
Mergers, reverse, 76–78
Microcaps and PIPEs, 68
Midway, 148
Millennium Chemicals, 151
Millstream Acquisition Corp., 74
Misonix, 27, 36
Morningstar, 76
Moses, Michael, 115
Motorcycle Centers of America, 78
Moving average, 134–135
Murstein, Alvin and Andrew, 19
My Story (Baruch), 194

Napster Inc., 60
NASDAQ futures, 101, 103
NASDAQ 100 ETF, 135–138
NASDAQ 100 index:
  additions to, 143–144
  deletions from, 144–145
  shorting, 101, 102–103, 104
NASDAQ Stock Market, 62
NASD violations, 164–165
National Bureau of Economic Research, 202
National Loan Exchange, 53
National Patent Development Corporation, 83
National Wireless Holdings (NWH), 28–35
Net asset value (NAV), 91
New River Pharmaceuticals, 76
Nierenberg, David, 97

NL Industries, 151–152, 153
Nusbaum, Roger, 197
NWH (National Wireless Holdings), 28–35

Occidental Petroleum, 77
Optimum Realty Corporation, 18
Option Expiration Friday method, 106–107
Oria, 158, 160, 161
Orion Capital, 18
Overstock.com, 76, 198
Ovitz, Michael, 23

Passive investors, 21
Pedigree of allocator, 190
People's Energy, 149, 150
P/E (price over earnings) ratio, 101–102
Pine Top Insurance, 30
PIPEs. *See* Private investments in public equities (PIPEs)
Pirate Capital, 41–42, 43
Pittman, John Jay, 112
"Playing the calendar," 71
Plummer, Michael, 115
Position, building, 22
Price over earnings (P/E) ratio, 101–102
Private investments in public equities (PIPEs):
- advantages of, 56–57
- deal types, 59–65
- death spirals and, 58–59
- Genitope example, 56, 57
- overview of, 5, 55–56
- performance of, 65–69
- Regulation S and, 57–58

Protein Polymer Technologies, 61
Psychology of risk and loss, 186
Pullman, David, 5–6, 117–119
Pullman Bonds, 117–119

QCharts, 202
QQQQ, 101, 143. *See also* NASDAQ 100 index
Quote.com, 201

RAE Systems, 78
Rainmaker Systems, 85, 86
Random Roger's Big Picture blog, 197
Rare coin collecting, 112–114
Ravenswood, 75–76
Reading and media sources, 6–7
Real estate bubbles, 13
Reference checks, 166
Registration of hedge funds, 161–162
Regulation S and PIPEs, 57–58
Rentek, Inc., 63
Reset, Inc., 58
Resettable convertible, 62–63
Resources:
- blogs, 196–199
- books about investment, 193–195
- for data, 201–203

Retail HOLDRs ETF, 138–139
Reverse merger, 76–78
Risk aversion, 1
Robbie Stephens, 55
Roberts, Lyle, 197
Rosato, Thomas, 97
Ross Stores, 144
Ruff, Howard, *How to Prosper During the Coming Bad Years*, 141–142
Rutledge, John, blog of, 198–199

Salon.com, 76
Salton, 147, 148
Scams, 157
Schmitt, Charles, 158
SEBL, 88–89
Secondary market for life insurance, 14–16
Secondary transactions, 56–57, 69
Securities and Exchange Commission (SEC):
- hedge funds and, 161–162
- reporting requirements of, 79
- searching filings of, 165–166
- 13D filing, 22–23, 27, 46, 80
- 13F-HR filing, 80

Securities and Futures Commission, 159
Securities Litigation Watch blog, 196–197

"Seeding risk," 186, 187
Seeking Alpha blog, 196
Segmentz, Inc., 84–85
Service provider checks, 166
Sevin, Irik, 36
Shamrock Holdings, 24, 25–27
Short-selling:
  advantages of, 105–109
  CSFB Tremont Dedicated Short Bias Index, 99–100
  overview of, 5, 99
  pitfalls of, 101–105
  volatility and, 101
Siebert, Muriel, 78
Sillerman, Robert, 78
The Silver Bears (Erdmann), 194
Smith, Adam, *Supermoney*, 193–194
Soros, George, 87
Sowood Capital Management, 97
S&P 600, 146–148
Spear, Leeds, Kellog, 87
Specchio, Michael, 31, 32, 33
Specialty acquisition corporations (SPACs), 72–74
Sports Entertainment Inc., 78
SPY index fund, 143
Star Gas Partners L.P., 36–41
Starting hedge fund:
  mistakes managers make when, 185–188, 190–191
  overview of, 6
Steel Partners, 42–43
Stockpatrol.com web site, 162
Structured equity line and PIPEs, 64–65, 66
Subprime auto finance, 10–11
Superior Galleries, 112, 114
Supermoney (Smith), 193–194

Talisman Partners, 50, 51–53
Taub, Bruce, 115, 116–117
TAXI Medallion Financial Corporation, 19–20
Taxi medallions, 18–20
Tax liens, 16–18
Tech Data Corp, 145
Terrapin Partners, 73
Tese, Vincent, 32
The10b-5daily.com blog, 197
Third Point, 27, 36
13D filings:
  billionaire, following using, 80
  reading and following, 27
  requirement for, 22–23
  reviewing, 46
13F-HR filing, 80
Time Warner Inc., 88
Tobias, Andrew:
  The Funny Money Game, 194
  Getting By on $100,000 a Year, 189–190
Trade factoring, 11
Trade Like a Hedge Fund (Altucher), 2–3
Trade Like Warren Buffett (Altucher), 3
Trader's Monthly (magazine), 185
Transparency, 161, 162
Trend *vs.* countertrend:
  Christmas system, 138–140
  moving average and, 134–135
  NASDAQ 100 ETF and, 135–138
  overview of, 6, 131–135
  unemployment, 141–142
Truscelli, Joseph, 31, 32
TRW Automotive, 61
Turner, Ted, 77–78
Turtletrader.com web site, 202

Undervalued, definition of, 22
Unemployment, fading, 141–142
United Industrial Corp., 42–43

Valuation methodology, 163–164
Value traps, 21–22
Valuing rare coins, 113
Vaultus, 76–77, 143
Veridicom International, 64

Waste Management Inc., 78
Wealth-Lab software, 201
Web sites:
  background checks, 164
  BackTrack Reports, 166
  cefa.com, 96

data, 201–203
etfconnect.com, 93–94
stockpatrol.com, 162
Weiss, Andrew, 97
Weiss, Jason, 73
Welch, Ivo, 202
Whitney Financial Group Inc., 30
Wiped Out: How I Lost a Fortune in the Stock Market While the Averages Were Making New Highs (Anonymous Investor), 195
Wiring money, 157–158
WR Hambrecht & Co., 75

XM Satellite Radio, 148

Yahoo! Finance message boards, 104–105
Yushiro Chemical, 42

Z-Seven Fund, 94–96
Zumwalt, J. Kenton, 93

HIF
DVM
PPT

PIV

HIY
PPT